The Ketogenic and Modified Atkins Diets

The Ketogenic and Modified Atkins Diets

Treatments for Epilepsy and Other Disorders

SIXTH EDITION

Eric H. Kossoff, MD
Zahava Turner, RD, CSP, LDN
Sarah Doerrer, CPNP
Mackenzie C. Cervenka, MD
Bobbie J. Henry, RD, LDN

New York

Visit our website at www.demoshealth.com

ISBN: 978-1-936303-94-6
e-book ISBN: 9781617052675

Acquisitions Editor: Beth Barry
Compositor: diacriTech

Demos Health is an imprint of Springer Publishing Company, LLC.

Library of Congress Cataloging-in-Publication Data
Names: Kossoff, Eric, author. | Turner, Zahava, author. | Doerrer, Sarah, author. | Cervenka, Mackenzie C., author. | Henry, Bobbie J., author.
Title: The ketogenic and modified Atkins diets : treatments for epilepsy and other disorders / Eric H. Kossoff, MD, Zahava Turner, RD, CSP, LDN, Sarah Doerrer, CPNP, Mackenzie C. Cervenka, MD, Bobbie J. Henry, RD, LDN.
Other titles: Ketogenic diets.
Description: Sixth edition. | New York, New York : Demos Medical Publishing, LLC, [2016] | Revision of: Ketogenic diets. c2010. | Includes bibliographical references and index.
Identifiers: LCCN 2015051252 | ISBN 9781936303946 | ISBN 9781617052675 (ebook)
Subjects: LCSH: Epilepsy in children—Diet therapy. | Ketogenic diet. | MESH: Epilepsy—diet therapy.
Classification: LCC RJ496.E6 K47 2016 | DDC 618.92/8530654—dc23 LC record available at http://lccn.loc.gov/2015051252

Printed in the United States of America by McNaughton & Gunn.
16 17 18 19 20 5 4 3 2 1

Important Note to Readers

This book introduces the ketogenic diet to physicians, dietitians, patients, and parents of children with difficult-to-control seizures who might benefit from the treatment. This book is not intended to be an instruction manual. A book cannot take into account the specific needs of any individual patient. As with any course of treatment for epilepsy, a decision to try the ketogenic diet must be the result of a dialogue between patients (or parents) and a neurologist.

THIS DIET SHOULD *ONLY* BE INITIATED **under the supervision of a physician and a trained dietitian or nurse.**

If you are reading this book, we assume that you are familiar with the basic descriptions of epilepsy and what they mean. This is not a book about seizures or epilepsy. This is about one form of treatment for epilepsy—dietary therapy.

This book is dedicated to the memory of Dr. John Freeman

In 2014, the world lost one of the biggest advocates, researchers, and believers in the ketogenic diet, my personal mentor, Dr. John Freeman. Dr. Freeman took over the ketogenic diet service at Johns Hopkins Hospital shortly after moving to Baltimore from San Francisco in the 1980s. The diet was being used, but only sporadically (and as a last resort). Dr. Freeman "kept the flame alive" as many other people have said over the years, writing articles, seeing children from all over the United States, and never letting the diet be forgotten at national meetings like the American Epilepsy Society. He would often be in line for the microphone at a lecture on epilepsy and would ask, "What about the ketogenic diet here?" Through his research and partnership with Jim Abrahams and The Charlie Foundation, the diet has truly become mainstream epilepsy care.

I had the amazing fortune about being in the right place at the right time when I was a child neurology fellow in 1999 and ran into John in the hallways of the Children's Center at Johns Hopkins one morning. It was the first day of ketogenic diet admission week, and John asked me to interrupt my rounds to follow him to the hospital floor. He asked me to meet a family from the Midwest who had traveled with their five-year-old daughter to Johns Hopkins to start the diet. He (purposefully) didn't give me any more history! I went into the room, introduced myself, and saw she was wearing a helmet and having drop seizures nearly every 5 minutes in front of me. It was difficult to watch. Afterwards I asked John what was going to happen and he told me she was fasting to start the diet. I had not heard much at all about the ketogenic diet previously and was skeptical about its likelihood of benefit. Dr. Freeman said, "Come back in 4 days and meet me here." Four days later, the same girl was seizure-free, her helmet was gone, and one of her anticonvulsants was gone. In retrospect, I believe she probably had Doose syndrome. I was flabbergasted, shocked, and hooked.

At that moment, I decided to focus on the ketogenic diet for research, my epilepsy fellowship, and later my neurology career. Dr. Freeman mentored and guided me through all of this, showing me how to implement the diet and investigate it scientifically. I was thrilled to eventually assume the leadership of the Johns Hopkins Ketogenic Diet team in 2005 when he retired and become an author of this book starting with the fourth edition.

Most importantly, I learned from John about just how unique and amazing this treatment can be. Using foods to combat epilepsy is incredible and he never grew tired of this. The ability for parents and patients to have some control over an inherently uncontrollable condition was not lost on him, and how powerful that control could be. At national and international conferences, he was always excited, enthusiastic, and full of ideas. I know for sure that Dr. Freeman was amazingly proud of just how far the use of the ketogenic diet has come, and equally thrilled to see it being used for adults and patients with cancer, both of which were personal interests of his. I will always hear his voice whenever I read some of the articles and chapters he's written, and his love and passion that transcended what is typical for a normal physician. Dietary therapy, this book, and my life would not have been as successful without him.

Eric H. Kossoff, MD

CONTENTS

SECTION IX: Appendices

FOREWORD I

There's a truism in medicine: It takes years for a new treatment to gain acceptance. That was the fate of the ketogenic diet—twice.

Developed in the 1920s, the ketogenic diet was finally gaining wider use as a treatment for seizures when an effective anticonvulsant in much-easier-to-administer pill form went on the market in 1939. The diet succumbed to that pill and a slew of others. Despite the fact that the new medications failed to halt seizures in many children, while the diet cured or helped two-thirds of those who tried it, within 50 years the diet had fallen into near-total obscurity. Then in the 1990s, a most unlikely team—a Hollywood movie director and a Hopkins professor—joined forces to start the battle for acceptance again. I was privileged to observe their efforts.

One of these fighters was Jim Abrahams, best known as part of a zany, creative Hollywood team that turned out comedies such as "Airplane" and "Naked Gun." But there was nothing funny about his desperate search for anything that might stop his toddler son Charlie's seizures.

What finally cured Charlie wasn't the $100,000 his dad spent on multiple medications and brain surgery, but a diet. Jim stumbled upon a brief mention of it in a Johns Hopkins Press book, *Seizures and Epilepsy in Childhood: A Guide for Parents.* A month after Charlie arrived at The Johns Hopkins Hospital to start the diet, he was seizure and drug free. Jim was overjoyed, of course, but he didn't see any humor in the situation. He was outraged and wanted to know: "Why don't doctors recommend the diet to their patients? Why don't more parents know about it?"

Jim's frustration was shared by my late husband John Freeman, Charlie's physician at Johns Hopkins and director of the pediatric epilepsy program there. John could offer the treatment because his group included dietitian Millicent Kelly, who had learned the diet before it was abandoned and could coach parents in its preparation. Most physicians didn't have this resource, and, frankly, either didn't know about the diet—or didn't trust it.

John thought he could alter doctors' mindset and make them see the diet's benefits again. He also appreciated that parents were the ones who had been most active in seeking out and working with the diet. He enlisted our daughter, writer Jennifer Freeman, to help him and Mrs. Kelly write a book aimed equally at parents and doctors. *The Ketogenic Diet: A Treatment for Epilepsy* was unusual that way, written in plain language and envisioned as a low-priced, accessible paperback rather than a fancy medical text. But he had a hard time nailing down a publisher; not only was its tone unusual but its audience seemed too limited.

Jim was sure that his communications skills, funding, and contacts could alter this situation. Furious that no one had told him about the diet, he dedicated himself to making others aware of it, launching The Charlie Foundation to Help Cure Pediatric Epilepsy to educate the medical profession and parents of children with epilepsy. He financed the design and publication of the book, brought in a film crew to make several videotapes introducing the diet to parents, to children—and to doctors—and mailed a copy to every pediatric neurologist in the country.

I'll never forget watching John and Jim trying to give away the videotapes to physicians at a medical convention. No takers. A diet to cure epilepsy must have seemed like snake oil to doctors accustomed to prescribing pills for their patients.

Jim was correct in thinking that communications was the key, but the route to the doctors proved to be through the parents—and Jim's neighbor, a producer for the TV news show *Dateline NBC*. In 1994, before the explosion of cable channels, three television networks still dominated, and a "Dateline special" on the diet reached an enormous audience. John called the response from parents "the deluge." Fortunately, he had anticipated that the nationally televised program would create far more demand for the diet than his center could meet.

"We had to put together a plan to meet the expected demand," he recalled in his memoir. "With The Charlie Foundation's help, we held a conference at which directors of seven other epilepsy centers from around the country came to Hopkins with their dietitians to learn about the diet. Together we developed a plan to evaluate the diet's effect on children with difficult-to-control seizures and to jointly publish the results."

Thanks to John and Jim, not only were other centers now prepared to handle the influx of patients generated by the TV program, but a built-in research component came with this sudden increase of patients on the diet. The first 1500 copies of the book sold out immediately, and Demos Press willingly assumed ongoing publishing.

Always a big thinker, Jim next produced a dramatic, made-for-TV film about a young Hopkins patient helped by the diet years earlier. The feisty mother in that story was played by Jim's good friend Meryl Streep. *First Do No Harm* aired in 1997. "Approximately 5000 phone calls later," John recalled, "we were again inundated with patients." Fortunately, by now the center's research coordinator had set up a database to keep track of the patients.

Jim and John carried their democratic vision for popularizing the diet even further, financing conferences where dietitians and parents had the floor as well as doctors. John supported the formation of parents' networks, with staff in addition to Mrs. Kelly on hand to help families work through problems.

The impressive research results, John believed, "answered many questions about the diet and have opened many new questions." He loved to point out that the ketogenic diet "opened whole new areas of research not only in the field of epilepsy, but in other areas as well." He would have been so pleased to see that some of these areas, from brain tumors to diabetes, Alzheimer's disease to Parkinsonism, are touched on in this book.

As scientists gain greater understanding of how the diet works to combat seizures, they are applying this knowledge to find new ways to achieve the same results. Ironically, the day may come when research may lead to a simple pill to replicate—not replace—a complicated diet. Children and adults disabled by recalcitrant seizures then will be able to lead a more normal life—thanks in part to two men who wouldn't give up.

Elaine Freeman

FOREWORD II

On March 11, 1993, I was pushing my one-year-old son, Charlie, in a swing when his head twitched and he threw his right arm in the air. The whole event was so subtle that I didn't even think to mention it to my wife, Nancy, until a couple days later when it recurred. She said she had seen similar incidents.

Nine months later, after thousands of a variety of seizures, an incredible array of drugs, dozens of blood draws, eight hospitalizations, a mountain of EEGs, MRIs, CAT scans, and PET scans, one fruitless brain surgery, five pediatric neurologists in three cities, two homeopaths, one faith healer, and countless prayers, Charlie's epilepsy was unchecked, his development "delayed," and he had a prognosis of continued seizures and "progressive retardation."

Then, in December 1993, we learned about the ketogenic diet and the success that Dr. John Freeman, Millicent Kelly, RD, and Diana Pillas had been having with it at Johns Hopkins Hospital as a treatment for children with difficult-to-control epilepsy. We took Charlie to Johns Hopkins. He started the diet. Charlie was seizure- and drug-free within a month. He never took another antiepileptic drug or had another seizure. Today he is a happy, healthy 24 years old. He has a Certificate in Early Childhood Education and works with preschoolers. He boxes twice weekly, has been playing piano for over 15 years, eats whatever he wants, has no recollection of his epilepsy, and very little memory of his five years on the ketogenic diet.

Back in 1994, when we realized that a vast majority of Charlie's seizures and most of his $100,000 of medical, surgical, and drug treatments had been unnecessary—even harmful—we founded The Charlie Foundation to help increase awareness and understanding of the ketogenic diet within the patient, medical, and scientific communities. Among our efforts, we financed the first edition of *The Epilepsy Diet Treatment*.

Twenty-two years later, as *The Ketogenic and Modified Atkins Diets: Treatments for Epilepsy and Other Disorders—Sixth Edition* is being released, the evolution of ketogenic diet therapies has been nothing short of astounding. The diet itself has become refined, palatable—even delicious. Syndromes for which it is most effective are being defined. The less restrictive modified Atkins diet, low glycemic index treatment, and modified ketogenic diet have opened availability to older children as well as the adult epilepsy population. Emerging science is beginning to reveal the significant benefits and mechanisms of ketogenic diets in the fields of brain cancer, autism, and cognitive disorders. Global interest has spiked dramatically.

Most importantly, tens of thousands of people are healthier.

The Ketogenic and Modified Atkins Diets: Treatments for Epilepsy and Other Disorders—Sixth Edition will continue to build on the near 100-year history of the ketogenic diet. By sharing timely and accurate knowledge, it will help its readers, both with epilepsy and with other neurological disorders, decide whether the diet is a viable alternative or adjunct to their current treatment. It is also a most valuable guide once diet therapy has begun.

Jim Abrahams, Charlie's Dad
Executive Director
The Charlie Foundation for Ketogenic Therapies

PREFACE

The ketogenic diet has figuratively and literally entered adulthood.

From its earliest beginnings in the 1920s, the infancy of the ketogenic diet was full of the turmoil of youth. Widespread use, even popularity, was the hallmark of the classic ketogenic diet in the 1920s and 1930s. Article after article came out of the Mayo Clinic and other hospitals, each one adding more patients and demonstrating efficacy for epilepsy. The unbridled enthusiasm of youth, however, often meets reality in adolescence. As the diet became a "teenager" in the 1950s through 1980s, it was more of a radical, unproven idea struggling to find acceptance in a big world of pharmaceuticals. Adults (and adult neurologists) ignored it, leaving it to its own devices in several select centers.

Young adulthood has been kind to the ketogenic diet, and just as college life for a teenager raises awareness of new ideas, unique possibilities, and brand-new directions, the ketogenic diet had a rebirth in 1994 with The Charlie Foundation's founding and the first edition of this book. Over the past 5 editions and 22 years, the ketogenic diet has finally gone from "voodoo" alternative medicine to respected, "nonpharmacologic" treatment for epilepsy. New ideas over the past two decades have included not just one but four dietary treatments, consideration for new-onset treatment instead of a last resort, and myriad different ways to start the diet. The emergence of powdered, premade ketogenic diet formulas have both revolutionized the use of this treatment for infants and those with feeding tubes, but using these powders as a baking mix have allowed for ketogenic foods to be created that are nearly indistinguishable from their carb-containing namesakes. As many neurologists familiar with the past 22 years of changes in the diet have said, "it's not your parent's ketogenic diet."

We believe the use of dietary therapy has truly entered adulthood today. This 6th edition reflects where the field is going, and it's an exciting future. For one, as evident in the title, the modified Atkins diet (often referred to as "MAD") is now 13 years old and this "alternative" diet has found its niche for teens, adults, and some other interesting uses when an outpatient, less restrictive dietary option is needed. An entire section of this book is now devoted to the MAD. Drs. Elizabeth Neal and Heidi Pfeifer have additionally revised their excellent chapters from the 5th edition on the MCT diet and low glycemic index treatments, respectively.

Perhaps most notably, this edition has increased its focus on the use of dietary therapy for adults. A mainstream concept in the 1930s, only to lapse into obscurity for seven decades, the use of the MAD has led to a rebirth in using diets for patients over age 18 years. Reflecting this change, two of our new coauthors, Dr. Cervenka and Ms. Henry, coordinate the Johns Hopkins Adult Epilepsy Diet Center and have written the sections on diets and adults that comprise a large portion of this book.

In 2011, the 5th edition had a single, very brief, chapter on the concept of using diets for conditions other than epilepsy. Now the research and clinical use has caught up to the interest from many patients. At the 4th International Ketogenic Diet Symposium held in 2014 in Liverpool, a large number of lectures were focused on this topic. Now an entire section of this book is devoted to discussions of using various forms of the ketogenic diet for cancer, autism, migraines, and dementia, with excellent guest authors providing their expertise. One can only predict the 7th and 8th editions of this book will see this section expand greatly.

Lastly, as evident by all the countries represented at the Liverpool meeting (and languages spoken in hallways and poster sessions!), the diet has truly gone global. The International League Against Epilepsy has taken notice of the use of dietary therapy and commissioned a Task Force to help bring it to developing countries. Chapters of this book are devoted to the international use of the diet and this edition is the first to be translated officially into another language (Spanish). Just as students graduating college often travel abroad to expand their horizons, the ketogenic diet has increased its scope internationally and is better off for it.

Despite all of the new ideas and uses that have been achieved in the ketogenic diet's adulthood, it is always wise to keep linked to its youth. This 6th edition is packed with chapters on epilepsy, tricks and tips to make the diet a success, and how to keep motivated when times get rough. One of the best ways to be successful is to have a great ketogenic diet team, and one of our star team members is our nurse practitioner Sarah Doerrer: she is also now a new coauthor. Never forget, however, that all dietary therapies must be done under the supervision of a neurologist and dietitian familiar with it. Just like any medical therapy, there are real risks involved.

We all hope you enjoy this book and it helps you appreciate just how far the diet has come in the past 100 years from infancy to middle age. It's been an amazing "maturity" and the diet is only getting more popular, increasingly researched, and easier for patients to do. Best of luck to you, your child, or your loved one as you embark on your ketogenic diet journey!

("Selfie" photo taken on the first day we started working on this edition!)

Zahava Turner, RD, CSP, LDN, Bobbie Henry, RD, LDN, Mackenzie Cervenka, MD, Sarah Doerrer, CPNP, Eric Kossoff, MD
(from left to right)

ACKNOWLEDGMENTS

We would like to express our appreciation for the invaluable help we received from the many contributing authors and reviewers of this book. Several authors were directly responsible for the information in prior editions. As demonstrated by their work on this edition, the world of the ketogenic diet is growing rapidly. These authors are from all over the world and their knowledge helped make this book a success. We would like to thank the following individuals:

- Dr. John Freeman
- Dr. Adam Hartman
- Dr. James Rubenstein
- Dr. Lee Peterlin
- Dr. Roy Strowd
- Dr. Jason Brandt
- Jim Abrahams
- Elaine Freeman
- Beth Zupec-Kania, RD
- Elizabeth Neal, RD, PhD
- Heidi Pfeifer, RD
- Jane Andrews, RD
- Jennifer Freeman
- Colette Heimowitz
- Millicent Kelly, RD
- Susie Gingrich, RD
- Jennifer Bosarge, RD
- Chef Neil Pallister-Bosomworth
- Gerry and Michael Harris
- Michael Koski
- Jason Meyers
- Emma Williams

The Ketogenic and Modified Atkins Diets

Overview of Diet Therapy

CHAPTER 1

Epilepsy Today and the Place of the Ketogenic Diet

WHAT IS A SEIZURE ANYWAY?

Many families who come to see us at Johns Hopkins have not even been told what epilepsy is. *Epilepsy*, other than being a scary word, just means more than one seizure. Some recent discussions suggest that it may also mean one seizure with a predisposition for more (e.g., an abnormal electroencephalogram or EEG). Recent statistics say that one in every 26 people has epilepsy, and that number is even higher for children. It is not rare. There are many children with epilepsy who are at the top of their class in math and science, and several more in colleges on varsity sports teams. However, other children are not so fortunate.

Epilepsy is not a very useful word for affected families unless it helps them put a name to their child's condition, a condition that in some cases does not have a clear resolution. There are many causes of epilepsy, so the name itself is not often helpful, except to get services or explain it to family members and neighbors. This is very frustrating, needless to say. The good news is that for situations when neurologists can't say definitively why a child is having seizures, they also can't say definitively if a child won't outgrow the seizures. Sometimes no news is good news, even when you have to tell other family members that you and your doctor "don't know why."

After a single seizure, we nearly always obtain an EEG and sometimes an MRI. In general, there is a 30% to 40% chance of a second seizure. On the other hand, there's a 70% chance that the child will never need to visit us (other than for social reasons) ever again due to being seizure free. It is for this reason that most neurologists do not start medications after just one seizure except in very unusual circumstances such as with a very abnormal EEG, or with a particularly severe seizure, or with persons desiring to drive a car.

Once a second seizure occurs, the risk flips, with a 70% chance of a third seizure. When this seizure will happen isn't clear, although typically people with abnormal EEGs are even more likely to seize sooner rather than later. Unless the two seizures are very far apart in time, we will often start medications to try and prevent more seizures.

MEDICATIONS

All the available medications are meant to help, not to cure. They are helpful in most people who start them, even at low doses, but they do not make the underlying epilepsy go away. Only time (and a little prayer) will lead to a cure for many of the people we care for. When seizures are impacting a child's quality of life, medications are not just a good idea, they are important. Twenty years ago, we only had a handful of medications. In 2016, we have more than 20 medications—double that of two decades ago.

Many of the newer medications have a kinder side-effect profile, although relatively few are approved by the Food and Drug Administration (FDA) for children, especially those under the age of 2 years. Neurologists will choose a drug depending upon the cause of the seizures and the seizure type. Drugs can be "first generation," such as Tegretol® and Depakote®, or "second generation," such as Trileptal®, Keppra®, and Topamax®. We are now on a "third generation" of drugs including Banzel®, Vimpat®, and Fycompa®. More and more frequently today, we are using the newer drugs earlier and in some cases even first.

Despite all these new medicines, it is not clear to us that the person with difficult-to-control epilepsy is much better off. New drugs have new mechanisms of action, but the chances of seizure freedom after two or three drugs have been tried is still low. Perhaps nowadays we tolerate side effects less often since there are other choices, but there still is a sizeable number of people who do not respond to seizure medications.

Sadly, about 10% don't respond to any drug. Many recent studies in both children and adults have shown that if two or three drugs don't work, stop wasting your time with a fourth or fifth drug and move onto other options. This is typically where the ketogenic diet is used.

WHAT ABOUT WHEN MEDICATIONS FAIL?

Even after one drug has failed, most neurologists nowadays think about whether brain surgery is an option. In some cases, it is. Although certainly facing some risk in the operating room, such persons have a very good chance (especially if there is something clear on the MRI, PET, or MEG scan) of having their seizures cured by surgery. However, there are even more people who are not clear candidates for surgery, as listed in Table 1.1.

When surgery is not an option and medications fail, patients are left with few options. These mostly include dietary treatments and electrical stimulation (either vagus nerve stimulation [VNS] or direct brain stimulation devices [e.g., NeuroPace®]). Depending upon the doctor, one of these therapies is typically recommended earlier than others. Most of the authors of this book lean toward dietary therapy first, as you would expect. Other hospitals, often those with less experience with diets or more familiar and comfortable with VNS, will recommend the diet only after VNS is unsuccessful.

TABLE 1.1

Why Surgery Would Not Be a Great Option

- Many different regions of the brain where the seizures originate
- Seizures coming from an important area of the brain (movement, language, or memory centers)
- Too risky for some people with other medical issues
- Source of seizures not clearly found despite an EEG with electrodes placed on the brain
- Some are generalized seizures (e.g., absence or Lennox Gastaut)
- Bleeding disorder
- Not able or willing to travel to a center that does surgery regularly
- Family (and child) not willing to take the risk

Our experience, similar to most centers, is that VNS is often a help but rarely a cure, and probably less commonly a cure than the ketogenic diet. The diet usually works quickly (studies suggest often within the first month of use), whereas VNS often takes months to work. The VNS is generally without major side effects (hoarse voice, cough, possible infection), other than the risk of general anesthesia required for the brief surgery. Most of our patients have had some improvement, but also seem more alert and interactive. We are very interested in the combination of both the ketogenic diet and VNS at the same time as using both together sometimes seems to work better than each alone (in limited research). We tend to rarely use VNS in children under the age of 3 years. The decision to try the diet or to insert a VNS is ultimately up to the parents and the doctors together. It's not wrong to try VNS first and don't feel bad if you did and it didn't work.

WHERE DO DIETARY TREATMENTS FIT IN THIS PLAN?

This is when the ketogenic and modified Atkins diets, as well as the low-glycemic index treatment, are commonly used. We have seen some dramatic results with diets for even the toughest of seizure cases. Diets are continuing to grow in use both in the United States and worldwide and the sixth edition of this book is a testament to that growth. Much of this success is a result of the work of The Charlie Foundation, a parent support group that has championed the use of dietary treatments in the United States since 1993 (www.charliefoundation.org). Further information about this wonderful group and other groups around the world is in Chapter 23. The diet can be given to young infants, teenagers, and adults. Side effects are generally few and often reversible should they occur; stopping the diet is not usually necessary.

WHAT ABOUT OUTSIDE THE UNITED STATES?

In the 1990s, as the ketogenic diet was starting to grow in popularity in the United States, other countries were also beginning to use this treatment as well; notable countries included England, Germany, Australia, and Canada. Since that time, there has been a virtual explosion of interest all over the world. In 2016, over 80 countries offer the ketogenic diet, with many countries having multiple centers! We still receive e-mails from parents in Europe and Asia stating that the ketogenic diet is "not available" in their country and they'd like to come to Baltimore, but this is rarely necessary today. Each country is more familiar with its own cultures and foods, so we usually refer these parents to appropriate ketogenic diet centers. Information about international use is in Chapter 33 and a list of these centers is provided in Appendix G and at the ILAE ketogenic diet website.

DOES IT WORK?

Multiple studies have shown that slightly more than half the children on the ketogenic diet will have their seizures improve by 50% (Table 1.2). About one third will have a >90% improvement. About 10% to 15% will be seizure-free, and when this occurs, everyone is thrilled. Studies show that the diet is particularly effective for conditions such as infantile spasms, myoclonic-astatic epilepsy (Doose syndrome), Rett syndrome, glucose transporter-1 (GLUT-1) deficiency syndrome, tuberous sclerosis complex, and children receiving formula only (such as through gastrostomy tubes or an infant bottle).

The diet is often used in conjunction with medications, but the rapid response (when seen) cannot be explained as simply natural improvement due to time

TABLE 1.2

Outcomes of the Ketogenic Diet: Johns Hopkins Patients, 1998

		TIME AFTER STARTING THE DIET		
NUMBER INITIATING	SEIZURE CONTROL AND DIET STATUS	3 MONTHS	6 MONTHS	12 MONTHS
Total: *N* = 150	100% seizure free	4 (3%)	5 (3%)	11 (7%)
	> 90%	46 (31%)	43 (29%)	30 (20%)
	50%–90%	39 (26%)	29 (19%)	34 (23%)
	< 50%	36 (24%)	29 (19%)	8 (5%)
	Continued on diet	125 (83%)	106 (71%)	83 (55%)
	Discontinued diet	25 (17%)	44 (29%)	67 (45%)

Source: From Freeman JM, Vining EPG, Pillas DJ, et al. The efficacy of the ketogenic diet—1998: a prospective evaluation of intervention in 150 children. *Pediatrics* 1998;102:1358–1363.

and medications "kicking in." When effective, the diet's success can be very dramatic and often leads to Internet success stories. Articles about children with 100% success stories have appeared in newspapers and websites around the country, with headlines such as "Michael's Magical Diet," "Cured by Butter, Mayo and Cream," "Epilepsy's Big Fat Miracle," and "High Fat and Seizure Free." These are the glowing reports of the dramatic success that the diet can achieve.

The diet is not as difficult as it used to be years ago. Ketogenic powdered formulas (e.g., KetoCal®) can be used as baking mixes to make foods that normally contain flour. We are not as strict as we used to be about calories, fluids, and the ratio. This is a big difference in this book's sixth edition compared to the earlier editions. KetoDietCalculator (Chapter 10) has made more recipes than ever available to families. The modified Atkins diet and low-glycemic index treatment are also available for those few who can't tolerate the ketogenic diet (and also for teens and adults). You and your child *can* do it.

DEFINING SUCCESS

Unfortunately, the ketogenic diet does not result in a success story for everyone. Almost half of all children who start the diet stop during the first year. The percentage of adults who stop the diet, even when it is helping, is even higher. Some stop because, despite the medical and support team's best efforts to "fine-tune" the diet, and despite the family's diligent efforts, the seizures have not improved sufficiently to make their efforts worthwhile. Some discontinue because of illness, noncompliance, or because the diet is "just too hard."

We have learned long ago that success for one family is not the same as success for another. For children, a 25% reduction in seizures may be great due to improved alertness and school performance. For adults, 25% reduction may mean they still can't get a driver's license and that's not good enough.

We have had people in whom the number of seizures is unchanged, but the parents strongly believe it is helping. The seizures might be shorter, less intense, or occurring only at night, for example. Some children are able to reduce medications and are more alert, despite the seizures not slowing down. Even though the total numbers of seizures may be discouraging to our ketogenic diet team, the parents may believe it's a success and want to stick with it. Ultimately, it is the patient and the family, and not just the neurologist, who must define the diet's success or failure.

WHEN SHOULD THE DIET BE USED, THEN?

Most experts (and insurance companies) believe diets should be considered after two or three medications have been tried. If seizures are well-controlled with medications and there are no side effects, the diet is *not* necessary. Children with infantile spasms and Doose syndrome may be exceptions to this rule, and we have used the diet first in those situations with excellent results. Details are in Chapter 6. Some adults have tried the diet before medications for different reasons, which we'll discuss in the section on adults.

However, for some people, even with seizures under fairly good control, medication may affect alertness and mental clarity, impairing their ability to learn and reach their full potential. Therapy for epilepsy is often a balance between seizure control and medication toxicity.

The point at which an individual's seizures are deemed out of control, or side effects are considered unacceptable, varies from person to person and from family to family. Most people (especially children) who start dietary treatment are having at least weekly (and usually many per day) seizures. In a study of parent letters written at the time the diet was started, we found that most mothers and fathers agreed and wanted seizures and medications reduced. Most were realistic and didn't expect seizure or medication freedom. Surprisingly, nine out of every 10 parents requested something else: typically improved alertness, less injury, or improved performance in school.

One hundred seizures a day is clearly too many, but are three seizures a month too many? Some children and families consider that limiting seizures to one a week a victory, while others consider one seizure every 2 months an intolerable state of affairs. Varying degrees of sedation, hyperactivity, and learning disabilities may be acceptable in exchange for seizure control. But what if you could control seizures without such side effects?

This is a question asked by many parents. Could my child learn better, faster, more easily without the toxicity of the medication? Would my child's behavior and attention improve if he or she weren't on anticonvulsants? What about an adult who is seizure free but can't concentrate at work? How can you tell when a child cannot be taken off medication without the chance of recurrent seizures?

The net result is that many children and their parents look beyond currently available medications for a satisfying solution to seizure treatment. For many parents, the ketogenic diet, which does not have the same level of cognitive and behavioral side effects of many anticonvulsant medications (especially older ones such as phenobarbital), offers a chance—sometimes an unattainable dream—of seeing their child free of medications and seizures. Even in those who discontinue the diet, however, most find the attempt at the diet worthwhile because, as they often say, "at least we know that we tried."

Success on the ketogenic diet requires the commitment, determination, and faith of the entire family. Thirty grams cream, 12 grams meat, 18 grams butter—the recipe begins to sound like witches' magic brew. There *is* mystery to it. No one understands fully how or why the ketogenic diet works. But it *does* work, and it has worked for almost 100 years.

CHAPTER 2

What Is the Ketogenic Diet?

The ketogenic diet is a medical treatment for controlling seizures by switching a body's primary metabolism to a fat-based energy source rather than utilizing glucose.

The body obtains energy from three major food sources:

1. *Carbohydrates:* Starches, sugars, breads, cereal grains, fruits, and vegetables
2. *Fats:* Butter, oil, and mayonnaise
3. *Proteins:* Meat, fish, poultry, cheese, eggs, and milk

Carbohydrates comprise approximately 50% to 60% of the average American's daily caloric intake. The body converts these carbohydrates to glucose, which is burned by the body to produce energy. When the supply of glucose is limited, as during fasting, the body burns its fat for energy. During prolonged starvation, if there is insufficient fat, then muscle is burned, thus compromising energy and good health.

The body maintains only about a 24- to 36-hour supply of glucose, and once that glucose is depleted, the body automatically draws on its backup energy source—stored body fat. This is a survival skill, inherited from our hunter–gatherer forefathers who may have had to go for prolonged periods between game kills and, during those times, used their stored fat as their energy source.

The ketogenic diet was designed to simulate the metabolism of this fasting. When a fasting person has burned up all glucose stores, he or she then begins to burn stored body fat for energy. After the initial fasting period, a person on the ketogenic diet derives energy principally by burning the exogenous dietary fat rather than from the more common energy source, carbohydrate (glucose), or from his or her own body fat. But unlike fasting, by providing exogenous fat the ketogenic diet allows a person to maintain this fat-burning metabolism as the primary source of energy (instead of glucose) over an extended period of time.

In the absence of glucose, the fat is not burned completely but leaves a residue of *soot* or *ash* in the form of ketone bodies, and these ketone bodies build up in the blood. The ketone residues are *beta-hydroxybutyric acid, acetone,* and *acetoacetic acid.* The beta-hydroxybutyric acid can be metabolized by the liver and by the brain as a source of energy. The acetoacetic acid is excreted in the urine (see Figure 2.1) and the acetone is excreted through the breath and imparts a sweet smell to the breath that has been likened to pineapple.

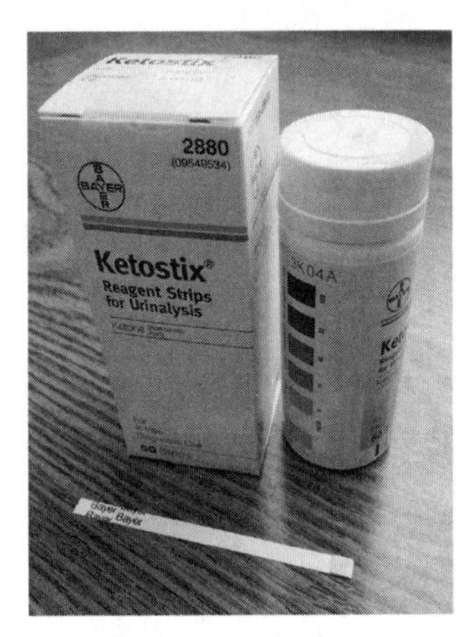

Figure 2.1. Ketone sticks (for urine testing).

When ketone levels are large enough, as indicated by a simple urine test, it is said that the body is *ketotic* (pronounced key-tah'-tic) or in a state of *ketosis.*

THE BASICS

REMINDER: The traditional ketogenic diet is a rigid, mathematically calculated, doctor-supervised therapy. This diet should only be attempted under close medical and dietary supervision.

The ketogenic diet simulates the metabolism of a fasting individual. A fasting person burns stored body fat for energy; a person on the ketogenic diet derives energy principally from the fat in the diet. But unlike fasting, the ketogenic diet allows a person to maintain this fat burning over an extended period of time. Traditionally, the diet has been initiated over 2 to 3 days after a 48-hour period of fasting (a limited amount of carbohydrate-free fluids are allowed during this period). More recent studies (discussed in Chapter 7) have questioned whether fasting, slow initiation, or even the traditional ketogenic diet itself is necessary for seizure control. At Johns Hopkins, in fact, we now do a 24-hour fast and 2-day introduction of the diet.

Foods

Common, but carefully selected, ingredients are used in meals that a child eats while on the ketogenic diet (see Chapter 31). With the help of a dietitian and careful calculations, the diet can be adapted to accommodate many foods and many cultures around the world (see Chapters 30 and 33).

The diet can also be started as a liquid formula for bottle-fed infants and children and adults with a gastrostomy feeding tube. For the caregivers of these tube-feeders, the diet can be fairly easy to administer because compliance is not an issue.

Can my child live a normal life while on this diet?

The answer is clearly YES! Here are examples of what some ketogenic meals might look like:

Sample Meal Plans

Breakfast 1	Breakfast 2
Scrambled eggs with butter	Bacon
Diluted cream	Scrambled eggs with butter
Strawberries	Melon slices
	Vanilla cream shake
Lunch 1	**Lunch 2**
Spaghetti squash with butter and parmesan cheese	Tuna with mayonnaise
Lettuce leaf with mayonnaise	Celery and cucumber sticks
Orange diet soda mixed with whipped cream	Sugarless Jell-O with whipped cream
Dinner 1	**Dinner 2**
Hot dog slices with ketchup	Broiled chicken breast
Asparagus with butter	Chopped lettuce with mayonnaise
Chopped lettuce with mayonnaise	Cinnamon apple slice with butter topped with vanilla ice cream
Vanilla cream ice pop	

Alternatively, breakfast might include a mushroom omelet, bacon, and a cream shake, or another special keto-recipe for cold cereal. Keto cereal was invented by the creative mother of a child who missed eating his bowl of cereal in the morning. The mother crumbled keto cookies into a bowl and poured cream over them. This made an excellent cold cereal that satisfied her son. Each meal will depend upon the desires of the child and the imagination of the parent.

MYTHS AND MISUNDERSTANDINGS ABOUT THE DIET

Contrary to the beliefs of some parents, the ketogenic diet is not "all natural," "holistic," "organic," or "pure." The ketogenic diet is a medical therapy used to treat seizures in children (and sometimes adults) and, like any medical therapy, it has side effects. In general, the ketogenic diet is better tolerated than most medications and has fewer potential side effects. The major side effects that can be seen with the diet are lack of weight gain, *slightly* decreased growth, *somewhat* high cholesterol, constipation, gastroesophageal reflux, kidney stones, and acidosis. All are manageable without having to stop the diet.

The ketogenic diet requires a lot of commitment and a lot of work initially. Even for families who become experts in preparing the diet and organizing their lives around it, the ketogenic diet is a big undertaking and can definitely be a substantial intrusion on a family's life. Anticonvulsant medications are far easier to use and if they work, they are probably a better choice than the diet. Physicians and families must always weigh the difficulties and benefits of the ketogenic diet compared to medications and their side effects and to seizures, and physicians usually recommend that an individual with seizures try one or two medications before turning to the diet.

A modified Atkins diet (discussed in Section III) is somewhat easier than the traditional ketogenic diet, but it is still not easy.

Common Misunderstandings About the Diet

- "The diet will completely control the seizures."

  Some children (about one in 10) do become seizure free. Others will have a reduced number of seizures. Still others may be able to cut down on the number of medications they must take. About half of the children who start the diet will derive some benefit from it and continue it while the other half do not. In any event, the diet is worth trying. If it is too difficult or provides inadequate control, you can always stop the diet (see Chapter 12) and return to trying medications.

- "My child will be able to get rid of all those poison medicines that have side effects and are not even approved for use in children."

  This is a result to be desired, but it is not a reality for everyone. Once the child is stable on the diet, the doctor can try to decrease or eliminate medication. The child does not necessarily need to be seizure-free to do this but the child's seizures should be reasonably controlled. Most children are on both the diet and medication(s). We see it as a "partnership" for most.

- "We will just try it for a few weeks, and if it doesn't work we'll go back to medications."

  We ask each family for a 3-month commitment. After starting the diet, it takes 3 months to tell if it's helping. Initiating the ketogenic diet requires too many changes and commitments on the family's part, and too much commitment from the whole keto team, to have someone not give it a proper chance.

- "The diet is all-natural and medications are not."

  Although most keto centers believe that the diet has fewer side effects than medications (and certainly fewer severe ones), the diet is neither healthy nor all natural. It is a medical therapy with risks and needs to be supervised. More information about side effects is in Chapter 24.

CHAPTER 3

How Does the Ketogenic Diet Work?

This chapter was originally written by Dr. James Rubenstein and revised by Dr. Adam Hartman, who is studying metabolism-based treatments in animal models. The authors appreciate their help with this chapter.

In 1994 when the first edition of this book came out, the answer to the question "How does the ketogenic diet work?" was "We don't know." Today, the answer is "There are many possible reasons, all of which are likely true." The amazing experimental results have led to new drugs being used (one called 2-DG, which blocks glucose, and current research is looking into another drug based on adenosine), and all seem to affect the body's metabolism. Many researchers refer to dietary therapy as "metabolism-based therapy," as these treatments change the way the body works and likely help make the neurons (brain cells) work *better*. Although many have tried, the evidence would suggest there is *no* single mechanism by which the diet works. Developing a pill that replaces the diet is highly unlikely. Starting a patient on the ketogenic diet essentially tricks the body into thinking it is maintaining a fasting state. The body is denied most carbohydrates, is given sufficient protein, and depending upon the dietary ratio chosen by the dietitian for the individual patient, is given large amounts of fat. The body quickly depletes its supply of easily accessed carbohydrate and turns to fat as its alternative energy source. Fasting accelerates the process, and as fats are burned without the presence of carbohydrates, ketone bodies accumulate and can be identified and measured in the blood, urine, and cerebral spinal fluid (Figure 3.1). The simplest way to identify if an individual has a large ketone supply is simply to smell the fruity aroma on the individual's breath. It is very dramatic.

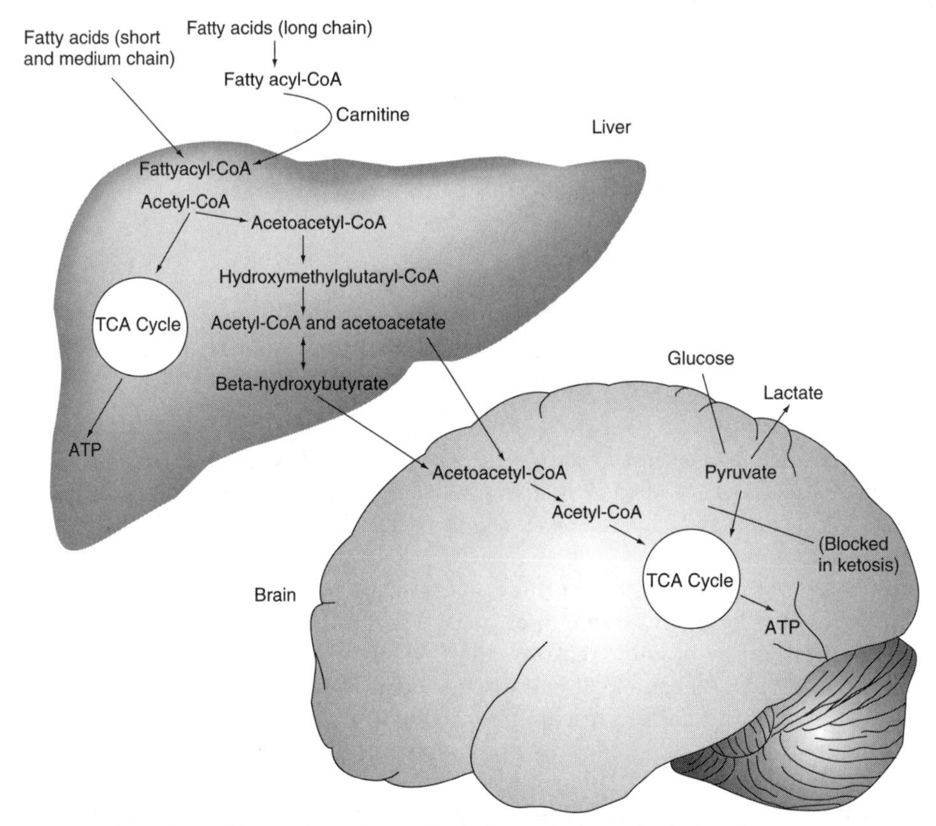

Figure 3.1. Breakdown of fatty acids into ketones by the liver and taken up by the brain for energy.

KETONES

Once the ketogenic diet is started, ketone bodies can cross the blood–brain barrier and enter the brain. There are three types of ketone bodies, which are by-products of burning fat for energy instead of carbohydrate. They are called acetone, acetoacetate, and beta-hydroxybutyrate. Some recent studies suggest that once they are in the brain, they can prevent ongoing seizure activity. This effect may occur either as a result of ketone bodies altering the ability of nerve cells to fire or their ability to change the activity of the cell's powerhouse, the mitochondria.

Because the ketone bodies are acids and cause acidosis (an increase in the amount of acid in the body), it has been proposed that the ketogenic diet works by creating an ongoing acidotic state that the body somehow compensates for, while it is also affecting one of the three factors. This was one of the first theories, but it has been largely disproven. Today we try to avoid acidosis because it can cause side effects!

We know that once the body realizes that certain levels of ketones are circulating in the blood, they "spill" into the urine and can be measured there. Interestingly, that does not always correlate with the actual amount of ketone bodies in the bloodstream. Levels of the ketone bodies in the blood and urine do not have a strong correlation with their levels in the brains of rodents (the brain, of course, is where the seizures are taking place), but as of now, we do not have a way to reliably measure these changes in people. Studies that have attempted to link blood (or urine) ketones with seizure control have not shown a consistent link.

OTHER POTENTIAL MECHANISMS

There are other ways that the diet might exert its antiseizure and neuroprotective effects. Areas currently being investigated include:

- the effect of chronic ketosis and fatty acids on brain energy reserves and mitochondria, the cell's powerhouse and one of the major components of cell death pathways;
- how the ketogenic diet alters the action of various neurotransmitter levels, which may play a role in explaining the efficacy of the ketogenic diet not only in treating seizures but also in treating a variety of other neurological and behavioral disorders;
- the role of adenosine and other neuromodulators in the mechanisms of action of the diet;
- the relative role of glucose stabilization versus high fats (with studies examining a drug currently called 2-DG that helps stabilize glucose and may help reduce seizures);
- the role of amino acids (the building blocks of proteins) in modulating seizure activity; and
- the importance of cellular metabolism-sensing pathways (in either neurons or their supporting cells) in altering sensitivity to seizures.

Unfortunately, our inability to explain exactly how the diet works has led many neurologists to remain skeptical about it. We tell these child neurologists that we do not know how many medications work either and most have many mechanisms of action like the diet! In fact, for many years, the drug Keppra® (levetiracetam), which is now one of the most popular drugs, had an "unclear mechanism of action" when described in advertisements. Despite that, it was very popular. The diet, just like many medications, probably has multiple mechanisms of action, and we suspect for some epilepsies a particular mechanism may be the most important. For example, for infantile spasms, maybe ketosis is critical, whereas for Doose syndrome it might be calorie restriction. Only time will tell, but finally, basic scientists are working together with clinical researchers to find ways to make the diet more effective in humans.

CHAPTER 4

History of the Ketogenic Diet

Fasting and prayer have been mentioned as treatments for seizures and epilepsy since biblical times and are mentioned again in the literature of the Middle Ages. Hippocrates in 400 BC described a man with seizures due to a burn injury who was successfully treated with "complete abstinence from food and water." Galen in 200 BC similarly recommended "abstinence from daily use of such food as engenders unhealthy humors." Of course, the famous quote from the Bible in Mark 9:14–29 states that Jesus cured a patient with epilepsy with "prayer and fasting." There were reports in the late 1800s from France of water diets being successful in reducing seizures.

However, it was only in June of 1921 in the journal *Medical Record* that fasting as a treatment for epilepsy was reawakened. At the American Medical Association meeting that year, Dr. Rawle Geyelin, a prominent New York pediatrician, reported the successful treatment of severe epilepsy by fasting.

Geyelin cited the case of a "child of a friend," age 10 years, who "for 4 years had had grand mal and petit mal attacks which had become practically continuous." At Battle Creek, Michigan, this child came under the care of an osteopathic physician (Dr. Hugh Conklin), who promptly fasted him, the first time for 15 consecutive days. Several subsequent periods of feeding, then fasting, occurred. "After the second day of fasting," Geyelin reported, "the epileptic attacks ceased, and he had no attacks in the ensuing year." Geyelin reported seeing two other patients, also treated by Dr. Conklin, who, after fasting, had been seizure free for 2 and 3 years. He further reported that he had fasted 26 of his own patients with epilepsy, 18 of whom showed marked improvement and two remained seizure free for more than 1 year. Dr. Geyelin stated that the best length of fasting was 20 days. This was the first U.S. report of the benefits of fasting for epilepsy.

It is of historical interest that the father of Hugh Conklin's patient, "HLH," reported by Geyelin, was Charles Howland, a wealthy New York corporate lawyer and the brother of Dr. John Howland, Professor of Pediatrics at the Johns Hopkins Hospital and director of the newly opened Harriet Lane Home for Invalid Children at Johns Hopkins in Baltimore.

In 1919, Charles Howland gave his brother $5,000 to find a scientific basis for the success of the starvation treatment of his son. These funds were used to create the first U.S. laboratories to study fluid and electrolyte balances in fasting children. Although these studies shed light on fluid and electrolyte balance in children and were the start of the investigational careers of many great pediatric physicians, Howland and his team were unsuccessful in finding how starvation helped to control seizures.

The following year, in 1922, Dr. Conklin published his belief that epilepsy was caused by intoxication of the brain by toxins coming from the Peyer's patches of the intestine. He had developed his "fasting treatment" program in order to put the patient's intestine at complete rest. He stated, "I deprive the patient of all food, giving nothing but water over as long a period of time as he is physically able to stand it . . . Some will fast for 25 days and come to the office one or more times every day for (osteopathic) treatment."

Dr. William Lennox, considered by many to be the father of U.S. pediatric epilepsy, writes of Conklin's fasting treatment as the origin of the ketogenic diet. Lennox, who later reviewed Geyelin's records, reports long-term freedom from seizures occurred in 15 of 79 of Geyelin's fasted children (18%).

During the early 1920s, phenobarbital and bromides were the only seizure medications available. Reports that fasting could cure seizures were therefore exciting and promised new hope for children and adults with epilepsy. These reports prompted a flurry of clinical and research activity at many centers.

THE DISCOVERY OF THE KETOGENIC DIET

Prolonged periods of starvation to hopefully control epilepsy were understandably unpleasant. The first article suggesting that a diet high in fat and low in carbohydrate might simulate the metabolic effects of starvation and its effects on epilepsy was published on July 27, 1921 in the *Mayo Clinic Bulletin*. Dr. Russell Wilder from the Mayo Clinic, its author, proposed that "the benefits of fasting could be . . . obtained if ketonemia was produced by other means. . . . Ketone bodies are formed from fat and protein whenever a disproportion exists between the amount of fatty acid and the amount of sugar." "It is possible," Wilder wrote, "to provoke ketogenesis by feeding diets which are rich in fats and low in carbohydrates. It is proposed to try the effects of such diets on a series of epileptics."

The calculation of such a diet, and the effectiveness of Wilder's proposed *ketogenic* diet, was reported by Dr. Peterman from the Mayo Clinic in 1924. Peterman's diet used 1 gram of protein per kilogram of body weight in children (less in adults) and restricted the patient's intake of carbohydrates to 10 to 15 grams per day; the remainder of the calories were ingested as fat.

The individual's caloric requirement was calculated based on the basal metabolic rate plus 50%. This is virtually identical to the standard ketogenic diet used today, almost 100 years later.

Of the first 17 patients treated by Peterman with this new diet, 10 (59%) became seizure free, nine on the diet alone. Four others (23%) had marked improvement, two were lost to follow-up, and one discontinued the diet. The following year, Peterman reported 37 patients treated over a period of 2.5 years: 19 (51%) were seizure free and 13 (35%) were markedly improved. These initial reports were rapidly followed by others from many centers. The currently used standard protocol for calculating and initiating the ketogenic diet was well discussed in a book by Dr. Fritz Talbot from Harvard published in October 1930. In many ways, Talbot's book was the first true ketogenic diet book (long before this book's first edition!).

Reports of the effectiveness of the diet appeared throughout the late 1920s and 1930s. In these reports, subjects varied and patients were followed up for varying lengths of time. As shown in Table 4.1, early reports of the diet even through the 1970s showed that 60% to 75% of children generally had a greater than 50% decrease in their seizures, 30% to 40% of these had a greater than 90% decrease in the seizure frequency, and 20% to 40% had little or no seizure control.

The ketogenic diet was widely used throughout the 1930s. In fact, the diet was widely used for conditions such as absence (petit mal) epilepsy, which has recently been rediscovered as a type of seizure that responds well to the diet. It was also used in adults. After the discovery of phenytoin (Dilantin®) in 1937, the attention of physicians and investigators turned from studies of the mechanisms of action and efficacy of the diet toward finding and evaluating new anticonvulsant medications. The era of pharmacologic treatment for epilepsy

TABLE 4.1

Reports From the Literature on Seizure Control Using the Ketogenic Diet

			SEIZURE CONTROL		
AUTHOR	YEAR	NUMBER OF PATIENTS	>90%	50%-90%	<50%
Peterman	1925	36	51%	35%	23%
Helmholz	1927	91	31%	23%	46%
Wilkens	1937	30	24%	21%	50%
Livingston	1954	300	43%	34%	22%
Huttenlocher[a]	1971	12	–	50%	50%

[a]Medium chain triglyceride diet.

had begun. When compared with the promise of the medications, the diet was thought to be relatively difficult to adhere to (versus taking a pill every day), rigid, and expensive.

As new anticonvulsant medications became available, the diet was used less frequently. As fewer children were placed on the ketogenic diet, fewer dietitians were trained in its rigors and nuances. Therefore, the diets prescribed were often less precise, less ketogenic, and less effective than they had been in previous years.

The diet, after years of popularity from 1920 to 1950, fell out of favor as new drugs came to market.

In an effort to make the ketogenic diet more palatable and less rigid, a form of the diet was developed using medium-chain triglyceride (MCT) oil (more about this in Chapter 27). The MCT diet has been recently revised by Dr. Elizabeth Neal and colleagues in the United Kingdom to lower the amount of MCT oil and has shown fewer side effects as a result.

Experiences such as these led to the widespread opinion that dietary treatment for epilepsy was cumbersome and difficult to tolerate. Many physicians also erroneously believed that parents and children would not be able to comply with the diet. Medicines, and the promise of even more effective medicines on the horizon, were further disincentives to using the ketogenic diet.

THE START OF THE MODERN ERA AND RENEWED INTEREST IN THE DIET

The ketogenic diet continued to be used six to eight times per year at Johns Hopkins Hospital beginning in the 1970s, under Dr. Samuel Livingston and his dietitian, Millie Kelly. Its use was mentioned in our papers on treating difficult seizure problems. Other centers in the United States used it as well, but not very frequently. It was not discussed at the American Epilepsy Society or perceived as serious medicine in textbooks.

In 1993, Charlie Abrahams, age 2, developed multiple myoclonic seizures, generalized tonic seizures, and tonic–clonic seizures that were refractory to many medications. As his father, Jim Abrahams, wrote in the initial foreword to this book, "thousands of seizures and countless medications later," when physicians were unable to help, Mr. Abrahams began to search for answers on his own and found reference to the ketogenic diet and to our hospital. Charlie was brought to Johns Hopkins on November 17, 1993, and within 1 week of starting the ketogenic diet, Charlie's seizures were completely controlled, his electroencephalogram (EEG) returned to normal, his development resumed, and he no longer suffered the side effects of antiepileptic medications.

Charlie's father wanted to know why no one had told him about the diet before. He found references to the high success rates discussed previously

Figure 4.1. Charlie Abrahams in April 1994–5 months after starting the ketogenic diet.

and determined that this information should be readily available so that other families of children with epilepsy could become aware of the ketogenic diet.

Charlie's father was a filmmaker and used his talents to expand awareness and the use of the ketogenic diet. He created The Charlie Foundation and funded the initial publication of this book. Charlie's story was covered in national magazines and on national television, starting with the news magazine show *Dateline NBC*, further raising awareness of the diet. After the *Dateline* program about Charlie aired in 1994, 1500 copies of the first printing of this book were immediately sold out.

When we told Jim Abrahams that Johns Hopkins could not conceivably handle the number of patients who would want the diet after the *Dateline* show aired, Jim and The Charlie Foundation funded five pediatric epilepsy centers to allow potential patients to come to Johns Hopkins for a meeting to plan a joint protocol to reevaluate the efficacy of the diet in children failing modern medications. Over the next few years, The Charlie Foundation also underwrote conferences to train physicians and dietitians from medical centers nationwide. Many more medical centers began to use the diet.

Jim created the made-for-TV film *First Do No Harm,* starring Meryl Streep, dramatizing the ketogenic diet. He also filmed our educational materials and produced videos teaching the diet to parents, dietitians, and physicians, and made the tapes available to those audiences. Meanwhile, Nancy Abrahams spent tireless hours coaching and helping other parents during their difficult times with the diet. She spoke at countless parent meetings and conferences, and she provided support for those in need.

After Charlie remained seizure-free for 2 years, he was allowed to come off the diet, but several months later he had a few further seizures. He resumed the diet in January 1996, and he again became seizure-free on a modified form of the ketogenic diet. Charlie has now been seizure-free, medication-free, and off the diet for years. He is a funny, happy adult.

Without Jim and Nancy Abrahams's persistence and their dedication to making knowledge of the diet available to other parents, physicians, and the public, there is no doubt the ketogenic diet would likely not have been rediscovered so dramatically and would certainly not have received the resurgence

Figure 4.2. Charlie Abrahams in 2008 with Millicent Kelly, RD.

in popularity it now enjoys. Another charity, Matthew's Friends, was started in the United Kingdom shortly after, and has expanded to South Africa, Canada, and Holland (see Chapter 23 for more on support groups). Considering that most centers around the world started their ketogenic diet centers shortly after the 1998 study funded by The Charlie Foundation, the influence of the Foundation is undoubtedly global. The past 20 years of progress are certainly due to their help.

THE DIET HAS A RENAISSANCE (1994 TO PRESENT)

The 20 years since the founding of The Charlie Foundation has seen a rebirth in interest in the ketogenic diet. Four clinical diets are available today and there are many different ways to start the diet with countless ways to combine and adapt these diets. Adults are being initiated on dietary therapy more frequently than in previous decades. We have gone from one ketogenic diet paper published per year in the early 1990s to now one paper (or more) per week.

Perhaps the next most influential year in ketogenic diet history was 2008. First, the "Consensus Statement" was published in the journal *Epilepsia*, which brought together 26 international neurologists and dietitians expert in the use of dietary therapy to create guidelines for prescribing ketogenic diets. This statement has been referenced over 200 times by other journal articles to date. It represents a coming-together of experts to provide clear, rational advice to other keto centers. Second, two randomized, controlled studies were published (one in *Epilepsia* from our group at Hopkins, and one in *Lancet Neurology* from Great Ormond Street Hospital in London). Both studies showed the ketogenic diet was better than placebo/standard antiepileptic drugs (and showed that this kind of complicated study design could be executed successfully even with a diet vs. a drug). Lastly, the first international ketogenic diet conference was held in Phoenix, Arizona, in 2008. This meeting has traditionally brought together 300 to 400 ketogenic diet specialists to share research, ideas, and collaborate to advance the study of the ketogenic diet. It was held again in 2010 in Edinburgh, 2012 in Chicago, and 2014 in Liverpool. The 2016 meeting is in Banff (to coincide with the publication of this edition).

Today, the diet truly is at a "tipping point" in history. Studies now prove that it works: Research is moving past that to look instead at how best to (safely) provide the diet, which patients benefit the most, and also nonepilepsy uses such as cancer, autism, dementia, and migraine (see Section VIII).

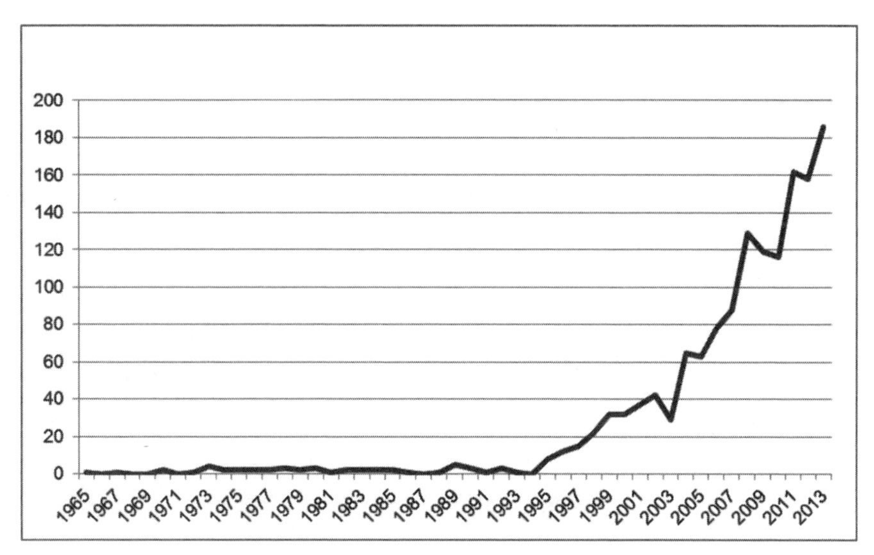

Figure 4.3. Publications over the years on the ketogenic diet, 1965 to 2014.

Figure 4.4. Organizing committee of the first international ketogenic diet conference in Phoenix, Arizona, 2008.

CHAPTER 5

Who Is a Candidate for the Ketogenic Diet?

Perhaps the most common question asked of us by parents and patients is whether or not we believe the ketogenic diet is likely to be helpful versus trying another medication (or surgery or vagus nerve stimulation [VNS]). Quoting the odds is helpful, but because everyone with epilepsy is different, is there a way to know who will respond to the diet and who will not? Most of the seizure medicines on the market now are initially used for partial (focal) seizures, and almost always in adults first. As most parents are no doubt aware, as time and familiarity with new drugs occur, these medicines are used not only for generalized seizures (which involve the entire brain all at once) but in young children as well. Sometimes figuring this out takes years. What about the ketogenic diet, which has been used for nearly a century now? For whom does it work best? When should it be tried? Who is it unlikely to help? The answers to these questions are becoming clearer as the diet is being used more. In the first edition of this book the answer was we didn't know. That is not true today!

WHEN IN THE COURSE OF EPILEPSY?

In general, the diet is used for people with intractable seizures, often occurring daily, that have failed at least two medications for seizure control. Does this mean the diet wouldn't be helpful earlier? What about if seizures are only monthly, but medications aren't working? Evidence would suggest the diet may still be helpful. For more information about using the diet as first-line treatment, read the next chapter.

When compared to many anticonvulsants, especially those of the *older* generation (e.g., phenobarbital, Dilantin®, Depakote®, Tegretol®), the diet, in our opinion, has a better side-effect profile. When compared to many of the newer drugs, the diet is certainly better established with more data, especially in kids, to support its use. We tell families that the diet is likely to work 50% of the time, with 10% to 15% of children becoming seizure free within 6 months. Trying drug number 3 or 4 is likely to work 30% of the time with 5% becoming seizure free.

The diet is about twice as likely to work for epilepsy as trying another new medication (after two to three medications have failed).

So why not try the diet? There are certainly some reasons against it, including the difficulty of the diet (no one would argue it's easier to take a pill or teaspoon of liquid medication). Many of the second- (and now third-) generation drugs have fewer (not zero) side effects than earlier drugs. With so many new drugs on the market, it's tough not to say "Why not give this new drug a try?," and we often receive e-mails and phone calls from neurologists referring patients for the diet who will say to us "How about trying a new drug first and then the diet if it doesn't work?" These concerns are real and there isn't a right or wrong answer. It really comes down to you and your family in deciding when it's the right time to try a dietary therapy.

WHO IS LIKELY TO BE A SUPER-RESPONDER TO THE DIET?

In general, we don't know for sure but we have our clues and hints from what other doctors have published so far. Parents often come to Johns Hopkins after they see a video, television special, or newspaper article that highlights an amazing "miracle" responder to the ketogenic diet. These children start the diet, are seizure-free within 1 to 2 weeks (sometimes after the fast), and are medication-free within months. Although wonderful to take care of, these children are not the norm (they are probably only about 10% of our patients on the diet). Based on our information from 1998, more than one quarter of patients will have a 90% or greater reduction in seizures, but all seizure types appear to be equally likely to respond. Children of a younger age tend to do slightly better as well.

A few years ago, we looked at 3 years of ketogenic diet patients to see who the "super-responders" were. We found out the same thing as we did many years ago: All seizure types, ages, weights, and severities of seizures of children were likely to be miracle responders. The only exceptions were children with *just* complex partial (focal) seizures, many of whom were possible surgery candidates but chose to try the diet first: They did not usually end up being seizure free immediately. This is not to say that many children with partial seizures don't do well on the diet; many had 90% or greater seizure reductions and were able to lower medicines, but the diet is rarely a cure in this situation. In this situation, if the diet is tried and ineffective after 3 to 6 months, and surgery is an option, we would suggest surgery be looked into at an epilepsy center.

In the earlier study, there were only a few children with Doose syndrome (myoclonic-astatic epilepsy). Our suspicion is that if we did this study again, now years later, this syndrome would turn out to be one in which children are likely to be super-responders. In fact, we often tell families of children in which this is a possible diagnosis that the response to the ketogenic diet is the best "test" for Doose syndrome we know. Keep reading for more information about Doose syndrome.

Today some centers are looking at genetics (not just for conditions like glucose transporter-1 [GLUT-1] deficiency syndrome) but for other findings that would suggest who is likely to be a super-responder. In addition, several groups have found that a quick improvement in the EEG will predict a longer-term response to the diet clinically as well. However, the best predictor right now is still the epilepsy condition. This is the reason why it's *so* important to figure out why a person has epilepsy in the first place.

SPECIAL DISORDERS

We have realized that there are some conditions that are very responsive to dietary therapy (and affected individuals should be started on the diet as soon as possible). Some of this research is from our center, some from other centers, and some combined. This list (Table 5.1) is by no means complete but does influence when we decide to try the diet earlier with some patients. These conditions are perhaps the most important.

TABLE 5.1

Conditions in Which the Diet Is Especially Likely to Work

- GLUT-1 deficiency syndrome
- Pyruvate dehydrogenase deficiency
- Myoclonic-astatic epilepsy (Doose syndrome)
- Infantile spasms (West syndrome)
- Dravet syndrome
- Tuberous sclerosis complex
- Rett syndrome
- Mitochondrial disease
- Children and adults receiving mostly formula

Infantile Spasms (West Syndrome)

In 2002, we published our experience using the diet for infants with one of the most terrifying epilepsy disorders: infantile spasms (West syndrome). In this condition, infants approximately 6 months of age develop the sudden onset of clustering body jerks, often when coming out of sleep, with a chaotic EEG and occasional loss of developmental skills. Treatments include steroids (ACTH or prednisolone) and vigabatrin, but these drugs have serious side effects, and vigabatrin requires lots of paperwork to prescribe nowadays. Knowing the diet can be provided via an infant formula and has fewer side effects, it's a natural choice. We found that nearly half of the 23 children we had treated, usually those with tough-to-control infantile spasms, had a 90% or better response, improvement on EEG, and better development by 6 months. Infants under age 1 year and who had failed no more than three drugs did better.

Based on this, we have now more than doubled our use of the ketogenic diet for infantile spasms and are seeing the same results—we had treated 104 children with infantile spasms by 2010 when we updated our results. About two thirds will have a >90% reduction in spasms. The earlier they were treated, the better. This is probably now the most common reason we start children on the diet at Johns Hopkins Hospital. We are also using the diet for new-onset infantile spasms (rather than steroids or vigabatrin). More on this in the next chapter.

Myoclonic-Astatic Epilepsy (Doose Syndrome)

In this disorder, children (often ages 3–5 years) present with the sudden onset of head drop seizures and occasionally cognitive decline. Although many neurologists can confuse this syndrome with Lennox–Gastaut syndrome (LGS), the EEG often shows periods of normal background, making this less likely. Traditional medicines such as Depakote® and Keppra® are only occasionally useful. We have used the ketogenic diet for 50 to 60 children over the past 20 years with typically dramatic success. Many patients with likely Doose epilepsy have also been similar responders on the modified Atkins diet, too. Dr. Douglas Nordli from Chicago and Dr. Sudha Kessler from Philadelphia have also seen this improvement with patients having Doose epilepsy, and both have published their experience in medical journals. It is not clear why children with Doose syndrome do so well with dietary therapy, but finding that out may someday help determine why the diet works. For more information, go to doosesyndrome.org.

Tuberous Sclerosis Complex

In a combined study from Johns Hopkins and the Massachusetts General Hospital, we found 12 children with tuberous sclerosis complex (multiple brain tubers, ash-leaf spots on the skin, heart and kidney tubers, epilepsy) that were started on the ketogenic diet did very well. Many had a history of infantile spasms in the past, but none at the time of starting the diet. All but one child had half their seizures improve, and half had >90% improvement. Five children even had several seizure-free months. Although there are a limited number of patients, Dr. Elizabeth Thiele and our group agree that the ketogenic diet is a good option for patients with tuberous sclerosis complex. We have used it as well for infantile spasms, but mostly after vigabatrin (which works extremely well for tuberous sclerosis) has been unsuccessfully tried. Interestingly, at least in our experience, having this condition also made it more likely for seizures to come back in those children who became seizure free on the diet (sometimes years later). In that way, it's possible that although the diet is a big help for tuberous sclerosis, it may be a more long-term treatment than for Doose syndrome or certainly infantile spasms.

GLUT-1 Deficiency Syndrome

In this rare condition, the molecule that allows glucose to cross into the brain to be used as fuel is missing. Children will often have seizures and cognitive delay until this is recognized, most often by noticing a very low glucose level in the spinal fluid after a spinal tap. In recent years, the availability of the genetic test for this (SLC2A1) has led to children with early-onset absence epilepsy (under age 3 years when it starts) to be recognized as occasionally due to GLUT-1 deficiency. Some children as well have been diagnosed due to a movement disorder (ataxia) with no seizures!

Logically, if the body cannot use glucose, then fat makes sense as a better alternative fuel. The ketogenic and modified Atkins diets are considered the best therapies for people with GLUT-1. Although other treatments are under investigation, including one using triheptanoin, the diet is still the gold standard treatment. More information about this disorder can be found on the Internet at www.g1dfoundation.org and in Chapter 6.

Dravet Syndrome

Formerly known as severe myoclonic epilepsy of infancy, Dravet syndrome is due to mutations in the gene for SCN1A. Children often present with seizures due to fever or heat in the first year of life, which eventually become prolonged. Developmental delay also occurs and medications are only partially helpful. The use of cannabis in a child with Dravet syndrome was profiled on CNN and has brought this condition to many people's attention. The ketogenic diet can be extremely helpful in reducing several kinds of seizures associated with this condition. For more information, see www.dravetfoundation.org.

Lennox-Gastaut Syndrome (LGS)

Perhaps no other condition is associated more with using the ketogenic diet than LGS. LGS may occur after infantile spasms and leads to frequent, often daily, drop, stiffening, and absence seizures. The diet has been used for this condition for many decades, but it was only in recent years that its true benefit was described. In a study from 2012, about 50% of children will have 50%

reduction in seizures (similar to overall seizure reduction with the diet) but only 1% stopped seizing entirely (less than overall). The diet can often lead to medication reduction, which is very important in LGS. For more information, see www.lgsfoundation.org.

Formula-Fed (Gastrostomy-Tube Fed) Infants and Children

Perhaps one of the easiest groups of children to place on the ketogenic diet is children who do not eat solid foods. If the diet is given just as liquids, it avoids all compliance issues. Infants on formula or who are breastfeeding will need to directly switch to one of several ketogenic formulas (see Chapter 8 for instructions), which can then be continued for months to years. As infants turn into toddlers, small amounts of solid ketogenic baby foods can be introduced after 1 to 2 months. Children that are fed using gastrostomy tubes (G-tubes) can also be started on the diet without compliance issues. In a study performed at Johns Hopkins, since 1998 more than a quarter of all patients started on the diet did so using formula only. Nearly 60% had a >90% improvement in seizures, double the average ketogenic diet patient. In any child in an intensive care setting for epilepsy, the diet can be easily started or continued via a temporary nasogastric tube.

In one study, children receiving all liquid ketogenic diets were twice as likely to have a >90% seizure reduction.

The formulas available are very palatable with a taste similar to most other infant formulas. It is easy to calculate for the dietitian and can be soy-based, milk-based, or even hypoallergenic. There is also less room for error and less education involved for parents. The presence of a gastrostomy tube also allows medications to be provided without carbohydrate sweeteners or flavoring. Patients who become ill on the ketogenic diet occasionally have acidosis and dehydration, but having a gastrostomy tube helps avoid this. Lastly, insurance companies often cover formula for children with gastrostomy tubes because it is being used as a medical therapy rather than for solely nutritional purposes.

OTHER CONDITIONS

There are several other conditions not described in detail here for which the diet may be very helpful. They include juvenile myoclonic epilepsy, absence epilepsy, Rett syndrome, and mitochondrial disorders. In these conditions, several articles have reported the ketogenic diet as leading to superb results. There are conditions, however, for which the diet is not a good idea. These conditions are presented in Table 5.2, which is reproduced in part from the 2009 consensus statement.

TABLE 5.2

Contraindications to the Use of the Ketogenic Diet

Contraindications
Absolute
Carnitine deficiency (primary)
Carnitine palmitoyltransferase (CPT) I or II deficiency
Carnitine translocase deficiency
β-oxidation defects
Medium-chain acyl dehydrogenase deficiency (MCAD)
Long-chain acyl dehydrogenase deficiency (LCAD)
Short-chain acyl dehydrogenase deficiency (SCAD)
Long-chain 3-hydroxyacyl-CoA deficiency
Medium-chain 3-hydroxyacyl-CoA deficiency
Pyruvate carboxylase deficiency
Porphyria
Relative
Inability to maintain adequate nutrition
Surgical focus identified by neuroimaging and video-EEG monitoring
Parent or caregiver noncompliance

DOES AGE MATTER?

Probably not, but there is a slight trend toward improved seizure control in younger children (see Table 5.3). Younger children often can maintain high ketosis for long periods and compliance is less of a problem. We feel, as do

TABLE 5.3

The Effect of Age on Outcomes of the Ketogenic Diet

AGE AT START OF DIET	NO. INITIATING DIET	>50% CONTROL AT 12 MONTHS
<2 years	*N* = 27	59% (1 seizure free)
2-5 years	*N* = 50	56% (4 seizure free)
5-8 years	*N* = 32	50% (4 seizure free)
8-12 years	*N* = 25	40% (1 seizure free)
>12 years	*N* = 16	31% (1 seizure free)
Total	*N* = 150	50% (11 seizure free)

Source: Adapted from Freeman JM, Vining EPG, Pillas DJ, et al. The efficacy of the ketogenic diet—1998: a prospective evaluation of intervention in 150 children. *Pediatrics* 1998;102:1358–1363.

other doctors, that infants may be one of the ideal groups for the diet for this reason. They certainly need extra care due to growth issues, but can do very well on the diet.

What about adolescents and adults? Most centers will tell parents that the diet is impossible to maintain for a teenager. In a study from both our group and Dr. James Wheless's at the University of Texas at Houston, we combined our teenage populations on the diet (45 teens in total) and found that compliance was very good, seizure reduction was similar to younger children, and side effects were low. Of the participants, 44% were able to stick it out for a year. Menstrual irregularities happened in almost half of teenage girls, but this is tough to separate out from the normal irregularities of this age and the effects of medications. In general, at present we tend to use the modified Atkins diet for most teenagers.

Adults can also do very well with the diet, typically using the modified Atkins diet. More information on this special age group is in Section IV.

There is no perfect age at which the diet is more likely (or less likely) to work.

TIME COMMITMENT

One of the only things that truly will lead to diet failure is a lack of commitment and time to make it work, which can be both the fault of the family and the physicians. The diet requires a significant investment of the *entire* family to spend a week to start and learn the diet in the hospital, calculate meal plans and weigh foods, and avoid cheating. A family in which the parents are divorced and one parent does not believe in the diet will nearly always be a ketogenic diet failure. Similarly, if grandparents or other caregivers do not agree that the diet is worth trying and make meals for children that will sabotage the diet, obviously this will not work. We try to have families demonstrate this commitment by (a) reading this book, (b) starting to cut carbohydrates and eat less "junk food" in advance, and (c) e-mailing us information we need to start the diet (3-day food records, labs, medical records, etc.). Good information about getting ready for the diet can also be found in the parent-written book *Fighting Back with Fat.*

Giving the diet at least 1 to 2 months to work before making any big medication changes is also crucial. Close communication with the physician and dietitian is not only a good idea, it's mandatory to make the diet work. The hospital team also must spend considerable time and energy to make the diet program effective with e-mail and phone contact with families, handling illnesses and providing support, and watching and monitoring for both expected and unexpected problems. It's sad when the diet is stopped by a family or adult and we feel it wasn't given a good shot. Often it is never tried again.

CHAPTER 6

Can the Diet Be Used Before Medications?

Despite its proven efficacy in the treatment of so-called intractable childhood epilepsy (seizure disorders that have failed to respond to the proper use of three or more anticonvulsant medications), the ketogenic diet is still regarded as a "treatment of last resort" by many neurologists and other physicians who manage seizure patients. As the diet gains more popularity around the world, studies have shown that some of the old myths about how the diet can be used are incorrect.

We now know that the ketogenic diet can be helpful in the treatment of both generalized and partial seizures, although it is less likely to be as completely effective in the localization-related (partial) epilepsies. It can be successfully implemented in a wide range of ages, including adults, without any clear influence of age on outcome. There is value in using dietary therapy short term in children who may ultimately require surgical intervention, especially when they are young children. And it can be helpful for absence epilepsy and other syndromes not seen as "severe"—the diet is still helpful for those conditions.

The ketogenic diet can be used as "first-line" therapy in certain situations, and actually there is agreement that it is the "treatment of choice" in specific epilepsy syndromes. The two prominent examples of first-line treatment are the glucose transporter-1 (GLUT-1) deficiency and pyruvate dehydrogenase complex deficiency (PDCD) syndromes. GLUT-1 deficiency syndrome is a rare disorder in which the brain cannot get its necessary energy through glucose metabolites because they cannot cross the "blood–brain barrier." By maximizing the body's level of ketones in a controlled and healthy way through the use of the ketogenic diet, a new energy source is made available to the brain so that the brain can function properly. Recent studies would suggest that the diet may not be a lifelong treatment for GLUT-1, and it could possibly be stopped in adolescence. About 80% of children on dietary treatment for GLUT-1 deficiency are seizure-free.

PDCD syndrome is a rare neurodegenerative disorder, usually starting in infancy, which is associated with abnormalities of the body's citric acid cycle. Proper production of carbohydrates is interfered with, and there is a resultant deficit in energy throughout the body, accompanied by a dangerous buildup of lactic acid. The result is damage to the brainstem.

In these two illnesses, the ketogenic diet acts as both an anticonvulsant treatment, as well as possibly treating other, nonepileptic, manifestations of the underlying metabolic derangement. Early consideration and confirmation of these two diagnoses offer the possibility of avoiding all or at least some of the devastating lifelong developmental conditions resulting from a disease, injury, or other trauma.

The evidence is similarly strong for the treatment of two other conditions: infantile spasms (West syndrome) and myoclonic-astatic epilepsy (Doose syndrome). Both conditions were included in Table 1 of the 2009 expert consensus statement on the ketogenic diet as "indications" for its use. For these conditions, paper after paper suggest the diet should *not* be a last resort.

West syndrome (infantile spasms) is one of the most studied conditions, with lots of information available. About half of the children who are started on the diet will have about 90% of the spasms go away, often for many months. What is most interesting is that the sooner the diet is started the better the outcome. Knowing this, why not use it first? We have done that—data from our center show that there is no difference in the time it takes to seizure freedom when comparing treatment with adrenocorticotrophic hormone (ACTH) versus the ketogenic diet. While the EEG improved and normalized faster with ACTH at 1 month in spasm-free babies, there was no difference at 2 to 5 months. Most significantly, the incidence of side effects was lower in the babies treated with the ketogenic diet, as well as the risk of the spasms coming back. We now use the ketogenic diet routinely here at Johns Hopkins as a first-line therapy (and not just for tough-to-control infantile spasms) and have done so in about 25 babies. Our experience suggests that, about half the time, it works within 10 to 14 days. If the diet is not helping, we suggest immediately stopping and moving on to steroids.

Figures 6.1 and 6.2. Carson Harris, one of our babies with new-onset infantile spasms at 6 months, was treated with the diet alone, and today, is now normal and off the diet. (See Chapter 23 for more information about The Carson Harris Foundation.) Courtesy of The Carson Harris Foundation.

Doose syndrome (myoclonic-astatic epilepsy) is an epilepsy syndrome of early childhood that is often resistant to medication and where the ketogenic diet offers a combination of virtually immediate seizure relief and long-term control. The Doose syndrome clinical and EEG pattern is clearly recognizable. Although up to this point in time medications are being used initially (typically Keppra® and Depakote®), the ketogenic diet may work best and then often allows the rapid discontinuation of medications, with seizure freedom even when the diet is stopped after 2 years. Multiple studies have shown that the diet is the *best* treatment for this condition, and nearly all these articles comment that the diet should be considered "sooner" versus as a last resort. At our center, we mention the diet as soon as the first visit and at times offer it before medications. If one drug fails, especially Depakote®, we strongly push the diet as the next choice. In fact, many ketogenic diet neurologists have suggested in meetings that if a study was ever done to test the ketogenic diet versus a new medication, Doose syndrome would be the perfect condition to use for the study (and we think the diet would win!).

There is also recently published research that reviews the usefulness of the ketogenic diet in status epilepticus, an acute life-threatening state where the brain is in a persistent state of continuous seizures. Early use of the ketogenic diet administered via gastric-tube (G-tube) feeding may be a rational therapy after one or two drugs have failed. In this case specifically, the diet is "easy" to do and therefore often considered earlier by neurologists, even those not as comfortable with typical, solid-food ketogenic diets (for more on formulas and calculating the diet with them, see Chapters 8 and 29). Seizures from tuberous sclerosis complex and Rett syndrome can be very difficult to manage with medication, and there appears to be a role for very early use of ketogenic diet therapy once those diagnoses are confirmed and seizures begin.

There are some barriers in the medical system to using the ketogenic diet before trying medication. First, dietitians and neurologists have to change their mindset about the diet and consider it an appropriate "emergency" treatment option. That means dropping everything to start the diet and not putting these children on a waiting list that might take months. This may even require that a dietitian and neurologist come in on a weekend! Insurance companies may disagree that the diet is an appropriate first-line treatment, and families might have to accept a financial burden if that happens. In these situations, we may forego the admission or more typically try the modified Atkins diet—these options avoid the insurance situation. Second, families (or adults trying the diet) would have to be patient (sometimes for months) and give the diet a chance to work. Although data would suggest that for infantile spasms the diet works within a week or two, in our experience the family is often very impatient if there is no benefit within days. The family would also have to understand that if the diet did *not* work, then they'd have to stop and move on to medications (especially for new onset West syndrome where time is of the essence). Similarly for some other epilepsy conditions such as childhood absence epilepsy, in which we've tried the diet first-line, the temptation to start one of the 20 to 30 anticonvulsant drugs with usually good efficacy (in the range of 50%–70% successful) is strong, especially if the diet is hard to follow. There isn't much published evidence that the diet is better than drugs in most of these epilepsies, so in our experience families eventually tire of the diet and move on to medications. Lastly, the education process for starting the diet would have to be shortened and streamlined. If not, a 3-day admission for education would certainly seem much more difficult than a 1-minute signing of a prescription. This book may help, along with the Internet and other resources, but the diet will need to be made easier and quicker for sure.

What is clear is that today, it is definitely not appropriate to think of the ketogenic diet only as a "last resort." Even if it is not being used first, it should be mentioned earlier in the treatment of epilepsy, certainly after two drugs have failed. At our center, we'll often mention it at the second or third visit as an option for children—something we keep "up our sleeves." Adults are increasingly reading about dietary therapy and asking about it before medications (see Section IV for details). By the time the seventh edition of this book is published, we suspect the diet will continue to be more widely used as an earlier therapy.

SECTION II

The Classic Ketogenic Diet

CHAPTER 7

Initiating the Ketogenic Diet: How Best to Do It?

At Johns Hopkins, initiating the ketogenic diet is a process, not an event. The journey begins before a child is accepted into the ketogenic diet program. For patients who have been seen in our pediatric epilepsy clinic, parents are informed about the diet, and the advantages and difficulties for their child are addressed. It is suggested that they read this book and become familiar with the diet before deciding to make the commitment. The Internet has become a huge resource for learning about recipes and foods, and making sure the diet is the right choice for a family.

Patients who live a distance from our center in Baltimore are asked to send the child's EEG and neuroimaging (head CT, MRI, etc.) reports and other medical records for review by the staff. Even those who live locally send records so we can review them and make sure the diet makes sense. In many cases, a 1-hour meeting between the neurologist and the family is incredibly important to make sure everyone understands (a) what the diet is, (b) what the commitment to the diet entails, and (c) what the expectations are for improvement in seizures, EEG, or medication reduction.

We have never had firm criteria for accepting or rejecting children for diet initiation at Johns Hopkins. In general, however:

- most children have more than weekly seizures (often daily);
- most children have abnormal EEGs;
- most families are willing to give the diet at least 3 months to work and everyone (including grandparents and other involved caregivers) is committed to try it;
- most children have tried at least two antiepileptic drugs without achieving seizure control (only on very rare occasions will we accept children whose seizures have been controlled but only at the expense of medication toxicity); and
- most parents have realistic goals and positive attitudes.

Because children with infantile spasms or Doose syndrome (a syndrome with drop seizures) may be more likely to respond to the diet than to medication, we are more likely to accept them for the diet earlier in the course of their epilepsy (read the previous chapter for more on this).

After being scheduled for diet initiation, parents are asked to keep a seizure calendar for the month before hospitalization and to read this book. We recommend that they tell their local child neurologist and pediatrician what is going to happen, especially if they live far away, because they are extended members of our team. Babysitters, caregivers, and even school nurses need to be on board for the journey.

Today, we *strongly* encourage that the families have e-mail access (for the often frequent e-mails to neurologists and dietitians) and Internet access (for KetoDietCalculator [see Chapter 10] and other websites). This allows for close monitoring of children starting the diet and rapid communication between the parents and the keto team. In some ways, in today's modern era, it's a requirement for starting the diet.

GETTING READY FOR THE DIET: THE KETOGENIC DIET TEAM

A *team* effort is needed to keep each child and family on track and help them to get through the challenges of the initiation and fine-tuning period. The ketogenic diet team at Johns Hopkins currently includes a physician and nurse practitioner, two dietitians, our parent support group, a pharmacist, a social worker, child life service, the floor charge nurse, and an office coordinator, who are all familiar with the diet. Each plays an important role in both initiating and maintaining the diet. This may not be the case at your ketogenic diet center and that may be perfectly fine, but at the very least, you need *both* a dietitian and neurologist to help you. The dietitian must allocate enough time not only to teach the diet while the family is in the hospital for diet initiation, but also to help the family with questions and dietary changes after discharge. Some medical centers also have a nurse or physician's assistant who can help the family through the many small crises that do not require medical attention.

If a center is going to start a child on the diet, it must also be prepared to adjust the diet and work with the family through the fine-tuning period for at least several months after discharge. We estimate that an average family requires 30 to 40 hours of dietary and illness counseling during the first year on the diet through e-mail and other correspondence. The child and family are, of course, essential partners in the keto team as well.

ADMISSION FOR THE START OF THE DIET

Growing evidence does suggest that the diet can be started on an outpatient basis, with families still coming in daily (sometimes with their child for clinic visits) to be educated and observed closely. This allows the child to sleep and eat at home, which is always more comfortable. However, even those centers that start the diet at home are very selective and only do this for very stable children, always without a fast.

At Johns Hopkins we still start the diet in the hospital for several reasons. If the child has a problem, there are nurses and doctors right there to help. It also allows for the intense hours of education to be planned and streamlined. We also believe the 3-day admission is a chance to get to know each family much better.

Lastly, we find that it is easier to admit four children simultaneously for initiation of the ketogenic diet than to admit one at a time. The advantage of admitting several patients at once is not only the efficiency of teaching the daily classes to multiple individuals, but also the support that families in the group can provide to each other as they go through the learning curve and the tribulations of diet initiation together. Without the group, there is a tendency for each parent to feel that he or she is the only person in the whole world who is burdened with such an overwhelming task. Families in each group often stay in contact after hospital discharge and are often brought back to clinic for follow-up on the same day. Groups are usually admitted every month, which allows us to get one group off to a good start before the next group comes in.

THE ADMISSION PROCESS

Just before admission to Johns Hopkins (other centers may have slightly different practices), a child is evaluated as an outpatient in clinic for an hour. Information is then e-mailed to the family to read and send back to us with details about food intake and medications.

Starting the diet at Johns Hopkins then requires 3 days of hospitalization at our center, often (but not always) beginning with fasting and followed by the gradual introduction of the high-fat meals (more on fasting later in this chapter). During the initial phase of the diet, which lasts several weeks, the body gradually adjusts to the smaller portions and lower calorie intake of the diet, as well as to digesting larger quantities of fat. Several weeks may be required for the child's energy level to return to normal. During this period, the family also becomes accustomed to weighing and measuring all meals and to reading food labels, and the child gradually becomes adjusted to eating only the foods of the diet and to not eating other foods.

THE FASTING DEBATE

Does the ketogenic diet need to be done in a hospital? Is fasting required to initiate the diet? There is debate about both of these questions. The ketogenic diet was originally begun by fasting patients for as long as 25 days and giving only water. In the 1960s, doctors at Johns Hopkins fasted patients until they had lost 10% of their body weight, usually for 10 days at the start of the diet. To make the diet more humane, we later developed a protocol using 48 hours of fasting, and then moved to our current protocol of just about 18 hours of fasting (from Sunday at midnight until Monday at 5 p.m.).

We believe that the initial fast is useful. The fasting jump-starts fat metabolism, resulting in rapid ketosis, and evidence suggests that the diet will work quicker (about 9 days on average) if a child is fasted. After 24 hours of fasting a child is usually in high ketosis, and any food looks good. Gradual introduction of the diet, starting with one third of the prescribed amount and increasing to two thirds and then to the full diet, enables the child to adjust to the fatty food and to achieve good ketosis (and often a reduction in seizures) before the child goes home.

Is a fast *absolutely* necessary? Definitely not. We review all children's cases before they are admitted and decide in advance if a fast is not safe. This may be because a child is felt to be too medically unstable, too young, or has significant issues with dehydration or nutrition to start. Good evidence from Dr. Bergqvist and her team at Children's Hospital of Philadelphia has shown that the long-term results are the same after 3 months, fasting or not. For most families, however, the quicker onset of seizure control is reassuring and a "bonus." We look at the 1-day fast as rapid "loading" of the diet. Remember, too, that fasting doesn't limit carbohydrate-free liquids, such as diet ginger ale, Fruit2O®, and water.

After fasting, we introduce the diet with a "keto shake" we like to call "eggnog," a milkshake-like meal that is easy to calculate and that may also be frozen into keto ice cream or microwaved into creamy scrambled eggs. KetoCal® can be used for the milkshake as well—more and more we are using this product in the diet. We have found that offering one third of a regular diet meal at initiation is unattractive: It amounts to a sprig of broccoli on one edge of a large plate, a thumbnail-size piece of turkey on another, and a swallow of cream. Initiating the diet with a keto shake avoids this unpleasant experience and also eliminates mistakes by our hospital's dietary service. However, there are some children who just do not like the "eggnog," no matter how hard we try! For those children, we may advance the diet to solid foods a bit earlier than the night before discharge (our usual time).

On Monday (the first day of admission) at 5 p.m. we start with half the typical daily calories (using the same ratio, often 4:1 for older children and 3:1 for those under age 2 years). On Tuesday at 5 p.m. the calories are doubled to "full" and solid foods (not the liquid) are provided by the kitchen. Children are then discharged Wednesday shortly after lunchtime. Some children do have to stay a bit longer if they are having difficulty with the diet, but this is extremely rare.

PROBLEMS WITH DIET INITIATION

When the previously described protocol is followed, most children do great. However, even without fasting, we have occasionally seen children become too ketotic and begin vomiting. Reversal of this condition requires a small amount of orange juice (about 30 ml or 1 ounce) to restore balance. We have rarely seen children develop symptomatic hypoglycemia (low glucose levels), with a decreased responsiveness, and sometimes pallor and sweating. This can also be reversed with a small amount of orange juice. These unusual but potentially serious side effects are one reason why we prefer to have children in the hospital during the diet initiation, where they can be closely observed and treated, if necessary.

Sometimes the problems at initiation are psychological. We are leery of making a parent deny food to their child for this prolonged period of time without the support of the medical staff and of other parents. Not feeding your child is very unnatural and difficult to do. We recognize not all children eat well in the hospital and often this improves when they are back in their own house (and own kitchen)!

We also find that the three-day hospital stay gives parents the opportunity to focus on the diet, to learn how to calculate meals, and to learn the purpose of what they will be doing. We feel that the intense (at least 2 hours per day) instructional process is a key element in our success. They also can meet other families starting the diet and make some contacts for support.

Have we tested each of these elements? No. Are they all necessary? We don't know. Can the diet be initiated without hospitalization? This has been done, too. If a family is able to come back for frequent classes, and they are more comfortable at home, on rare occasions we have started the diet on an outpatient basis without a fast, with good success. This is actually commonplace in some countries like England and some centers have developed a "low and slow" method in which they introduce the diet over days to weeks. However, for the vast majority of children, at Johns Hopkins we continue with the protocol that has brought our patients such success: 3 days of hospitalization with 3 to 4 hours of teaching each day.

On the third day after hospital admission (Wednesday typically), the child is discharged home. The families are ready for the journey ahead. This marks the end of the initiation process and the beginning of the *fine-tuning* phase.

FINE-TUNING THE DIET

Fine-tuning the ketogenic diet begins after discharge and is usually done by phone or e-mail. It involves the dietitians adjusting the various components of the diet—calories, liquids, fats, recipes, ketogenic ratios, and so forth—to achieve the best level of ketosis for optimal seizure control and best compliance. Fine-tuning can be an important part of achieving success on the diet for some children and is discussed further in Chapter 11.

SPECIAL EQUIPMENT TO HAVE BEFORE YOU START

The essential pieces of equipment for the ketogenic diet are a gram scale and reagent strips to test ketones in the urine. The urine ketone test strips are also important for the modified Atkins diet along with a carb-counting paperback book (or app). The rest of the items listed in this section are things that other patients and parents have found helpful.

Gram Scales

The gram scale is the main calculating tool for the diet, so it is extremely important. Parents must either buy a gram scale or make sure that the hospital plans to supply one for the family to take home. Providing this service at the hospital ensures that all parents get an accurate scale while saving them the time and effort of searching for one on their own. The scale should be accurate, should display weights in one-tenth gram increments, and should be portable.

Scales can be obtained through office supply or kitchen supply stores. Electronic digital scales, although slightly more expensive, are more accurate to the gram than manual scales. Examples of suitable scales include the Pelouse™ electronic postal scale and the Ohaus™ portable electronic postal scale. Many centers will provide these scales free of charge to families during the admission, so check first before you buy one.

Urinary Ketone Strips

Strips for testing ketone levels in the urine are commonly available in drugstores, often located with glucose tests used by diabetic patients (made by Bayer™ and available over the counter). These can be generic (e.g., Walgreens, CVS, Walmart) as well. A box of 50 keto strips should cost no more than $10 to $15 in the United States and can be less expensive if purchased in bulk or by using generic brands. Children on the ketogenic diet test urine periodically with these keto strips, usually daily the first week or two, then more sporadically. We ask our families to bring a box of keto strips with them to the hospital for the admission week.

Optional Equipment That May Be Useful

Parents have found a variety of equipment helpful while their children are on the ketogenic diet. The following is a list gathered from many parents. It is meant as a source of ideas. All of this equipment is optional. Parents may buy these supplies as needed:

- Large collection of small plastic storage containers
- Bendable straws for drinking every drop
- Sippy cups for smaller children
- Screw-top plastic beverage containers
- Small rubber spatulas to be used as plate cleaners
- 1-, 2-, 4-, and 6-ounce plastic cups
- Measuring cup marked with milliliters or a graduated cylinder for weighing and measuring

- 10-ml syringe
- Pyrex custard dishes for microwave cooking and freezing meals
- Ice pop molds
- 6-in. nonstick skillet for sautéing individual portions with easy cleanup
- Travel cooler and/or insulated bag (useful to take home keto shakes from the hospital)
- One or two small thermoses for school and travel
- Toothpicks for picking up morsels of food to make eating fun
- Blender
- Milkshake mixing wand or small hand beater
- Portable dual-burner electric camping stove for trips
- Masking tape for labels
- Microwave oven

To repeat, it is not necessary to own a lot of equipment before starting the diet. This list simply contains items that families have found helpful. Parents will gain more insight as to what equipment they will need as well as specific brands of food that are acceptable during their in-hospital ketogenic diet education. The only supplies that are absolutely necessary before starting the diet are a scale that measures in grams (to weigh foods) and strips for testing ketone levels in the urine, which may be purchased or obtained from the hospital.

SPECIAL FOODS

Heavy Whipping Cream

The fat and carbohydrate content of available cream will affect the calculation of the diet, so it is important to find out what is available in a given neighborhood and to tell the dietitian before the child's diet is calculated. Most are 36% fat. Make sure that there is no sugar added!

If you have any doubts about the macronutrient content (fat, carbohydrate, and protein) of your local cream, call the dairy directly. Dairies are required by law to know the fat percentage of the cream they supply. Remember, labeling laws do not require companies to list anything less than 1 gram of carbohydrate, protein, or fat, although fractional grams can affect the ketogenic diet! Once you find an acceptable brand, stick with it. Some local dairies will help to ensure that your local store stocks large containers of heavy whipping cream. Call your local dairy if you have any questions. We are indebted to Wawa dairies in the mid-Atlantic area, as they have provided heavy whipping cream free-of-charge for several years to families of children on the ketogenic diet. If you live in an area that has Wawa dairies, make sure to let your dietitian know.

OTHER FOODS AND FLAVORINGS

Many parents use flavorings to make the diet more fun for kids. These include the following:

- Baking chocolate
- Fruit-flavored, sugar-free, caffeine-free diet sodas or waters
- Pure flavoring extracts, such as vanilla, almond, lemon, maple, coconut, and chocolate. Make certain that they are pure, and check for alcohol content. Pure flavorings may be ordered from Bickford Flavorings
- Sugar-free flavored gelatin such as Jell-O or Royal
- Nonstick spray such as Pam or Mazola No-Stick for cooking
- Carbohydrate-free, calorie-free sweeteners. Saccharin (1/4 grain tablets of pure saccharin) is fine, despite some parents concern about artificial sweeteners. In fact, these sweeteners are often very important to maintaining a child's compliance and making foods more normal. Splenda and Stevia are also okay; liquid versions of these are probably best

This list, like the equipment list, is intended as a source of ideas, not a must-buy-right-away order. The rest of the diet ingredients should be pure, fresh, simple foods: lean meat, fish, poultry, bacon, eggs, cheese, fruit, vegetables, butter, mayonnaise, and canola or olive oil.

READ THE LABEL (OFTEN)! When using processed foods be sure to read the label carefully every time. Manufacturers often change the formulations of their products without prior notice. Therefore, each time you buy a processed food product, even if you have used it before, you must read the label very carefully. Remember that labeling laws do not require disclosure of macronutrient contents less than 1 gram. Call the manufacturer if you have any questions.

BEWARE OF HIDDEN CARBOHYDRATES

Pay close attention to any foods or medicines that may contain carbohydrates. Nonsugar carbohydrates include mannitol, sorbitol, dextrin, and many ingredients ending in "-ose," such as maltose, lactose, fructose, sucrose, dextrose, or Polycose®. All of these are carbohydrates and can possibly be broken down into glucose. They should be used sparingly when on the diet, and on the modified Atkins diet we calculate these "sugar alcohols" as part of the daily carbohydrate limit. Many foods, candies, and gums that are billed as "sugar-free" are NOT carbohydrate-free and cannot be used on the ketogenic diet. When in doubt, avoid it.

Consuming carbohydrates can lower ketosis, which does not always cause breakthrough seizures and often the children do fine without problems, but it can cause seizures. The good news is that when isolated breakthrough seizures occur, they nearly always can be eliminated again once the source is traced and removed.

MEDICATIONS

Medications play an important role in the ultimate success of the ketogenic diet. Appendix A gets into more detail about this topic. Most children remain on antiepileptic medications (usually lower doses or fewer medications, however) while on the diet. Starches and sugars are frequently used as fillers and taste enhancers in all forms of medication—particularly liquid medications.

Difficulty in prescribing medications for a child on the ketogenic diet often arises from the fact that many common over-the-counter and prescription medications are not available in a sugar-free form. A pharmacist who is willing to get to know the ketogenic diet and the child and to work with the family for the duration of the diet can be a critical and valuable asset, helping to interpret labels and calling manufacturers if necessary.

CHAPTER 8

Calculating the Ketogenic Diet

Calculating the ketogenic diet requires a combination of a full nutritional assessment and an understanding of the child's medical condition, mixed with experience and intuition. In each case, a child's individual needs must be taken into account. At Johns Hopkins, we meet as a group a week in advance of every ketogenic diet admission week and discuss each patient's needs (ratio, possibility of fasting, calories, medications, etc.). Because each child is different, this really helps guide management.

ESTIMATING CALORIC NEEDS

Calculating the caloric requirements of an individual child requires consideration of both the child's current and desirable weight as well as the patient's activity level. However, calculating the caloric needs of children going on the ketogenic diet should not be any different than calculating their needs as if they were on a regular diet. The dietitian needs to look at the history of weight and length gain over the years and evaluate the child's current eating habits and patterns before estimating the child's nutritional needs. A three-day food record with the exact amounts of food eaten plus a growth chart or detailed weight history are essential in figuring out a child's caloric intake. We often match the ketogenic diet calories to the prior three-day food record calories.

The caloric needs for patients on the ketogenic diet is calculated using the Dietary Reference Intakes (DRIs) or whichever calculation the dietitian feels will meet the patient's needs. However, you can use the Recommended Daily Allowance (RDA) to evaluate estimated caloric needs (see Table 8.1). The goal of the ketogenic diet is to provide optimal seizure control and maintain adequate nutrition for growth. The ketogenic diet may be beneficial when a patient maintains his or her growth percentiles and doesn't gain weight or lose weight too rapidly.

Underweight children need to gain weight in order to have sufficient fat reserves to burn for ketosis between meals and obese children may need to

TABLE 8.1

Estimating Energy Requirements (EER)

RDA AGE	kcal/kg	Protein/kg
0-5 months	108	2.2
0.5-12 months	98	1.6
1-3 years	102	1.2
4-6	90	1.1
7-10	70	1.0
Males:		
11-14	55	1.0
15-18	45	0.9
19-24	40	0.8
Females:		
11-14	47	1.0
15-18	40	0.8
19-24	38	0.8

Note: EER (kcal/day) = Resting Energy Expenditure × Activity Factor × Stress Factor.

Abbreviation: RDA, recommended dietary allowance.

Source: Recommended Dietary Allowances, 10th ed., National Academy of Sciences, National Academy Press, 1989.

lose weight. Severely handicapped children may be less than the average for their age in size and weight. That is just the start—because a child's activity level is also an important determinant of caloric needs, a very active child may need more calories than a less active one. Profoundly handicapped children, who sometimes are very inactive, usually require fewer calories.

There is limited evidence that calorie restriction makes much of a difference in seizure control. Although this may be true in animals put on ketogenic diets, we don't always see that in children. In fact, on the modified Atkins diet, many children eat *more* calories than before they were treated! However, there are some children who seem to respond to cutting calories. Every child is different (see Table 8.1).

PROTEIN

Recommended daily protein allowances are calculated for average children of a given height and weight and an average activity level. The goal is to reach as close to the RDA for age of protein as possible. In adolescents it may be difficult to achieve the proper fat-to-carbohydrate ratio if 1 gram of protein per kilogram of bodyweight is given. In this case we may use as little as 0.75 gram of protein per kilogram. Growth is closely monitored every 3 to 6 months and is used as a guide of adequate nutrition. The evidence, however, suggests that the biggest impediment to growth is over-ketosis, rather than insufficient protein.

FLUID ALLOTMENT

Anecdotally, in the past it was thought that a fluid restriction on the ketogenic diet may help with seizure control. This probably was due to concentration of the urine and, therefore, apparently higher levels of urine ketosis. Recent studies and years of evidence have determined that fluid restriction has no effect on seizure control. Therefore, we try and maintain as close as possible to 100% of fluid maintenance values. These numbers are based on the child's weight in kilograms and are more of a fluid volume goal rather than a restriction.

BODY WEIGHT	FLUID ALLOTMENT
1-10 kg	100 ml/kg
10-20 kg	1000 ml + 50 ml/kg for each kg >10 kg
>20 kg	1500 ml + 20 ml/kg for each kg >20 kg

Fluid intake should be individualized and increased with an increase in activity or a hot climate. Children in warmer countries may need more fluids than those in colder climates. Fluids are encouraged during illness. Monitor your child for signs and symptoms of dehydration such as cracked lips, decreased urination, and a dry mouth.

JAMES: A CASE STUDY

The case of James illustrates the thought process of a dietitian evaluating an individual coming in for ketogenic diet initiation:

James is a 4-year 7-month-old male with a history of infantile spasms (myoclonic seizures) and developmental delay. Seizure onset was at 12 months of age. Seizure frequency is 100 to 150 jerks/day.

CURRENT MEDICATIONS: Topamax® 75 mg BID, Depakote® 375 mg TID. Supplements: Flintstone Gummy multivitamin/mineral.

LABS: No current labs available.

FEEDING ABILITY: Needs help feeding himself—no problems with chewing, swallowing, and so forth. No history of pneumonia or aspiration.

James's mother reports his appetite to be poor and states that he is a "picky eater." James normally eats a great deal of starches (pasta, bread, etc.) as well as vegetables. He does not like meat very much. He eats three meals and two snacks daily. Food preferences were recorded. Activity is low to normal—James participates in physical therapy once a week and recess at school. His bowel movements are normal for the most part. There are no known food allergies or intolerances.

THREE-DAY FOOD RECALL: Average intake 1290 kcal, 42 grams protein, vitamin/mineral consumption adequate with the exception of calcium.

WT: 18.4 kg (40.5 lb.)

HT: 111.8 cm (44 in.)

WT FOR AGE: 50% to 75%

HT FOR AGE: 75% to 90%

WT FOR HT: 25% to 50%

James's growth pattern has been relatively normal—both height and weight were proportional following the 75% to 90% curve until 6 months ago. His mother said that James has been the same weight for 6 months now, despite an increase in height. She attributes his lack of weight gain to a decreased appetite since the addition of Topamax®.

PHYSICAL ASSESSMENT: No physical signs of deficiencies. James appears to be well nourished.

Assessment

James does not appear to be at nutritional risk at this point. Despite not gaining weight for 6 months, he looks healthy and is consuming what is recommended for age for protein and macro- and micronutrients (with the exception of calcium intake of only 700 mg). Caloric intake is obviously a bit too low as seen by the lack of weight gain and the fact that James is under his ideal body weight. It is reasonable to start him at his current caloric intake (and increase later if necessary) at a 4:1 ratio. We do not want him to lose weight, and the high ratio will allow us to provide the fat needed for ketosis via the diet.

Initial Diet

1300 kcal, 4:1 ratio, 1400 ml total fluid daily. To be given in three equal meals and two snacks of 75 kcal during the day.

KCAL: 1300 (70.7 kcal/kg body weight)

TOTAL PROTEIN: 24.5 grams

TOTAL CARBOHYDRATE: 8 grams

TOTAL FAT: 130 grams

TOTAL FLUID: 1400 ml (100% of estimated maintenance needs)

Parent, Neurologist, and Nutritionist Goals

1. Seizure control.
2. Maintaining current growth curve. Increasing kcal in small increments (5%–10% of kcal every 2–4 weeks) should be sufficient to attain this goal provided that seizures are well controlled. James will probably not only have improvement of appetite, but hopefully of activity as well if his seizures can be controlled.
3. Maintaining optimal nutritional status (maintaining growth and overall nutritional status long term).
4. Weaning medications once the diet is fine-tuned satisfactorily.

Plan

1. Implement diet, educate parents.
2. Attain biochemical indices to check nutritional status (visceral protein status, anemias, electrolytes, hydration, renal function, etc.).
3. Discuss Topamax® wean with physicians after 1 month of the diet. Weaning this medication aggressively might help improve James's appetite.
4. Order multivitamin/mineral supplement that meets 100% of the patient's recommended micronutrient needs.
5. Continue to track height, weight, seizure control, and so on, via phone/e-mail/fax.
6. See James at 3-month follow-up visit.

GENERAL RULES FOR INITIAL KETOGENIC DIET CALCULATION

1. Decide on an optimal level of calories. This should be done using a thorough medical and nutritional history and the dietitian's and physician's professional judgments. Variables such as the child's activity level, frame size, medical condition, recent weight gain or loss, and so forth, must be taken into account.
2. Set the desired ketogenic ratio. Most children ages 2 to 12 years old are started on a 4:1 ketogenic ratio. Medically compromised children may be started on a 3:1 ratio of fat to combined protein and carbohydrates. Children under 2 years of age and adolescents are usually started on a 3:1 ratio.

3. Fluid levels should be set at 100% of maintenance for healthy, active children. Fluids can be increased for fragile children and infants under 1 year of age.
4. Always strive to attain RDAs for protein (and never allow protein to fall below World Health Organization [WHO] standards).
5. The ketogenic diet must be supplemented *daily* with calcium, vitamin D, and a carbohydrate-free complete multivitamin with minerals. The diet is not nutritionally sufficient without supplementation.

Because this book is written for both parents and medical professionals, and because we believe that the diet works best with informed parents as part of the team, we believe it is important to know as much about the diet as possible. However . . .

The ketogenic diet should never be attempted without careful medical and nutritional supervision.

How a Dietitian Calculates the Diet: Another Example

1. **AGE AND WEIGHT.** Fill out the following information:

   Age ________

   Weight in kilograms ________

   Mary has been prescribed a 4:1 ketogenic diet. She is 4 years old and currently weighs 15 kg (33 lb). Her dietitian has determined that this weight is appropriate for Mary.
2. **CALORIES PER KILOGRAM.** After a full medical and nutritional assessment, a dietitian will assign a calorie-per-kilogram level for diet initiation.

   The dietitian has set Mary's diet at 72 kcal/kg. (Note that this figure involves a dietitian's judgment; it is usually based on comparing the child's current intake with the RDA.)
3. **TOTAL CALORIES.** Determine the total number of calories in the diet by multiplying the child's weight by the number of calories per kilogram.

   Mary, age 4 and weighing 15 kg, needs a total of 72 × 15 or 1085 calories per day.
4. **DIETARY UNIT COMPOSITION.** Dietary units are the building blocks of the ketogenic diet. A 4:1 diet has dietary units made up of 4 grams of fat to each 1 gram of protein and 1 gram of carbohydrate. Because fat has 9 calories per gram (9 × 4 = 36), and protein and carbohydrate each have 4 calories per gram (4 × 1 = 4), a dietary unit at a 4:1 diet ratio has 36 + 4 = 40 calories. The caloric value and breakdown of dietary units vary with the ketogenic ratio:

RATIO	FAT CALORIES	CARBOHYDRATE PLUS PROTEIN CALORIES	CALORIES PER DIETARY UNIT
2:1	2 g × 9 kcal/g = 18	1 g × 4 kcal/g = 4	18 + 4 = 22
3:1	3 g × 9 kcal/g = 27	1 g × 4 kcal/g = 4	27 + 4 = 31
4:1	4 g × 9 kcal/g = 36	1 g × 4 kcal/g = 4	36 + 4 = 40
5:1	5 g × 9 kcal/g = 45	1 g × 4 kcal/g = 4	45 + 4 = 49

Mary's dietary units will be made up of 40 calories each because she is on a 4:1 ratio.

5. **DIETARY UNIT QUANTITY.** Divide the total calories allotted (Step 3) by the number of calories in each dietary unit (Step 4) to determine the number of dietary units to be allowed daily.

   Each of Mary's dietary units on a 4:1 ratio contains 40 calories, and she is allowed a total of 1085 kcal/day, so she gets 1085/40 = 27 dietary units per day.

6. **FAT ALLOWANCE.** Multiply the number of dietary units by the units of fat in the prescribed ketogenic ratio to determine the grams of fat permitted daily.

   On her 4:1 diet, with 27 dietary units/day, Mary will have 27 × 4, or 108 grams of fat per day.

7. **PROTEIN + CARBOHYDRATE ALLOWANCE.** Multiply the number of dietary units by the number of units of protein and carbohydrate in the prescribed ketogenic ratio, usually 1, to determine the combined daily protein + carbohydrate allotment.

   On her 4:1 diet, Mary will have 27 × 1, or 27 grams of protein and carbohydrate per day.

8. **PROTEIN ALLOWANCE.** The dietitian will determine optimal protein levels as part of the nutritional assessment, taking into account such factors as age, growth, activity level, medical condition, and so forth.

   Mary's dietitian has determined that she needs 1.2 grams of protein per kilogram of body weight (18 grams total).

9. **CARBOHYDRATE ALLOWANCE.** Determine the carbohydrate allowance by subtracting protein from the total carbohydrate + protein allowance (Step 7 minus Step 8). Carbohydrates are the diet's filler and are always determined last.

   Mary's carbohydrate allowance is 27 – 18 = 9 grams of carbohydrate daily.

10. **MEAL ORDER.** Divide the daily fat, protein, and carbohydrate allotments into the desired number of meals and snacks per day. The number of

meals will be based on the child's dietary habits and nutritional needs. It is essential that the proper ratio of fat to protein + carbohydrate be maintained at each meal.

Mary's dietitian has decided to give her three meals and no snacks per day:

	DAILY	PER MEAL
Protein	18 g	6 g
Fat	108.0 g	36.0 g
Carbohydrate	9 g	3.0 g
Calories	1085	361

Note: **This example is simplified for teaching purposes. In reality, most 4-year-olds would be prescribed one or two snacks in addition to their three meals. The snacks would be in the same ratio (4:1) and the meals reduced by the number of calories in each snack.**

11. **LIQUIDS.** Multiply the child's desirable weight by the value shown on the chart listed earlier in this chapter to determine the daily allotment of liquid. Liquid intake should be spaced throughout the day. Liquids should be noncaloric, such as water, or decaffeinated zero-calorie diet drinks. In hot climates the cream may be excluded from the fluid allowance (in other words, liquids may be increased by the volume of the cream in the diet). The liquid allotment may also be set equal to the number of calories in the diet.

    Mary, who weighs 15 kg, is allowed 1000 + (50 × 5) = 1250 ml × 0.9 = 1125 ml of fluid per day, including her allotted cream.

12. **DIETARY SUPPLEMENTS.** The ketogenic diet is deficient in some nutrients. Multivitamin and mineral supplements are required. In choosing a supplement it is important to consider carbohydrate content. Children who are not medically compromised can usually be adequately supplemented with an over-the-counter, reputable multivitamin and mineral supplement and a separate calcium supplement. Most children do well with commercially available supplements, although these have been alleged to lack some micronutrients.

CALCULATING MEAL PLANS

Calculating the meal plan, in contrast to the diet prescription, is a fairly straightforward procedure. There are currently two different ways of calculating the meal plans: by hand or by computer.

The hand calculation method uses exchange lists and rounded nutritional values for simplicity. This method is cumbersome, time-consuming, and based to a certain extent on nutritional averages. It is, however, the method that was used at Johns Hopkins and elsewhere with much success before the availability of personal computers. It is important that dietitians become familiar with the hand calculation method in order to fully understand the logic of meal planning, and in case a computer is not available in a pinch.

There are several computer programs available at many centers that are used by the dietitian to create meal plans. One such program is KetoDietCalculator. Because the computer program uses data about the precise nutritional content of specific foods, whereas the hand calculation method relies on averages in order to simplify the math, the computer program may result in slightly different numbers of calories and grams for a given meal than the hand calculation method.

No program should be initiated or changed without the oversight of a dietitian to be certain that the nutritional information is up to date.

Generic Group A and B vegetables and fruits can be exchanged with both methods of meal calculation. It is easy for parents to switch from one Group A vegetable to another, or one 10% fruit to another, depending on the child's whims or what is available in the grocery store. The exchange lists assume that there will be some variety in the diet. If the child only likes carrots and grapes—which contain the highest carbohydrate levels on the exchange lists—then the child could end up with less than optimal seizure control. In this case the meal plans should be recalculated specifically for carrots and grapes.

The precision of the computer calculations shows the minor differences between the content of, say, broccoli and green beans. For most children these minor differences are of little importance. Therefore, once the computer has calculated a meal plan, and assuming that the child is doing well on the diet, exchanges may still be made among the foods on the fruit and vegetable exchange lists. If better seizure control is needed, however, in some cases it may be achieved through the use of specific meal plan calculations instead of exchange lists.

With the availability of the computer program, we no longer use meat exchange lists. The fat and carbohydrate contents of meats vary too greatly. The exchange lists are still used with hand calculations.

The dietitian provides parents with a set of basic meal plans before they go home from the hospital.

AVERAGE FOOD VALUES FOR HAND CALCULATIONS

	GRAMS	PROTEIN	CARB	FAT
36% Cream	100	2.0	3	36
Ground beef	100	23	–	16
Chicken	100	31.1	–	3.5
Tuna in water	100	26.8	–	3
10% Fruit	100	1.0	10.0	–
Group B vegetable	100	2.0	7.0	–
Fat	100	–	–	74
Egg	100	12.0	–	12
Cheese	100	30.0	–	35.3
Cream cheese	100	6.7	3.3	35
Peanut butter	100	26.0	22	50

***Note:* A food contents reference book, such as Bowes & Church's *Food Values*, is helpful for current information on specific foods. The fat content of heavy cream should be consistent (e.g., 36%), and butter should come in solid, stick form, not whipped or low calorie.**

CROSS MULTIPLICATION: THE KEY TO USING THE FOOD LIST

Sample Calculation

1. Jeremy, a 9-year-old boy, is to be placed on a 4:1 ketogenic diet. His actual weight is 32 kg, and his height is 134 cm. According to the standard charts, he is at 50% for height and 90% for weight.
2. The dietitian estimated Jeremy's calorie allotment at 60 calories per kilogram. One of the dietitian's goals was to have Jeremy gradually achieve his ideal weight. Toward this end, Jeremy's total calorie allotment is set by multiplying his ideal weight by 60: 29 × 60 = 1740 calories per day.
3. Each of Jeremy's dietary units will consist of:

   4 grams fat (9 calories per gram) = 36 calories

   1 gram carbohydrate + protein (4 calories per gram) = 4 calories

   Total calories per dietary unit = 40 calories
4. Jeremy's dietary units will be determined by dividing his total daily calorie allotment (Step 2) by the calories in each dietary unit: 1740 calories/40 calories per dietary unit = 43.5 dietary units per day.

5. Jeremy's daily fat allowance is determined by multiplying his dietary units (Step 4) by the fat component in his diet ratio (4 in a 4:1 ratio): 43.5 × 4 = 174 grams fat.
6. Jeremy's protein needs are at a minimum 1 gram of protein per kilogram of body weight. His ideal weight is 29 kg, so he needs at least 29.0 grams of protein daily.
7. Jeremy's daily carbohydrate allotment is determined by multiplying his dietary units (Step 4) by the 1 in his 4:1 ratio, then subtracting his necessary protein (Step 6) from the total: 43.5 – 29 = 14.5 grams carbohydrate per day.

Jeremy's complete diet order will read as follows:

	PER DAY	PER MEAL
Protein	29.0 g	9.7 g
Fat	174.0 g	58.0 g
Carbohydrate	14.5 g	4.8 g
Calories	1740	580

Note: **Most children are now given a meal plan that includes one or two snacks, which would diminish the quantity of food in the three main meals.**

CALCULATING A MEAL	JEREMY'S TUNA SALAD
1. Calculate the whipping cream first. Heavy whipping cream should take up no more than half of the carbohydrate allotment in a meal.	1. Jeremy is allowed a total of 4.8 grams carbohydrate per meal. To use half of this carbohydrate allotment as cream, calculate the amount of 36% cream that contains 2.4 grams of carbohydrate. Jeremy should eat 80 grams of 36% cream, which contains 2.4 grams of carbohydrate.
2. Calculate the rest of the carbohydrates (fruit or vegetables) by subtracting the carbohydrate contained in the cream from the total carbohydrate allotment.	2. For his remaining 2.4 grams of carbohydrate, Jeremy can eat 35 grams of Group B vegetables, or twice as many Group A vegetables.

(continued)

CALCULATING A MEAL	JEREMY'S TUNA SALAD
3. Calculate the remaining protein (chicken, cheese, or egg) by subtracting the protein in the cream and vegetables from the total protein allowance. The total amount of protein may occasionally be off by 0.1 gram (over or under) without adverse effect.	3. The 34.3 grams Group B vegetables and 80 grams 36% cream contain a total of 2.3 grams protein (0.68 + 1.6 = 2.3). Jeremy is allowed 9.7 grams protein per meal, so he can eat as much tuna as contains 9.7 - 2.3 = 7.4 grams protein. Referring to the food values chart, this works out to be 28 grams tuna.
4. Calculate the amount of fat to be allowed in the meal by subtracting the fat in the cream and protein from the total fat allowance.	4. Jeremy has to eat 58 grams fat with each meal. The cream and tuna contain 29.3 grams fat, leaving 28.7 grams of fat to be mixed in with his tuna fish. Jeremy will get 39 grams mayonnaise, which contains 28.9 grams fat. (Note that mayonnaise actually has fewer grams of fat than oil does and also contains some protein and carbohydrate. The hand calculation method does not account for these variations.)

CALCULATING A MEAL PLAN

	WEIGHT	PROTEIN	FAT	CARBOHYDRATE
Tuna	28 g	7.4 g	0.5 g	–
Group B vegetable	33 g	0.7 g	–	2.3 g
Fat	39 g	–	28.9 g	–
36% cream	80 g	1.6 g	28.8 g	2.4 g
Actual total	9.7 g	58.2 g	4.7 g	
Should be	9.7 g	58.0 g	4.8 g	

The 4:1 ketogenic ratio of this menu may be double-checked by adding the grams of protein + carbohydrate in the meal and multiplying by 4. The result should be the amount of fat in the meal, in this case 58 grams. Since (9.7 + 4.8) × 4 = 58, the ratio is correct.

NOTES ON JEREMY'S LUNCH

- Jeremy likes his cream frozen in an ice cream ball (slightly whipped), flavored with vanilla, and sprinkled with a little cinnamon.
- Jeremy's mom arranges the vegetables in thin-sliced crescents or shoestring sticks around the tuna.

- If Jeremy doesn't like as much mayonnaise with his tuna, some of his fat allowance in the form of oil can be calculated and whipped into the cream 1 hour after it goes into the freezer. The fats on the exchange list can be used interchangeably—a meal's fat can be provided as all mayonnaise, half mayonnaise and half butter, or the oil may be calculated and mixed with the butter, depending on the child's taste and what makes food sense. In the case of hiding fat in ice cream, oil works nicely because it is liquid and has little flavor.

SOME COMMON QUESTIONS AND ANSWERS

Q. *How do you add extra ingredients to a meal plan when calculating by hand?*

A. Take the tuna salad meal as an example. Suppose Jeremy wants to sprinkle baking chocolate shavings on his ice cream and bacon bits on the tuna salad. You would add a line for bacon and a line for baking chocolate in your hand or computer calculation. Then choose a small quantity, perhaps 5 grams of bacon and 2 grams of baking chocolate, and fill in the values for protein, fat, and carbohydrate of each. The quantities of other ingredients would then have to be juggled downward until all the columns add up to the proper totals. Bacon, which contains protein and fat, will take away from the meal's tuna and mayonnaise allotment. Baking chocolate, which is primarily fat and carbohydrate with a little protein, will take away from the amount of Group B vegetables in the meal. As the overall carbohydrate allotment is very small and the nutritive value of chocolate is less than that of vegetables, no more than 2 grams of chocolate should be used in a meal on the 4:1 ratio. With the accompanying computer program, an additional ingredient may simply be filled in on a blank line and the other ingredients adjusted until the actual totals match the correctly prescribed ones.

Q. *When is it necessary to make calorie adjustments?*

A. Weight should be monitored on a weekly basis for the first month, and height on a monthly basis. Infants should be weighed and measured accurately at the pediatrician's office about every 2 weeks. At least during the first 3 months, the ketogenic diet team should be informed monthly of a child's height and weight changes and any other relevant information. Once a child is started on the diet, changes in the diet order are usually made in response to the child's own performance—weight loss or gain, growth in height, seizure control, and so forth. We evaluate in this manner and may make adjustments based on these factors throughout the child's time on the diet.

Q. *How often should a child eat on the ketogenic diet?*

A. The number of meals and snacks included in a child's diet should approximate prediet eating habits (when possible) and the family's schedule, and should always take into account the child's nutritional needs. Infants will need to be given about six bottle feedings a day. Toddlers will probably need three meals and one or two snacks. Older children might need three meals and only one snack. Some children gain better ketosis overnight and achieve early morning seizure control by having a bedtime snack. Snacks are sometimes used to test how many extra calories are needed for a child who is losing weight and whether the extra calories cause any seizure activity problems.

Q. *Is it necessary to use half of the carbohydrate allotment as cream?*

A. Using up to half of the carbohydrate allotment as cream is a guideline, not a hard and fast rule. It's meant to replace milk for children who drink milk, and cream can be an easy way to fit a lot of fat into the diet in a way that most children enjoy. However, children who do not like milk do not have to drink the cream; they will just have to have more mayonnaise, butter, or oil. Some children like to eat fat, some don't. Some children love cream, some don't. As long as the diet makes food sense, there is no need to use half of the carbohydrate allotment as cream.

A DIET ORDER TEST

Lily is 24 months old and weighs 12 kilos. She is 86.5 cm tall. Both her height and weight are at the 50th percentile. She is going to start on a 4:1 ketogenic diet. What will her diet order read?

1. At age 2 years, Lily's calorie per kilogram requirement will be approximately 75 calories per kilogram. (As indicated previously, calorie requirements vary with the metabolism and activity level of the child and must be individually assessed.) Her ideal weight is the same as her actual weight, 12 kg. So Lily's total calorie allotment is 75 × 12 = 900 calories per day.
2. Lily's dietary units will consist of 40 calories each, the standard for a 4:1 diet.
3. Lily's dietary units are determined by dividing her total calorie allotment by the calories in each dietary unit. So she will have 900 / 40 = 22.5 dietary units per day.
4. Lily's daily fat allowance is determined by multiplying her dietary units (22.5) by the fat component in her ratio (4 in a 4:1 ratio). She thus will be allowed 22.5 × 4 = 90 grams fat per day.
5. Lily's protein and carbohydrate allotment is 22.5 grams per day, determined by multiplying her dietary units (22.5) by the 1 in her 4:1 ratio. As a young, growing child she may need 1.1 to 1.5 grams of protein/kg. Her weight is 12 kg, so allowing 1.2 grams of protein per kilogram per day makes her protein allotment 14.4 grams per day.
6. Lily's daily carbohydrate allotment is determined by subtracting her protein allotment (14.4 grams) from the total protein and 1 carbohydrate allowance (22.5 grams): 22.5 – 14.4 = 8.1 grams carbohydrate per day.

Lily's complete diet order will read as follows:

	PER DAY	PER MEAL
Protein	14.4 g	4.8 g
Fat	90.0 g	30.0 g
Carbohydrate	8.1 g	2.7 g
Calories	900	300

Note: **As mentioned previously, most 2-year-olds eat one or two snacks in addition to their three meals a day. This example has been simplified for teaching purposes.**

A MEAL TEST

For dinner, Lily would like to eat grilled chicken with fruit salad and a vanilla ice pop. How would you calculate this meal?

1. Start from the per-meal diet order. Lily is allowed a total of 2.7 grams carbohydrate per meal. To use half of this allotment as 36% cream, her ice pop should contain 45 grams cream, which will provide 1.35 grams carbohydrate.
2. To provide her remaining 1.35 grams carbohydrate, she can have 13 grams of 10% fruit.
3. The 10% fruit and 36% cream contain a total of 1.03 grams protein. Lily's total protein allotment for the meal is 4.8 grams, so she can eat as much grilled chicken as will provide 4.8 – 1.03 = 3.77 grams protein. This works out to 12 grams chicken.
4. Lily is allowed 30 grams of fat in each meal. The chicken and cream contain a total of 16.5 grams fat. Lily should eat 17 grams of butter or mayonnaise to provide the additional 13.5 grams fat allotment.

Lily's dinner plan will read as follows:

CHICKEN CUTLET WITH FRUIT SALAD

	WEIGHT	PROTEIN	FAT	CARBOHYDRATE	CALORIES
36% Cream	45 g	0.9 g	16.2 g	1.4 g	155
Chicken breast	12 g	3.7 g	0.3 g	–	18
10% Fruit exchange	13 g	0.1 g	–	1.3 g	6
Butter	17 g	0.1 g	13.8 g	–	125
Actual total		4.8 g	30.3 g	2.7 g	304
Should be		4.8 g	30.0 g	2.7 g	300

Notes on Lily's meal: The chicken can be pounded to be very thin to make it look bigger on the plate. The fruit salad will be pretty if composed of small chunks of water-packed canned peaches and fresh strawberries. Lily thinks it is fun to pick up the chunks with a toothpick. The cream can be diluted with some allotted water, sweetened with saccharin, flavored with four or five drops of vanilla and frozen in an ice pop mold in advance of the meal. Lily loves butter; she will eat it straight or it can be spread over her chicken. A small leaf of lettuce can be added to the meal for extra crunch.

Calculating the ketogenic diet is much simpler nowadays with the use of computer programs. It's important to know how to calculate by hand, however. For dietitians it's also important to utilize time efficiently using the ketogenic diet programs available.

CHAPTER 9

All Those Crazy Supplements!

One of the most important goals for parents starting their child on the ketogenic diet is to reduce their child's medications. Parents are surprised when they start the diet that we write more prescriptions than when they came in! Nevertheless, most of these are supplements essential for maintaining the diet and vitamins and minerals to keep their child safe.

A child on a regular diet should be able to meet all of his or her vitamin and mineral needs just from eating a regular diet. However, the ketogenic diet is very high in fat and very low in carbohydrates, essentially eliminating a huge component of a regular diet. Vitamins and minerals are found naturally in fruits, vegetables, and animal proteins. However, in the United States, all grains are enriched with vitamins and minerals. Through eliminating pastas, cereals, and bread and limiting fruits and vegetables, you are eliminating essential vitamins and minerals. The Dietary Reference Intakes (DRIs) have been established and provide recommendations for both macro nutrients (carbohydrate, protein, and fat) and micro nutrients (vitamins and minerals). It is provided free of charge as a PDF download at this website: iom.edu/Reports/2006/Dietary-Reference-Intakes-Essential-Guide-Nutrient-Requirements.aspx.

MULTIVITAMINS

It is essential for all children on the ketogenic diet to be supplemented with a complete pediatric multivitamin meeting all of the DRIs for their age. There are a couple of vitamins that are low in carbohydrates that can either be purchased over the counter at a local pharmacy or via the Internet.

Some of the common vitamins that we use are Centrum® (Wyeth), Kirkman's Children Hypoallergenic Multi Vitamin® (Kirkman), Nano VM® (Solace Nutrition), FruitiVits (VitaFlo®), and PhlexyVits® (Nutricia). Most general complete multivitamins are still low in calcium, requiring additional calcium supplementation. Nano VM® Fruit Vits and Phlexy Vits® are the only vitamins that usually do not need additional calcium, however, they typically need to be ordered over the Internet with a prescription. These are completely carbohydrate free or low-carbohydrate powdered supplements that can be mixed with fluids or small amounts of calculated applesauce or keto yogurt. The other vitamins can be chewed, swallowed, or crushed with water to provide via gastrostomy tube.

Formula-fed babies and older kids getting formula through a gastrostomy tube might not need additional supplementation. Compare the vitamins and minerals in the formula for the amount being provided to the DRIs, and supplement only those vitamins that do not meet 100% of the child's daily needs.

CALCIUM AND VITAMIN D

A lot of epilepsy medications are associated with bone loss and calcium metabolism. Many studies have shown that common medications for epilepsy lead to significant reduction in bone mineral density. However, it is unclear if supplementing more calcium and vitamin D than is required will help with calcium absorption. On the ketogenic diet there are very few calcium sources through foods. The only dairy that is eaten is cheese, and it's limited. Therefore, adding a calcium and vitamin D supplement will ensure that your child is getting at least the DRIs for his or her age.

Calcium is essential for the structures of bone and teeth and is also involved in vascular and neuromuscular functions. It is the most abundant mineral found in the body. Calcium is found in dairy products, such as milk, yogurts, cheeses, and ice cream; green leafy vegetables, such as broccoli and kale; and calcium-enriched foods, such as orange juice. Despite dairy products being high in fat they still have protein and some carbohydrates in them, making them difficult to use for the ketogenic diet. Heavy cream, the fat skimmed off of milk, contains minimal calcium. Therefore, calcium supplementation is essential on the ketogenic diet. The Institute of Medicine has a list of the calcium guidelines per age (see Table 9.1).

Some common calcium supplements that we use are found in most pharmacies or are available for purchase on the Internet. For tablets that can be crushed or swallowed, we use Nature Made brand of either 500 or 600 mg calcium plus vitamin D. There is an oral suspension from Roxanne called Calcium Carbonate 1250 mg for 5 ml oral suspension, and there is a powdered supplement from Now Foods called Calcium Citrate powder that can be mixed into liquids.

Vitamin D (calciferol) is also involved in bone health and is not found naturally in many food products. It is synthesized in the skin through sun exposure, and it aids in calcium and phosphorus absorption. Vitamin D can be found in fatty fish, fortified milk, and other fortified foods such as breakfast cereals. The Institute of Medicine recently published new guidelines for vitamin D intake. The range is 400 to 600 International Units (IU) per day, but a child should not exceed 2500 to 4000 IU per day (see Table 9.2).

You can purchase vitamin D from Now Foods or Carlson, in doses ranging from 100 IU to 1000 to 2000 IU per day.

TABLE 9.1

Calcium Guidelines From the Institute of Medicine

AGES	RECOMMENDED DIETARY ALLOWANCE (mg/day)	UPPER LEVEL INTAKE (mg/day)
1-3 years old	700	2500
4-8 years old	1000	2500
9-13 years old	1300	3000
14-18 years old	1300	3000

TABLE 9.2

Vitamin D Guidelines From the Institute of Medicine

AGES	ESTIMATED AVERAGE REQUIREMENT (IU/day)	RECOMMENDED DIETARY ALLOWANCE (IU/day)	UPPER LEVEL INTAKE (IU/day)
1-3 years old	400	600	2500
4-8 years old	400	600	3000
9-13 years old	400	600	4000
14-18 years old	400	600	4000

ORAL CITRATES

Due to recent studies based on known side effects on the diet, many centers are providing oral citrate supplements. At Johns Hopkins we prescribe a potassium citrate (Polycitra K®) to all of our patients starting the diet. Since supplementing each patient we have seen a significant reduction in the amount of kidney stones by nearly seven times, as shown in a study by Dr. Melanie McNally, in 2009. Oral citrates work to alkalinize the urine and solubilize urine calcium. They increase the pH in the urine, which increases urinary citrate and essentially decreases the amount of kidney stones. Polycitra K® is a powder supplement that can be added to water, and it is recommended to drink a lot of fluid as well to prevent kidney stones. For most children we dose it 2 mEq/kg/day; for a young child we may give 15 mEq twice daily (half of a 30 mEq packet); and for an older child 30 mEq twice daily (a full packet twice daily). Other supplements, such as Citra K® and sodium bicitrate, are fine and can be substituted if the pharmacy doesn't have Polycitra K®.

MIRALAX AND GASTROINTESTINAL MEDICATIONS

Constipation and gastrointestinal intolerances to the ketogenic diet are both common side effects while on the diet. There have not been any studies looking at beginning antireflux medications when starting the diet, however, a high-fat diet can cause gastroesophageal reflux and may be helped by starting an anti-reflux medication.

Constipation is one of the common side effects of the ketogenic diet. It is a diet very low in fiber, fresh fruits, and vegetables, and sometimes fluids. There are ways to help with constipation through foods using oils, medium chain triglyceride (MCT) oil, and avocados, adding some prunes to the meals, exercising, and drinking enough fluid. But when that doesn't work, Miralax® is usually the safest and most effective way to treat constipation. It is another powder that gets added to water, but this one has no flavor! Some families report benefits with using George's Aloe Vera®, but there are no studies regarding its efficacy, and it is not approved by the Food and Drug Administration (FDA).

CARNITINE

Carnitine is a compound synthesized by the amino acids lysine and methionine and required for fatty acid to be transported into the mitochondria during the breakdown of fats for the making of metabolic energy. The active form of carnitine that is needed is called L-carnitine. The body makes enough carnitine on its own to help turn fat into energy; however, some children on a high-fat diet cannot produce enough carnitine on their own or have issues transporting it across the cell.

There are some clinicians that start all children beginning the ketogenic diet with carnitine and some that test levels and only give carnitine if the levels are low. Symptoms of carnitine deficiency can be fatigue and lethargy. The consensus of multiple centers is to test the carnitine level before the diet is started and then check every three to six months while on the diet and only supplement if there is a deficiency or symptoms. Carnitine is another pill or liquid to take on top of everything else and can be expensive, so we use it at Johns Hopkins only when necessary. Carnitor® is the brand name product, but a generic product works fine (just make sure it's sugar and carb-free). It comes in 330 mg capsules or 1000 mg/10 ml liquid.

MCT OIL

Medium chain triglyceride (MCT) oil is an oil compared to the regular household oils that are long chain triglycerides. In the 1970s, MCT oil was introduced as a modification to the classic ketogenic diet. MCT oil was thought to produce higher ketosis; it is absorbed better than long chain fats and is carried directly to the liver. Because MCT oil was thought to be more ketogenic, less fat is used compared to the classic ketogenic diet, allowing for more protein and carbohydrates on the diet. Originally MCT oil would provide 60% of total prescribed calories, but this caused gastrointestinal distress and was reduced to 30% to 40% of total energy with long chain fats providing the other 30% of energy. The first double-blind study was conducted comparing the classic ketogenic diet to the MCT oil diet, and it showed no difference in the two groups attaining 50% to 90% seizure reduction. There is more information about MCT oil and the MCT diet in Chapter 27.

Because MCT oil is not sold in the supermarket and needs to be obtained online or from a specialty health food store, it is not a supplement that is usually started at the initiation of the classic ketogenic diet. It may be started for a variety of reasons such as high cholesterol and triglycerides or to increase ketosis, and can be started in various doses of 5 to 25 grams at each meal or per day.

Coconut oil is one of the only oils available in most supermarkets in the health food section that contains MCT oil; depending on how the oil is extracted it can be 80% to 100% MCT oil. Many families are choosing to use coconut oil instead of other oils due to the higher MCT content. Coconut oil can be used in place of all oils and is very heat stable and good for cooking and frying.

OMEGA-3

Omega-3 fatty acid (alpha linolenic acid) is an essential fatty acid; the body does not make it by itself, and it has to be consumed through food, but it is still necessary for human health. You can find Omega-3 in fish, such as sardines, tuna, and salmon; some plants; and nut oils. Omega-3 is a polyunsaturated fatty acid, plays a vital role in brain function and normal growth and development, may reduce the risk of cardiac diseases, and is anti-inflammatory. The highest concentration of Omega-3 is found in the brain and is important for cognition, behavioral functions, and performance.

For children, the recommended range of Omega-3 is to have 0.6% to 1.2% of total fat intake be from polyunsaturated sources. Because the ketogenic diet is very high in fats, making the right choices for foods and fat sources should provide more than an adequate amount of Omega-3. There is no established amount of Omega-3 that is too much to consume in one day, but the FDA recommends that total dietary intake of Omega-3 fatty acids from fish not exceed 3 grams per day for adults. Therefore, there is no reason to supplement with Omega-3 or assume that your child is deficient in Omega-3 fatty acids. However, one of the forms of Omega-3 is an oil and can easily be added into the diet.

SELENIUM

Selenium is an antioxidant nutrient that is involved in the body's defense against oxidative stress. One of the side effects of not eating enough selenium is cardiomyopathy, which is a weakening of the heart muscle or a change in the structure of the heart muscle. Regular diets provide adequate selenium through foods; however, because the ketogenic diet is restrictive it might not provide enough. Foods that contain selenium are Brazil nuts, tuna, beef, chicken, turkey, and enriched grains. Because we supplement every child with a multivitamin including selenium on the ketogenic diet, we rarely see a selenium deficiency; however, the clinician must look at the vitamin that is chosen to determine if there is enough selenium for that child, and if not, then an additional selenium supplement is added.

SUMMARY

To make the ketogenic diet work for your child it is imperative that you provide your child with all of the prescribed supplements. Sometimes it's very difficult to force your child to take another pill or drink the flavored water, or even use a syringe to get in all of these supplements. We understand that. Your keto team will work with you to find a supplement that works best for your child, such as a crushed pill versus a powder, but sometimes there are no other forms and that extra supplement is what is preventing your child from kidney stones or another side effect of the diet. There are many websites and chat rooms that talk about additional supplementation for children with all types of chronic illness. Do not start anything new unless you speak to your keto team and discuss the pros and cons of that supplement.

CHAPTER 10

KetoDietCalculator

This chapter was written by Beth Zupec-Kania, RDN, from The Charlie Foundation for Ketogenic Therapies.

Computer technology is valuable in assisting with the management of diet therapies for epilepsy. KetoDietCalculator is a unique program that computes and stores diet information (see Figure 10.1). It was designed to calculate diets quickly whether you are in the middle of preparing a meal or are creating a series of new meals. The program is available online (www.ketodietcalculator.org), which makes it readily accessible wherever there is Internet access.

KetoDietCalculator may be used to create variations of the ketogenic diet. It has the flexibility to calculate the ketogenic diet ratios (5:1, 4:1, 3:1, 2:1) as well as the MCT (medium chain triglyceride) oil diet, modified Atkins, and the LGIT (low glycemic index treatment) (approximately 1:1). The program may be used to design diets for any age group and can be modified to the specific dietary needs of an individual. KetoDietCalculator can be utilized to create meals with baby foods, solid foods, liquid diets (formulas), or any combination of these.

The advantage to using an Internet-based system is that the food database is updated instantly and regularly. The database includes several hundred foods. The U.S. Department of Agriculture's Food Composition Database is the main source of macronutrient data for naturally occurring foods. Commercial food product information is obtained directly from the manufacturers. The carbohydrate content of medications and supplements is also obtained directly from the manufacturers. Registered professional users may add foods, supplements, and medications to their database.

KetoDietCalculator is intended for use by people who are under the supervision of a health care team, and some features of the program are only viewable by these professionals. The program is free to health care providers who are then able to grant access to families. Health care providers may register for the program via the website (www.ketodietcalculator.org). Once registered, a username and password are provided as well as instructions for navigating the program. The providers can then grant access to caregivers by creating a separate username and password. Access to the program is secure, and caregivers

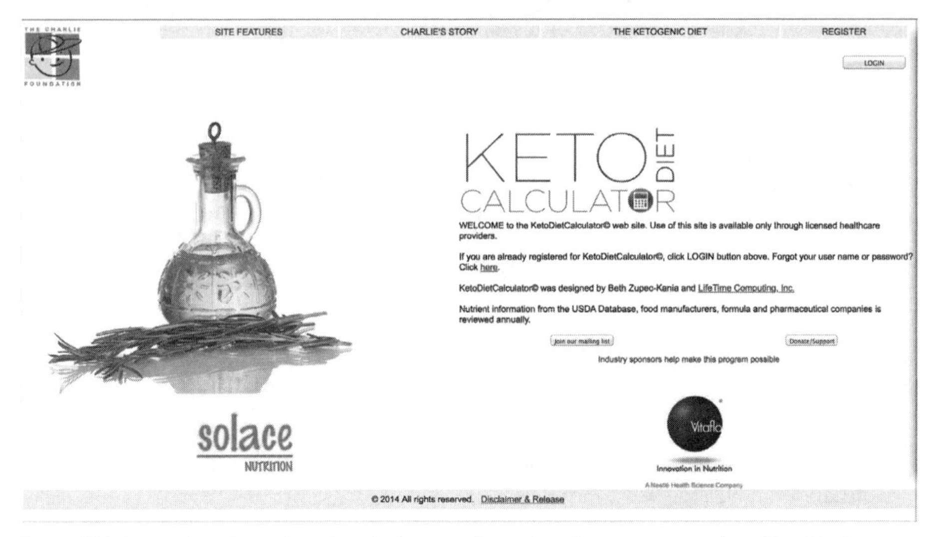

Figure 10.1. Screenshot of www.ketodietcalculator.org. Reproduced with permission from The Charlie Foundation.

are able to view only their diet (and not the diets of other people). The following features are available through the caregiver access:

Create and Display Meals	Create and Display Snacks
Weekly Menu Planner	Fluid and Diet Schedule
Handouts	View Tables

The menus that are provided in the program display gram weights of foods that are specific to the classic ketogenic diet and the MCT oil diet. These values may be converted to household measures for liberal diets, as shown in the table at the end of this chapter.

DIET CALCULATION

Prior to creating meals or snacks, the dietitian must enter a *Diet Calculation*. The Diet Calculation is tailored to the needs of the each individual and should be adjusted during the course of therapy by the dietitian. The Diet Calculation includes a calorie level, the ratio of the diet, and the appropriate amount of protein to provide the recommended dietary allowance (RDA) for the individual based on his or her weight and age. A sample Diet Calculation is shown in Table 10.1.

Once the Diet Calculation has been created; the total protein, carbohydrate, and fat are equally divided into the number of meals that are to be consumed daily. Three meals a day is the most typical diet plan, however, this can be tailored to the needs of the individual. For example, a 1-year-old may consume four meals daily.

TABLE 10.1

KetoDietCalculator Calculation Screen

DIET DATE	2/23/20XX		DAILY	PER MEAL
Age range	1-3	**Fat**	96.77	32.26
Desirable weight	15 kg	**Protein**	18	6
Recommended calorie range	1000-1125	**Carb**	14.26	4.75
Daily calories	1000	**Dietary units**	32.26	10.75
Diet ratio	3:1			
Feeding route	Oral			
Meals per day	3			

CREATE AND DISPLAY MEALS

After the Diet Calculation is complete, the next step is to design meals. The user may select from a list of *Standard Meals*. The Standard Meals are meals that are typical to the diet and consist of at least two foods that are high in fat, one high in protein, and one source of carbohydrate. The following list is a sample of the Standard Meals that are found in the program. Recipe instructions are included with certain meals.

Examples of Standard Meals

Breakfast sausage with fruit
Cheesecake
Chicken and spinach casserole
Chicken vegetable soup
Crabmeat salad with garlic dressing
Hot dog with vegetable
Lean meat with vegetable
Pork stir-fry
Scrambled eggs with avocado
Tuna salad with fruit

Once selected, the program automatically calculates the gram weight of each food in the meal; see Table 10.2.

This Standard Meal is created with the inclusion of two food groups. Group B vegetables are vegetables of similar carbohydrate content, and lean meat includes meat of similar protein and fat content. These food lists are accessable from the Handout link within KetoDietCalculator.

TABLE 10.2

Example of a Standard Meal: Top of Form

FOOD ITEM	GRAMS		FAT	PROTEIN	CARB	CALORIES	UNITS	RATIO
Cream, 36%	60	▲▼	21.6	1.2	1.8	206		
Group B vegetable	41	▲▼	0	0.82	2.87	15		
Lean meat (from list)	17	▲▼	2.84	3.96	0	41		
Butter	10	▲▼	8.11	0.09	0.01	73		
	Actual		32.55	6.07	4.68	335	10.75	3:1
	Recommended		32.26	6	4.75	333	10.75	3:1

Meals may be individualized to suit preferences by changing the amounts of food using the up/down arrows. The user may also delete foods or add new foods to the meal. When these changes are made, the user must then manually correct the meal to match the recommended values shown at the bottom of the meal calculation.

The example in Table 10.3 illustrates the Standard Meal shown in Table 10.2 with the addition of a new food. In order to account for the avocado that has been added to this meal, a reduction in the cream and butter has been made. The vegetable and meat have also been adjusted.

A single meal may be edited in numerous ways to suit the preference of the individual. For example, if the user wanted to choose a specific meat and vegetable instead of using the choices in the Standard Meal, the meal could be easily adjusted by deleting those items then adding new foods. Once these new foods are selected, the meal can again be edited to meet the *recommended* values at the bottom of the calculation.

When a user edits a meal, the dietitian is notified to review and verify these edits. This notification occurs in the Main Menu of the dietitian's program. Once the dietitian has verified the meal, it becomes a printable meal. Without this verification, the meal cannot be printed. This is a cross-check system that helps to prevent the user from preparing meals that have not been reviewed. The printed version of the previous meal follows. Instructions may be added to the meals to clarify how the food items should be prepared.

TABLE 10.3

Example of a Standard Meal With Editing

FOOD ITEM	GRAMS		FAT	PROTEIN	CARB	CALORIES	UNITS	RATIO
Cream, 36%	55	▲▼	19.8	1.1	1.65	189		
Group B vegetable	37	▲▼	0	0.74	2.59	13		
Lean meat (from list)	16	▲▼	2.67	3.73	0	39		
Butter	8	▲▼	6.49	0.07	0	59		
Avocado, California or Mexico (Hass)	20	▲▼	3.08	0.39	0.37	31		
	Actual		32.04	6.03	4.61	331	10.64	3:1
	Recommended		32.26	6	4.75	333	10.75	3:1

LEAN MEAT WITH VEGETABLE AND AVOCADO

GRAMS	
55	Cream, 36%
37	Group B vegetable (from list)
16	Lean meat (from list)
8	Butter
20	Avocado, Hass

Instructions: **Sauté sliced roast beef in butter in a small skillet until lightly browned. Pour remaining butter over warm vegetables. Serve cream as beverage or add diet caffeine-free root beer (free food). Serve sliced avocado with meat and vegetable.**

CREATE AND DISPLAY SNACKS

In addition to meals, snacks can also be created in KetoDietCalculator. The calculation of a snack is similar to creating the calculation of a meal. It requires that the dietitian choose a calorie value and ratio. Standard snacks can be selected from a list of typical ketogenic snacks. They may also be modified to meet preferences. There are several innovative snacks recipes in this feature, which allow the user to test new items.

Table 10.4 is an example of a snack calculation from home-prepared ketogenic diet chocolate brownies. The recipe instructions (not shown) are provided with this snack. Once prepared, a brownie is cut to the gram weight identified to meet the desired calories and ratio.

TABLE 10.4

Example of Brownies Snack in KetoDietCalculator

FOOD ITEM	GRAMS		FAT	PROTEIN	CARB	CALORIES	UNITS	RATIO
Chocolate brownies	22	▲ ▼	10.01	2.09	1.08	103	3.17	
		Actual	10.01	2.09	1.08	103	3.17	3.16:1

WEEKLY MENU PLANNER

After creating several meals and snacks, the user may plan a calendar of menus using the title of the meal or snack. The *Weekly Menu Planner* feature is helpful for organizing meals and snacks for upcoming days or weeks. This is especially helpful when there is more than one caregiver involved in managing the diet. First, the user selects a date from the calendar, then is prompted to select from the list of meals or snacks that were previously created and verified. A week of meals is illustrated in Table 10.5. The number that appears after the meal titles references the recipe for the meal.

TABLE 10.5

Week of Meals on the Ketogenic Diet

MEAL	SUN FEBRUARY 8	MON FEBRUARY 9	TUE FEBRUARY 10	WED FEBRUARY 11	THU FEBRUARY 12	FRI FEBRUARY 13	SAT FEBRUARY 14
AM meal	Keto pancakes - 5	Sausage/ fruit - 17	Keto shake - 22	Cheesecake - 8	Quiche - 14	Keto shake - 22	Omelet - 11
Mid-day	Hot dog/ celery - 3	Mac-N-cheese - 4	Cheese/ veg - 9	Taco - 21	Tuna salad - 15	Turkey salad - 6	Chicken/ veg - 26
PM meal	Spaghetti - 16	Stir-fry - 13	Veg soup - 10	Beef/veg - 18	Chicken salad - 2	Pizza - 12	Pork/veg - 24

FLUID AND DIET SCHEDULE

Another feature that assists caregivers with organizing the diet is the *Fluid and Diet Schedule*. This tool is intended to plan a daily routine of meal and snack times, nutritional supplements, medications, and beverages. It calculates the amount of fluid that is recommended for good health. The user can adjust the schedule during diet therapy as needed. This schedule is also available in a special format for individuals who are receiving their nutrition in liquid formulation, such as bottle feeding or feeding tubes.

ADDITIONAL FEATURES

KetoDietCalculator also includes supportive features to assist health care providers in the management of diet therapies. These are only viewable through the health care access portal of the KetoDietCalculator.

- Vitamin and mineral supplement database with micronutrient and carbohydrate content
- Medication database with carbohydrate content
- Help Line—a question and response field for help with KetoDietCalculator

KetoDietCalculator was designed in 2002 by Beth Zupec-Kania with David Chase of LifeTime Computing and has since received weekly editing and additions to its database, as well as annual updates to maintain the integrity of its digital framework. Use of this program has grown each year and is currently accessed by medical centers in 45 countries with several thousand users worldwide. The program is housed on a secure server. The Charlie Foundation for Ketogenic Therapies (see Chapter 23) provides funding for regular upgrades and maintenance. Cambrooke Therapeutics, Vitaflo, and Solace Nutrition provide supportive funding. For further information, you can e-mail Beth Zupec-Kania at ketokania@gmail.com.

Gram Conversion to Household Measure

5 grams = 1 teaspoon (tsp)
15 grams = 1 tablespoon (tbl)
30 grams = 2 tablespoons
60 grams = 1/4 cup
120 grams = 1/2 cup
180 grams = 3/4 cup
240 grams = 1 cup

CHAPTER 11

Fine-Tuning the Diet

Fine-tuning the ketogenic diet typically occurs during the first few months of beginning the diet. However, it can also occur after years have gone by as a way to make the diet more effective. This can be an important part of individualizing the diet for your child, be it changes in calories, ratios, fluid allotments, or other variables such as medication dosing. Most changes can be done by e-mail and phone when necessary.

We encourage close communication with the ketogenic diet team as the dietitian adjusts the various components of the diet—calories, liquids, fats, recipes, ketogenic ratios, and so forth—to achieve high ketosis and the best meals for tolerability for the child and the family. This support can be crucial as the family searches for the proper foods, learns to read and interpret labels, becomes accustomed to preparing the diet, and integrates the diet into their lifestyle. A myriad of questions arise as a child's body becomes accustomed to the diet and as the meals are prepared—we expect many e-mails in the first few months! Support for fine-tuning is particularly necessary when seizure control improves initially but the family is hoping for even better seizure control.

Initiating the diet means not only changing the foods that are consumed but also changing the parents' and family members' attitudes and expectations about food and mealtimes. This is particularly true for small children where the small number of calories calculated is overestimated at the start or just seems "too small" and is increased by the parent who does the cooking, with resultant weight gain for the child and lack of optimal seizure control. We often make changes based on a child's body mass index and hunger level—if a child is happier and healthier, the child may be more compliant with the diet as well. Our studies show that calories do not usually affect seizure control (more on this later), so if the child is hungry, we will often give more ketogenic food.

Sometimes a child refuses to eat the cream or becomes too constipated. Adjustments to the child's diet must then be made. It takes at least a week to see if a change is effective, so you have to be a bit patient. Because only one change should be made at a time, it may take several months of fine-tuning to see how much benefit the diet will provide for that child.

There is often a bit of trial and error by the dietitian to find the *right* diet for the child. Although usually we start with a 4:1 diet for children over 2 years of age, lower ratios may be better for some (especially babies). Some centers now will start with lower ratios (e.g., 1:1 or 2:1, such as the modified Atkins diet) and gradually increase ratios monthly to get to 4:1. This has been described as the "low and slow" approach and was pioneered by Jennifer Fabe from Canada. Many centers do things differently and that's okay!

Each family is asked to make a three-month commitment to attempting the diet in order to allow it time to work. We ask this even before the family comes into the hospital to initiate the fasting phase of the diet. Of our families, 83% remain on the diet for at least 3 months. Every family is told that they may discontinue the diet any time they wish after the 3-month trial. However, because the initiation of the diet is so very labor-intensive for the family and ketogenic diet team, this investment of time, effort, and money is not worthwhile if the diet is not given a good trial. Of course, if there is an emergency (unremitting vomiting, pancreatitis, etc.) in which the diet has to be stopped sooner than 3 months, please don't feel bad. The diet is not the right option for every child.

Our data suggest that if the diet is going to work, it will do so within that first 3 months. Some other research suggests that the first 3 months may be the most important with stricter diets (e.g., 4:1 better than 3:1 and 10 grams/day better than 20 grams/day with the modified Atkins diet) and more likely to lead to seizure control. In this regard, although the first few months may involve this fine-tuning, we often loosen up on our restrictiveness after that. This isn't always the case, though, and even some children who have been on the diet for decades require some "tweaking" of their diet now and then.

In this chapter we discuss some ideas to fine-tune the diet. Some are designed to boost ketosis, but recognizing that ketosis is not clearly why the diet works; other ideas may work in different ways (e.g., cutting calories).

EXPECTATIONS

Fine-tuning does not always lead to total freedom from seizures. During the initiation of the ketogenic diet and afterward, it helps if a family's expectations are realistic so that they are not setting themselves up for disappointment. Virtually all families have heard of Charlie and been to The Charlie Foundation's website. Charlie Abrahams came to Hopkins severely impaired by his seizures and medications and within one week was cured. This impression of the speed in which the diet works is reinforced by the story of another child with uncontrollable seizures in the Meryl Streep film, *First Do No Harm*. That child was also flown to Johns Hopkins and sent home cured.

These stories are both based on truth, but they are not typical, and certainly not universal.

- Not everyone is cured by the ketogenic diet.
- Not all of those whose seizures are substantially helped by the diet have that happen during the brief hospital stay.

- Not all children are able to come off medication and remain seizure free. Medications and the diet are often a "partnership."

We spend a lot of time with families during the initiation week reviewing their personal goals. Every family has different goals. For most, it's fewer seizures. For others, the primary reason to start the diet is fewer medications. For nearly all, it's a brighter, more alert child! We may also look at the EEG over time to see if there is improvement. Think about what *your* expectations are before you start the diet—you may even want to write them down, keep them somewhere safe, and look at them again in 6 months.

The most important thing for a parent to remember during the fine-tuning period is this: *You can, and you will persevere!* If your child is doing well at the start of the diet, that's terrific. But most children do not immediately have seizure improvement. Only after working carefully with the ketogenic diet team for several months will you have enough information to decide if there is sufficient improvement in your child to continue with the diet.

Breakthrough seizures do not necessarily mean that the diet has failed; further fine-tuning may likely be beneficial. If seizures are less frequent or less severe, it may be hoped that further improvement will be achieved as the diet is adjusted.

THE IMPORTANCE OF SLEUTHING

To master the fine-tuning process, parents and the ketogenic diet team become adept at tracing the cause of any problem that arises. It is also important not to make a change based on one bad day—the next day could be much better with no changes to the diet! Colds and illnesses can make seizures worse and then go away after a week or so. We usually make diet changes if things are worsening over a week or more. It is hard (but important) not to jump to conclusions that the diet isn't working after one bad day.

If a child is having persistent seizures and/or problems on the diet, the parents and the rest of the diet team should try to become mystery solvers. It often takes a detective's spirit to locate the source of a problem and fix it. Important questions to ask:

- Is there an opportunity for the child to eat extra nonketogenic food at school or while playing at a friend's house?
- Are new commercial foods being used? They often contain hidden carbohydrates.
- If commercial foods are used, are they the exact brands and items called for in the menu? For example, different brands of bologna may have different fillers and different carbohydrate contents.
- Check the label—has the manufacturer changed ingredients?
- If calculations were made by computer, are the database entries for the ingredients correct?

- Is the child sick with a common virus or bacterial infection? Infections may trigger seizures both in children on the diet and those on medications. Wait until the infection is gone then reassess how the child is doing.
- Is everything being measured on a gram scale except free fluids? Sometimes, after the diet seems to be working well, parents become lax and measure foods by eye rather than by scale.
- Are vegetables being weighed cooked or raw as specified?
- Are the peaches packed in water, as they should be, rather than in glucose-containing syrup or fruit juice?
- Is there a soft-hearted grandparent in the picture who is encouraging the child to cheat"just a little"?
- Did the medication change (either on purpose by the neurologist or by a pharmacy mistake)?
- If ketones seem lower, are the ketostrips fresh (sometimes if >1 year old they can test lower)?

It is not possible to list every problem and solution in this book, but the principle to remember is *be a sleuth.* Think it through. Don't give up. Look for clues. Was there a change in the number or kind of seizures at a certain time of the day or week? Did the problems begin following a certain meal plan or a specific family event? Sometimes the best thing to do can be to wait a week and see if seizures return to the prior number. If nothing is found that caused the worsening of seizures, allow the natural history of epilepsy (ups and downs of seizures) to play to your advantage. Things could get better just with time rather than increasing a medication.

If a problem develops after good seizure control has been established, parents should examine every aspect of their child's food and liquid intake, play habits, pharmaceuticals, and time with babysitters and relatives. The dietitian should listen to a parent describing exactly how each meal is prepared. If the dietitian cannot solve the problem, the physician may need to get involved.

REMEMBER: Illness, ear infection, the flu, or urinary tract infection may cause breakthrough seizures. See if a child is sick and if the cause of breakthrough seizures might be temporary illness before changing the diet. Illness is the most common cause of breakthrough seizures.

MEASURING KETOSIS

Although we don't know for sure that ketones matter for everyone, they seem to for some children. Looking at a seizure calendar and trying to correlate seizures and ketones can help your ketogenic diet team see if your child is "ketone sensitive." If that is the case, then changing the diet (if ketones are low) may be beneficial.

We teach parents to check ketones daily by using a urine dipstick. This is an easy, cost-effective method for monitoring the level of ketosis. The paper stick, when dipped in the child's urine, turns color depending on the amount of ketones in the urine. The ketogenic diet has traditionally been fine-tuned to maintain the child's urine at 3 to 4+ ketones, which turn the stick a dark purple color (80–160 mmol/L). As mentioned before, make sure the ketone sticks are fresh. Be aware that many neonates and babies only can achieve trace or small ketosis on the diet (despite many attempts to make the diet higher in fat or lower in carbs).

For babies and young children who are not yet toilet-trained, urine is collected by placing cotton balls in the diaper. Once the child has urinated, the cotton balls can be squeezed onto a dipstick for testing. For older children on the diet, peeing on a dipstick becomes second nature. For older children that are not continent, you can use the cotton ball approach, or periodically use a urine collection bag, available in physician offices.

The weakness of urinary ketone testing is that it is actually ketones in the brain, not those in the urine, that may influence seizure control. Ketones in the urine can seem lower if tested after a child drinks a large quantity of liquid. They may vary with the time of day and often reflect several days of metabolism. These ups and downs, however, may have only an indirect relation to seizure control.

Preliminary evidence using blood ketones suggests that once the blood ketone level rises to more than 2 mmol, the urine ketone level becomes 4+. That is the highest level the dipsticks can measure. There are some children who report that when they have checked blood ketones using meters, they have seen higher levels (>4 mmol/L) correlate with better seizure control. Therefore, in *some* situations, blood ketones may be important. However, we don't usually recommend that our parents go home with blood ketone meters in all cases. We see this as generally an unnecessary sticking of children. We sometimes do check serum ketones with the rest of the blood work at clinic visits if we think the urine ketones may be unreliable (or a child has "no ketones" but we smell it on their breath).

COMMON PROBLEMS AT THE START OF THE DIET

For the first 2 to 3 weeks after the hospital discharge, the child and the family will have had the chance to adapt to the diet as it was initially calculated. This is the time we start making the small changes we call fine-tuning that may make a difference in a child's level of seizure control. The most common areas to be explored for fine-tuning potential are the following:

- Caloric intake
- Distribution of meals
- Misuse of free foods
- Menu preparation

- Illness
- Ketogenic ratio
- Fluid intake
- Processed food content
- Function or use of gram scales
- Food values used in calculations

"FREE" FOODS

There are no foods on the ketogenic diet that are actually "free," meaning available on an unlimited basis. What are often referred to as "free" foods are those that can be eaten occasionally in small quantities without being calculated into the daily ketogenic menu plans.

Free foods include 25 grams of lettuce; one walnut, macadamia nut, or pecan; three filberts; or three ripe (black) olives. Most other foods, such as sugar-free Jell-O or any carbohydrate-based snack food, cannot be used at all without being calculated into the diet.

Any added foods outside of meal plans can make a difference in seizure control. Children who eat free foods every day may find that they affect seizure control. For children who continue to have seizures on the diet, free foods should be the first thing restricted during the fine-tuning process.

SPECIFIC FOODS

Initial menus for the diet are usually calculated using "generic" fruits and vegetables but designating specific meats and fats. The use of processed foods such as hot dogs and deli meats may cause a drop in urine ketones and result in a rise of seizures. The content of these foods is hard to assess. The labeling of their content is not exact. They are usually high in carbohydrates and sodium and relatively low in protein. Therefore, while fine-tuning the diet of a child with continued seizure activity, parents are requested to withhold processed foods for one month to see if this has an effect. Most of our children do fine with these foods (in fact, we have one child who ate nothing but hot dogs every day!), but if they are new and seizures have increased, be aware and let your dietitian know.

FATS

Not all fats are equal. A child who is having difficulty producing sufficient ketosis may need to have the type of fats in the diet adjusted. It may help to reduce or remove the less-dense fats such as butter and mayonnaise and substitute canola, flaxseed, olive, or medium chain triglyceride (MCT) oil (Table 11.1). MCT oil is more efficiently metabolized, helping to produce a deeper ketosis. We use MCT oil for only a portion of the fat allowance, however, because when

TABLE 11.1

The Protein, Carbohydrate, Fat, and Calorie Content of "Fats" (kcal)

	GRAMS	PROTEIN	FAT	CARB	KCAL
Butter	100	0.67	81.33	0.00	735
Margarine, stick corn oil	100	0.00	76.00	0.00	684
Mayonnaise, Hellmann's	100	1.43	80.00	0.70	729
Corn oil	100	0.00	97.14	0.00	874
Olive oil	100	0.00	96.43	0.00	868
Canola oil	100	0.00	90.00	0.00	810
Flaxseed oil	100	0.00	100.00	0.00	900
Peanut oil	100	0.00	96.43	0.00	868
MCT oil	100	0.00	92.67	0.00	834
Safflower oil	100	0.00	97.14	0.00	874

ingested in large quantities it often causes gastrointestinal disturbances such as diarrhea or vomiting.

We suggest using as much as possible oils that contain a high-fat level per gram and little or no carbohydrate or protein. When using MCT oil we begin with 5 grams per meal, or 15 total grams daily, for children who need to go into deeper ketosis. This may be increased slowly, as tolerated, until seizure control seems as good as possible with minimal side effects.

FREQUENCY OF MEALS AND SNACKS

Not only is the *quantity* (calories) and *quality* (ketogenic ratio and nutritional content) of food important, but also sometimes the *timing* of food intake can influence the success of the ketogenic diet.

An individual on a normal diet stores energy for short-term use as glycogen and fat. During periods between eating or during starvation, the body first burns carbohydrate from food recently eaten, then burns carbohydrate that it has stored as glycogen, and finally begins to burn fat. Burning fat, in the absence of carbohydrates, will result in ketosis.

Children on the ketogenic diet have virtually no carbohydrate in their diet, and they consume few calories, so they have virtually no stores of glycogen. Therefore, they depend on fat for their energy.

A child who is at the desirable weight has very little stored fat and, therefore, is dependent upon the fats he or she eats at each meal. If too long a time passes between meals, the child may run out of fat to burn. The child's body will then burn some of its stored protein, but this will make his or her ketones decrease, and seizures may result. In this way, we'll give extra snacks here and there, especially at times of the day with more seizures (e.g., nighttime).

Children usually have breakfast in the early morning and eat lunch around noon, but dinnertime is very variable. Some children are fed supper as early as 5:30 p.m. and then go to bed at 7:30 to 8:00 p.m. This means that they will not have eaten for 12 to 14 hours before their breakfast. This makes little difference to a child on a normal diet who has plenty of energy reserves stored as glycogen and fat. But a child on the ketogenic diet may not have sufficient reserves to maintain ketosis overnight. If a child eats dinner later or has a 10 p.m. snack at bedtime, the body is less likely to run out of ketones during the night. This may help to control early morning seizures.

COMMON PROBLEMS IN THE FIRST MONTHS ON THE DIET

Hunger

Because the physical quantity of food on the diet (the bulk) is smaller than in a normal diet, many children will feel hungry during the first week or two of the diet until they adjust. This may be especially true of overweight children, who will have their diets calculated to include some weight loss. However, ketosis itself decreases the appetite, so children are much less likely to be hungry when consistently high levels of ketones are reached, usually within a week of starting the diet.

If a child initially complains of being hungry, try to determine which of the following are true:

- The child is really hungry.
- The child has not yet adapted to the smaller portion.
- The child wants the pleasure and comfort of eating.

Sometimes it is not the child who is hungry at all, but rather the parents who feel pity for the child or guilt about the small portions and who project their feelings about the diet onto the child. Other times, in the complex emotional atmosphere of diet initiation, a child's cries of hunger are actually declarations of rebellion against the parents. In any case, most children will lose their feelings of hunger once they adjust to the food they are consuming and achieve consistently high ketosis. Remember, in many cases the amount of calories is EQUAL to what they were eating before (that's how we do it at Johns Hopkins nowadays).

We recommend that parents deal with hunger without trying to add extra calories to the diet, at least for the first few weeks. Tricks to modify hunger without increasing calories include:

- Drinking decaffeinated diet soda or seltzer instead of water for at least part of the liquid allotment

- Freezing drinks, such as diet orange soda mixed with cream, into ice pops
- Eating a leaf of lettuce twice a day with meals
- Making sure that foods, such as vegetables, are patted dry so that water is not part of the weight
- Recalculating the diet plan into four equal meals, or three meals and a snack, while maintaining a constant level of calories and the proper ketogenic ratio
- *Decreasing* calories slightly to raise ketosis and suppress hunger

Irritability

Children who are on the diet become irritable and cry for many reasons just as other children do. It is not always due to the diet. When problems appear in a child on the ketogenic diet, don't always assume that the diet is the cause of the problem. A child may be irritable from the hospital stay or from the difficulty of making such a radical adjustment in his or her life. The child may rebel against the extra attention and pressure to which he or she is being exposed, or may be coming down with the flu or a cold. A cautious approach to fine-tuning over several weeks or months after the start of the diet will make it easier to remain on the diet.

Thirst

Thirst is not a common problem for children on the ketogenic diet because ketones also decrease thirst. However, it is important to watch the child's urine output, particularly in hot weather, because extra fluid may be needed. In general, we do not restrict fluid any longer, so this should not be a problem.

It seems to be important for many children to space the consumption of liquids throughout the day and not to give a thirsty child a big drink all at once, as this can sometimes cause breakthrough seizure activity and can also leave the child thirstier later on. Some parents give their child a regular dose of water or diet soda (with no caffeine) every one to two hours during the day. Other children seem to be able to drink larger amounts of liquid with no seizures.

In hot climates or during summer months, the cream in the diet need not be counted as part of the allotted liquid. In effect, this raises the liquid allowance by the quantity of the cream.

CHANGING THE DIET'S KETOGENIC RATIO

Raising the diet's ratio (fat:[protein + carbohydrate] grams) increases the amount of fats consumed, with the goal of increasing ketosis and thereby resulting in better seizure control. If a child is continuing to have seizures, and if careful, thorough sleuthing has not revealed a cause, then raising the ketogenic ratio may be considered. This is probably the *most* common way to "fine-tune" the diet. We raise ratios in 1-point increments, from 3:1 to 4:1, or 2:1 to 3:1. We rarely go higher than this. On occasion, we'll use half-point ratios (e.g., 3.5:1 or 4.5:1), but these have really not been studied and we don't think they make much of a difference.

Occasionally the ratio is decreased during the fine-tuning period if the child becomes anorexic and will not eat, if the child remains too acidotic, is experiencing frequent illnesses, or is having digestive difficulties on the diet. Most children over age two years start the diet on a 4:1 ratio. They are then adjusted downward slowly after their first year on the diet.

Overweight children are an exception to this rule. We frequently start them on a diet on a 3:1 ratio with restricted calories to facilitate weight loss. As they lose weight, they burn their own body fat, and this produces high ketones for them. As overweight children approach their desirable weight, they have less of their own body fat to burn, so we may need to increase the ratio to maintain the same high level of ketones. Adolescents often need a 3:1 ratio to provide sufficient protein within their caloric restrictions. Very young children and infants are also usually started on a 3:1 diet to allow more protein for their growth.

CARNITINE

There is a lot out there on the Internet about carnitine. In general, most people make enough carnitine to burn long chain fatty acids and do not need supplementation. However, we do check free carnitine levels at clinic visits, as do most ketogenic diet centers today. If the free carnitine levels are <15, and especially if a child is sleepy or sluggish, extra carnitine (330 mg capsules [or 3 ml of the 1000 mg/10 ml solution], given three times a day) can be helpful. There is no proof that giving carnitine will also help reduce seizures and some reports suggest it could even make things worse for some children! However, we all have a few cases where the parents say that it helped. We will sometimes try a one-month trial of carnitine for a child who had control on the diet but lost it over time. If it doesn't help, then we'll stop the carnitine.

INTERMITTENT FASTING

Based on some research in mice, Dr. Adam Hartman in our group found that intermittent fasting (skipping some meals here and there) worked for seizure control. Surprisingly, this was NOT the same as the ketogenic diet, as people believed 100 years ago when it was first created. We still fast children to start the diet, but Dr. Hartman's research found that they are two completely separate things and BOTH work to help control seizures.

As a result of his interesting work in mice, we tried intermittent fasting (skip breakfast and lunch on a day—do that twice a week) in six children on the ketogenic diet. All six had improvements in their seizure control, but wanted to fine-tune their diet to do even better. We found that four of the six did improve further with the fasting, but it was only temporary. Eventually it became too hard and hunger set in. We're still interested in this idea, and are working on ways to make it better and less difficult. It also is unknown if this would work for children NOT on the ketogenic diet.

FINE-TUNING THE MODIFIED ATKINS DIET

The modified Atkins is a lower ratio ketogenic diet that induces ketosis with less restrictiveness. Carbohydrates are reduced to 10 grams per day (20 grams per day for adults) and fats are encouraged. Fine-tuning details for this diet are provided in Chapter 16.

THE DECISION TREE

The first thing to look for when breakthrough seizures occur is whether the child has had an opportunity to eat something that is not on the diet. Someone may have given the child food or the child may have helped himself or herself. One child was slipping out of bed at night and raiding the refrigerator. Another girl had a seizure on Sunday, and her mother found to her dismay that a well-meaning grown-up at church had given her a lollipop.

The level of urinary ketosis may vary with the time of day. It is usually lower in the morning and higher later in the day. This natural variation in the level of ketones as measured in the urine does not necessarily indicate a problem if it is not accompanied by seizures.

We will at times test the system in a child with low ketones by fasting the child for 24 hours. If the ketones rise after this fast, then we will decrease calories. With the exception of weight gain correlated to growth in height, weight gain on the diet is an indication that calorie levels are set too high. At an excess of 100 calories per day, it takes an entire month before any weight gain is seen. Therefore, some caloric adjustments can be made based on low-ketone levels.

Sometimes better control may be achieved by using a 4.5:1 ratio for a period of time. The higher the diet ratio, the more restricted food options get, so the implications of raising the diet ratio should be seriously considered before it is prescribed.

THE MOST COMMON cause of breakthrough seizures in a child who is getting the proper food and liquid volumes is illness or fever.

An isolated seizure during illness requires no action on the part of the parents. Repeated breakthrough seizures can be the presenting sign of kidney stones, urinary tract infection, gastroenteritis, or other childhood infections. See Chapter 24 for greater detail on managing acute illness during the diet.

The ketogenic diet decision tree in Figure 11.1 can be used as a guide to investigating breakthrough seizures. This tree has been in use since the first edition of this ketogenic diet book and still is very helpful!

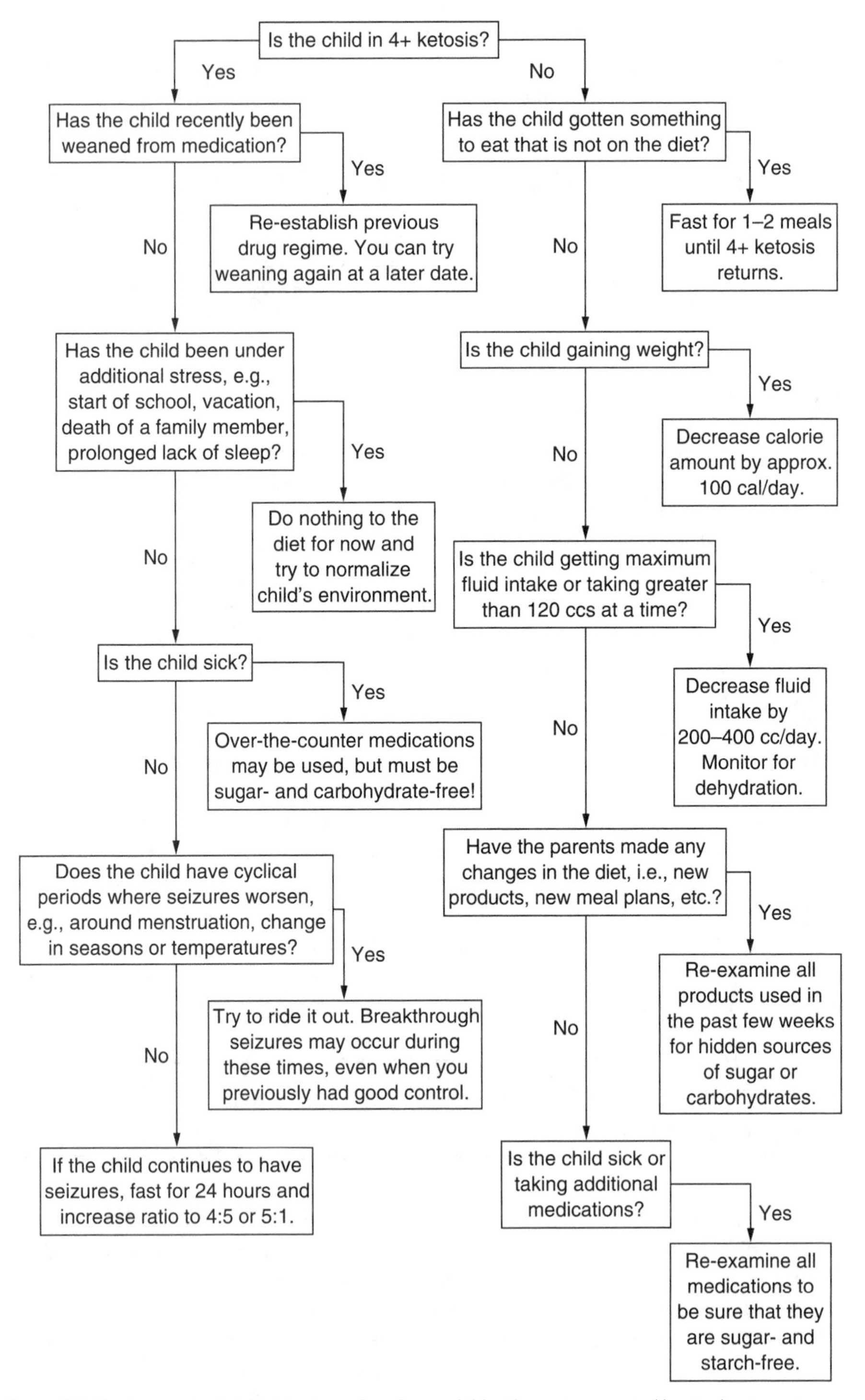

Figure 11.1. The ketogenic diet decision tree—for when a child with previous control begins having seizures.

TOP TRICKS MONTHS AFTER STARTING THE DIET

Sadly, we also see children who come back after initially good seizure control and find that without any obvious diet-related problems (or illness), the seizures have returned. This is obviously disappointing and this "honeymoon" situation is frustrating for neurologists and dietitians as well. It is probably the number one reason we see children for consults from other ketogenic diet centers. Sometimes children just honeymoon to the diet as they had in the past to medications. However, there are some tricks we use, one at a time, to see if we can regain some control. Some have been mentioned earlier in this chapter already. They are listed in Table 11.2.

TABLE 11.2

Tricks to Regain Lost Seizure Control

- Lower (or sometimes raise) calories by 100 calories/day.
- Add carnitine (usually 330 mg three times a day).
- Check serum anticonvulsant levels and increase them. Sometimes as children get bigger their levels drift downward.
- Reduce anticonvulsants! Although this seems counterintuitive in children who are having more seizures, sometimes it works. We have seen improvement, specifically in those on valproate and clonazepam, by reducing them.
- Fast occasionally for 12 hours (assuming the child has done this during the ketogenic diet admission previously).
- Add MCT oil. In a way, this is a different diet (see Chapter 27) and might help.
- Increase the ratio temporarily to 4.5:1 (if at 4:1) or more permanently to 4:1. Realize, however, that studies to date show ratio changes months after starting the diet are not usually helpful.
- Lower the ratio! One of our previous dietitians, Jane McGrogan, RD, taught us this trick. Again, it may seem counterintuitive, but some children do better at lower ratios with less ketosis.
- Spread out foods over the day. Sometimes ketones can dip later in the day if meals are too far apart.
- Change the formula (if the child is formula fed). Sometimes a new formula is absorbed differently for some children and this can help.
- Intermittently fast (2 days a week, 2 meals per day skipped on those days).
- Take away artificial sweeteners and prepackaged meals.

DOES IT REALLY HELP?

In 2014, after we began seeing more and more children coming to Johns Hopkins for second opinions on the ketogenic diet from other centers, we realized that fine-tuning was the number one reason they came. Perhaps from reading this book or talking to other parents, families thought that fine-tuning *should* work. However, does it really help?

A very eager (and hard-working!) medical student, Jessica Selter, approached me to help try and answer this elusive question. In order to do this, Jessica combed through the charts of 200 consecutive children seen at our ketogenic diet center over six years. She reviewed thousands of e-mails and phone calls and found 391 distinct fine-tuning changes that were made (mostly done in order to improve seizures). Most of them were listed in Table 11.2. She then looked to see if those changes worked (either a >50% seizure reduction after that change or even seizure freedom).

She found some good news and bad news. The good news was that 42% of the time, there was some reported improvement (even mild). Less commonly, but still reasonably (one in five), there was a big change (>50% reduction). It also didn't matter when the change was made—even children with fine-tuning after years on the diet still saw improvement occur (don't give up!). As a result, we no longer say "it's too late to try and fine-tune." Another interesting finding was that younger children were more likely to respond to fine-tuning (maybe they need higher ketones).

The bad news was that only 1 in 30 became seizure-free from a diet change. No one method as listed in Table 11.2 was the best, but if anything, calorie changes were not very helpful. Since this research, we are much less likely to cut calories alone as a method of fine-tuning. We also found that adding a medication, although not always done for keto kids, could be helpful—24% of the time it helped (slightly more often than a diet change, in fact).

How does this help us? Well, it suggests that fine-tuning is worth trying (especially in babies), and changes can help even after years of the diet, but there's a limit. After many fine-tuning changes have been made, don't forget about medications. As we've said before, the diet and medications are often a "partnership." We've had families refuse medications because "nothing worked" only to find that a new drug, just introduced onto the market, really helps. That doesn't mean the diet is a failure and should be stopped: The diet may be doing half the work and medications the other half.

THE LIMITS OF FINE-TUNING

Improvements in behavior, mood, mental alertness, and a general sense of well-being are additional benefits that the diet often brings. If parents set a goal of total seizure control, they may be setting themselves up for disappointment. Total control may not be possible.

After trying the diet for the initial three-month period, and after working with the ketogenic diet team to figure out if greater control can be achieved by adjusting food or medications, parents of children who have not responded to the diet or who have improved only moderately have to make a decision. This is also true for children with improvement on the diet who eventually see those benefits wear off over the years, and fine-tuning didn't add anything additional. These parents must weigh the benefits of the diet for their child against its burdens. Then they have to decide whether it is worthwhile for them to continue the diet.

CHAPTER 12

Going Off the Diet

You have come to the end of what may have been a long journey. We know this is tough for any family. For children who are seizure free, there is anxiety and fear about seizures coming back. For children who have not improved with the diet, there is sometimes a sense of depression at this having been the "last resort" (which it is not!). For those in between (50%–99% improved), it's a mix of all those emotions.

In prior editions of this book, this chapter was brief and there was little real research to guide our recommendations. That has changed and we can now be more specific about the odds of a child coming off of the diet successfully. Despite that, every decision is a difficult one and needs to be made using a team approach: parents, neurologists, and dietitians together. Make only one change at a time. Do not wean the diet and medications at the same time! You also do not need to add a medication if the diet is being weaned. We are also generally not in favor of weaning the diet before big life events, trips, school examinations, and so forth. Plan ahead—in most situations, weaning the diet is not an emergency. Also make sure to have your neurologist's phone number or e-mail readily available in case the wean does lead to worse seizures.

WHEN TO STOP THE DIET?

This question is truly up to the parents of the individual child. We will rarely "give up" on the diet in less than a month unless seizures are worsening or the child is having serious metabolic problems we can't fix. The data would suggest that the diet will start to work within 4 to 6 weeks for most children (if it *is* going to work). However, we usually tell parents to give it at least 3 months just in case their child is a "late bloomer."

If it does work, there is no set time in which the diet must be stopped either. Even in super successful cases, most centers will start seriously considering the risks of the diet compared to benefits after 2 years. In many children, we suspect the diet has "done its job" and without it seizures will be no different than with it. The only way to find out for sure is to wean the diet! For some children, our suspicion will be correct: Seizures will be no different. For others, it will not be: Seizures will get worse. Of course, it is important to be in close contact during the diet wean and have a plan already in mind for what to do if the seizures do worsen.

Some children who have responded exceptionally well to the diet start to come off it before the two-year mark is reached. This decision is often suggested by the parents and agreed to in consultation with the physicians. We have done this in cases of Doose syndrome and infantile spasms, sometimes even after 6 to 12 months. For children with infantile spasms we treat with the diet before medications; if the diet works, we stop after 6 months.

Can the diet be continued longer than 2 years? Yes! The child who has had a good, but incomplete response to the diet and for whom the diet is not a burden may continue the diet on a visit-by-visit basis. We have had children who have remained on the diet as long as 26 years. A lot depends on side effects, too. But many families find the diet is easy and part of their routine … and their child needs to eat anyway! The parents are really the primary decision makers at our center in determining when to stop the diet.

THE DOWNSIDE OF LONG-TERM DIET USE

The long-term consequences of remaining on the ketogenic diet for many years have been studied recently, and although most children do very well, there can be problems. We recently studied about 30 children who had been continually on the ketogenic diet for 6 to 11 years. The risk of kidney stones is about one in four with long-term use, so this needs to be closely monitored. No child had very significantly elevated cholesterol levels (above 400 mg/dl). Studies have shown that lipids and triglycerides are elevated during the diet to levels that would normally be considered to increase the threat of stroke or heart disease after a lifetime of exposure. Bone fractures do occur more often in children on the diet for over 6 years (one in five). However, the potential threat of stroke or heart disease after a limited exposure of 2 or even 10 years of a high-fat diet does not appear to occur. Any health threat would have to be evaluated in relation to alternative health risks posed by uncontrolled epilepsy, such as increased seizures or increased long-term intake of anticonvulsant medications, but it is important for the clinician and family to weigh the pros and cons of remaining on the diet. It may be important to test and see what the diet is still doing five years down the road by having the child come off the diet. Many parents are scared to take their child off the diet, but it is not a treatment without risks, and it has to be discussed yearly at each clinic visit to decide whether or not remaining on the diet for many years is beneficial to that patient.

HOW DO I WEAN THE DIET?

Previous editions of this book and even the 2009 consensus statement suggested that weaning the diet over "several" months was "traditional," but there has never been proof that a slow wean is best. It is usually tapered slowly as there is concern that a quicker discontinuation would lead to dramatic worsening (e.g., some children may cheat with carbs and have a seizure). However, we have all seen children stop the diet abruptly during a hospitalization or emergency and do fine. In some children, we would taper the diet by lowering the ratio every few days. They also would often do perfectly fine.

A study done in 2010 at Johns Hopkins Hospital (Dr. Lila Worden et al.) looked at our experience in how to discontinue the diet—the first time this has ever been done. Interestingly, how it was done was different depending upon who the Hopkins neurologist was! About a third of the time it was stopped in 1 to 7 days. Another third was stopped over 1 to 6 weeks. The other third was more traditional, and the diet weaned over several months. In general, as would seem obvious, the children weaned more slowly tended to be those who had done better (i.e., seizure free and fewer medications at the time of the wean). If the diet didn't work, parents were anxious to stop it—as soon as possible.

The big surprise was that it didn't matter how quickly the wean was done. For one in 10 children, seizures get worse (>25% increase in seizures), no matter the speed of the wean. Details from this study are in Table 12.1.

These results have changed how we wean the diet—we are much quicker in weaning the diet than we used to be. Tapering the diet over months no longer seems necessary—we now typically will reduce the ratio every one to two weeks. If a child is in the hospital in a safe setting, generally for an emergency problem, we may discontinue the diet abruptly as well.

Our current recommended wean (for most children on a 4:1 ratio) is presented in the following list:

Weeks 1-2:	Reduce to 3:1
Weeks 3-4:	Reduce to 2:1
Weeks 5-6:	Reduce to 1:1
Weeks 7-8[a]:	Start a regular diet

[a]Remain on multivitamin, calcium, and oral citrate supplements during the wean until the diet is over. Keep in close contact with your ketogenic diet team!
Can make these changes weekly, if desired.

Meals with lower ketogenic ratios are increasingly similar to regular meals. A 1:1 ratio will seem almost like a normal diet compared with the 4:1. There will be room for a lot more meat and vegetables and even the possibility of some carbohydrates.

Once a child has been weaned down to a 1:1 ratio and has been on that ratio for 1 to 2 weeks, we recommend that regular foods are introduced and the patient is then off the ketogenic diet.

TABLE 12.1

Number Who Worsened by Discontinuation Rate

OUTCOME	IMMEDIATE (1-7 DAYS)	QUICK (1-6 WEEKS)	SLOW (>6 WEEKS)
Overall	11%	11%	19%
<50% seizure reduction	3%	9%	9%
50%-99%	26%	22%	36%
Seizure free	25%	9%	10%

If seizures worsen with the last few steps, we generally will go back to a 1:1 ratio. This is close to the modified Atkins diet (Section III). We have many children in whom this happened, and they stayed on the modified Atkins diet for an additional several months to years. They generally found it easier than the ketogenic diet and were willing to keep carbohydrates reduced.

WILL MY CHILD GET WORSE DURING THE WEAN?

Back in 2007, we looked at this question for children who were seizure-free and stopped the diet. Thirteen of 66 children (20%) had seizures return, sometimes years later. The seizures were most likely to come back in those who had (a) an abnormal EEG around the time of weaning the diet, (b) an abnormal MRI for any reason (e.g., stroke or brain malformation), or (c) tuberous sclerosis complex. That doesn't mean we don't try to wean the diet in these seizure-free children—but we do it carefully. The study mentioned previously looked to see if any factors led to seizures worsening in *all* keto children (not just those who were seizure free). The only factor that seemed important was having a 50% to 99% seizure reduction. Children who were either seizure free or <50% improved rarely got worse. When Dr. Worden and colleagues looked specifically at those children with 50% to 99% improvement, the only factor that seemed more likely to lead to seizures getting worse was being on more anticonvulsant drugs (1.4 drugs vs. 0.8).

In other words, if your child is still having seizures on the diet after a few years but is definitely better, he or she is at a bit higher risk to have seizures worsen when weaned from the diet. There is a higher risk if they are on more seizure medications. You can still try to wean the diet, just do it carefully!

WE HAD BEEN DOWN TO A 1:1 RATIO for a few months when one day the doctor said, "Why don't you take him out for an ice cream sundae—you're off the diet!" Well, I couldn't quite do that but we did take him for a steak and potato dinner. Then about an hour later I got him a little dish of mint chocolate chip ice cream. It was very dramatic for me to see him eat a real meal. And for him, too—his little eyes were watering. It was a tear-jerking experience. We had finally made it! He used to be an extremely picky eater, but now he just really enjoys eating.

AFTER HE HAD DONE PERFECTLY for a year and a half on the 4:1 diet, we had done 6 months on the 3:1, and then a couple of months on the 2:1, when his sixth birthday was coming up. We asked him what he wanted, and he said pizza. Well, you're nervous as can be, but he was doing so well that we decided to stop the diet on his birthday, before the full 6 months of the 2:1 were up. We invited all the neighborhood kids in, and I put candles in the pizza. After he took the first bite, he looked up at me and said, "Dad, this is the best birthday present I've ever had."

ANXIETY AND RELIEF

It is natural for a parent to feel anxious when a child is going off the diet. After all that time spent planning and measuring food within the accuracy of a gram, it's hard to kick the habit! All we can tell nervous parents is that ending the diet is to their child's advantage once the child is seizure free for 2 years. The ketogenic diet therapy's goal is to treat a problem—seizures. Once the problem is gone, the therapy should also end.

GOING OFF THE DIET WAS VERY LIBERATING. At last we could go places without planning and thinking about every meal. We could spend a day at the mall. She could go to parties and eat what the other kids were having. It was great. We still see our neurologist, but it's in a regular epilepsy clinic every few months. We ran into our dietitian at the mall several years later and gave her a big hug!

We know this is a tough moment for you. The diet is not like anticonvulsants—it requires lots of time and energy from parents and children. It also requires lots of work by the neurologists and dietitians who use it. We also find it hard to take our patients off the diet, and yes, we're nervous, too! Our final bit of advice is this: (a) one change at a time, (b) keep in close contact with your keto team, and (c) have a plan just in case the seizures get worse. Good luck!

The Modified Atkins Diet (for Children)

CHAPTER 13

When and Why Should I Use Alternative Diets?

What is an "alternative" diet anyway? When we talk about alternative diets, we are referring to the modified Atkins diet (MAD) and the low glycemic index treatments (LGIT). These diets were invented in the early 2000s and were first touched upon in the fourth edition of this book, with more information in the fifth edition. These diets are now much more widely used and, in fact, the MAD is now part of this book's title! Note: The medium chain triglyceride (MCT) diet is another ketogenic diet that provides fat in a slightly different way than the classic ketogenic diet but is not considered an alternative per se (covered in Chapter 27). There are other diets also being looked at, including the "specific carbohydrate diet," "paleo," "gluten-free, casein-free," but we will not cover them in this book. Suffice to say that creative families, dietitians, and neurologists are looking at **many** ways to provide ketosis by changing foods!

The key benefit to these two major alternative diets, and the primary difference between them and the classic ketogenic diet, is to achieve seizure control but in a less restrictive way for patients (and in this section, we will focus on children). Both diets are similar to each other and also similar to the ketogenic diet; both require medical supervision. We look at them as more tools in your toolbelt, rather than competition. Both diets are about 10 years old and well proven: Studies suggest they do work well with similar results to the ketogenic diet.

Big similarities include that all are high fat and low carbohydrate. Both the MAD and LGIT require commitment from a parent and family, as well as the child. Children still will be eating different foods, and their lifestyle will change somewhat. Cookies, candy, and cupcakes are still pretty much forbidden. Eggs, bacon, and cream are still encouraged (although a bit less so with the LGIT). Lab tests including cholesterol need to be checked before starting and every few months while on these diets.

These diets do have differences, primarily in regard to strictness. They allow more protein and calories are not closely monitored. Both diets are started in the clinic without a fast. Neither diet requires gram scales or weighing of foods, although portion sizes are important to monitor. Side effects do occur and include elevated cholesterol and constipation, but overall, compared to the ketogenic diet, these side effects seem to be a bit less frequent, especially in terms of the child's risk of growth suppression and development of kidney stones.

The biggest food difference between the ketogenic diet and alternative diets (MAD and LGIT) is the unlimited protein and calories.

HOW CAN I CHOOSE?

Every child and every family is different. There is no right or wrong answer to which diet your child (or you) should start. The best thing to do is read this book and information on the Internet about these diets and look at recipes. Talk to other families that have done it and ask them. Making a decision does not mean you are stuck with one diet; you can always switch between them if necessary (more on that later in Chapter 16). Some centers offer just one diet, but most large ketogenic diet centers will offer several. However, they may have preferences based on age or epilepsy type, as do we (details to follow). Our current general decision tree is described in the next section.

DECISION ALGORITHM FOR CHOOSING BETWEEN THE KETOGENIC AND MODIFIED ATKINS DIET AT JOHNS HOPKINS HOSPITAL

There are some situations in which we do not generally recommend "alternative" diets, and tell families to use the classic ketogenic diet. One situation is children with gastrostomy tubes. There is no "Atkins" formula, while ketogenic diet formulas (see Chapter 29) are easy to use and come in premade 3:1 or 4:1 ketogenic ratios. The formula can be made into a 1:1 or 2:1 ratio if necessary as well. Therefore, there is no advantage to the less-restrictive MAD for these children: A formula is a formula! A second situation is in an infant. Despite the availability of ketogenic formulas, infants are a bit more "high risk," and we feel that careful calculations of calories and protein with the ketogenic diet may add a level of supervision that is needed for these patients. Similarly, any child with nutritional compromise or fragility may be better served with the close dietitian support of the ketogenic diet. Lastly, families in which there is an obvious need for the extra help and guidance of a dietitian in creating meal plans and recipes often do better with the ketogenic diet. Although the alternative diets allow flexibility, we have some families that find them too "vague" or "uncertain" and prefer the unequivocal nature of the ketogenic diet.

Similarly, there are some situations in which we strongly encourage the MAD or LGIT. The first: These diets are better for most teenagers and adults. In fact, our adult epilepsy diet center nearly universally offers the MAD (see Section IV). The second is for a patient with an epilepsy that is less intractable (only failed one medication or theoretically zero and patients with "benign" epilepsies such as absence epilepsy or juvenile myoclonic epilepsy) in which it is unlikely that an insurance company would approve the hospital admission to start the ketogenic diet. Rather than fighting the battle (or paying out-of-pocket), we may try the MAD first. We may choose to start the MAD in a clinic visit as it's easier to get going. Also, some children have had difficulty with the fat intake (either due to restrictiveness or tolerating it), and we'll then try the LGIT, which has less fat. Finally, there are situations in which there is a long wait before admission to the hospital for the diet (i.e., months) and getting the MAD started immediately is in the child's best interest.

However, many children could potentially benefit from multiple approaches. We let the families play a big role in that decision, making sure they've read this book and understand the pros and cons of each diet.

The one thing that we cannot emphasize enough is that no matter what diet you choose, you should do it preferably with both a neurologist and dietitian available. All of us in the ketogenic diet community have seen issues where children are started on an "alternative" diet thinking it's easy and simple, but are either given no support or misleading information. Neither this book nor any other book about the MAD or LGIT is meant to substitute for a well-trained ketogenic diet team. If you read something that seems wrong, or your neurologist or dietitian seems confused about something related to the diet, pause and double check. There is nothing worse than a child doing poorly on a diet started by the parents and then parents forever thinking that diets will not work. They are often upset years later when it is retried and much more successful.

CHAPTER 14

The History of the Modified Atkins Diet for Epilepsy

THE PIONEER PATIENTS

A 9-year-old boy was on the ketogenic diet since age 5 for his intractable absence seizures. He also had significant behavior problems, which the diet was helping, but it still was difficult to keep him compliant with the diet. In August 2001, on her own, his mother switched him to the Atkins diet. His seizures remained under control with fewer episodes of cheating. Seizures worsened when his mother added carbohydrates, so the ketogenic diet team's natural impulse was to put him back on the stricter ketogenic diet. After 2 more years of dealing with food battles, his mother switched him back for the second time to the Atkins diet, which he remains on to some degree today, now 10+ years in ketosis.

In March 2003, a 7-year-old girl named Casey (permission to use her name granted!) was 1 month away from her scheduled week-long admission for the ketogenic diet. Her seizures were occurring 70 to 80 times per day, and she had failed eight antiepileptic drugs. In preparation for the ketogenic diet, we suggested a gradual reduction of high-carbohydrate items, such as bread, pizza, cake, and breakfast cereal in order to get Casey used to the foods that would be given on the diet. Her mother asked for more information to help reduce carbohydrates, so we suggested buying *Dr. Atkins' New Diet Revolution* and reading about the induction phase. That was on a Friday; by Monday her seizures had totally stopped.

Needless to say, we were shocked. When we saw her in clinic later that week, her urine ketones were large. Our dietitian calculated that she was receiving about 10 grams per day of carbohydrates, which we recommended she continue. We also started a multivitamin and calcium supplementation and began to check her cholesterol periodically. After 1 month of seizure freedom, we canceled her admission for the ketogenic diet. Casey remained on the modified Atkins diet (MAD) for about 4 years before seizures returned and she eventually stopped the diet to pursue epilepsy surgery (which did eventually lead to seizure freedom). She is now 19 years old and about to graduate high school.

Figure 14.1. Casey starting the diet age 7 and Casey today age 19.

After these first two children, others were tried on a MAD of 10 grams/day of net carbohydrates. Details about these children and adults can be found in the next chapters. Although the induction phase of the Atkins diet allows 20 grams/day of carbohydrates, our dietitian believed that the ketogenic diet generally allows 5 to 10 grams/day, and therefore 10 grams/day was a more appropriate starting point for children. She felt the Atkins diet was likely approximating a 1.5:1 to 2:1 ratio, which has turned out to be true. However, it is important to realize that this is NOT just a 1:1 ketogenic diet.

IS THE ATKINS DIET THE SAME AS THE KETOGENIC DIET?

Since the creation of the Atkins diet in the 1970s, families that were told to start the ketogenic diet often asked "Is this the Atkins diet?" Our typical answer was "Of course not!" Although we were quick to point out the many differences, there were just as many similarities.

The Atkins diet was created in the 1970s by the late Dr. Robert C. Atkins as a means to combat obesity. It has become very popular since the year 2000, as a result of several high-profile articles in the *New England Journal of Medicine*, the clear failure of the obesity epidemic to improve with the "accepted" low-fat diet, and the widespread availability of pre-packaged low-carbohydrate snacks and meals in stores and restaurants. Similar to the ketogenic diet, it encourages fat intake and restricts carbohydrates. Foods on the Atkins diet are very similar to what is eaten on the ketogenic diet. Both diets can induce weight loss, although with the Atkins diet, it's the major goal compared to the ketogenic diet! For many years the medical community described both diets as voodoo medicine, unsafe, unlikely to work, and dangerous . . . but has recently changed its mind. A high-profile *TIME* magazine cover article about this in June 2014 was even titled "Eat Butter." Fat is no longer a bad word.

TYPICAL 2 DAYS OF FOOD FOR A CHILD ON 10 GRAM/DAY MAD

Day 1

Breakfast

Scrambled eggs
Bacon (two strips)
36% heavy whipping cream diluted with water to make milk

Lunch

Bologna/ham, lettuce, Dijon mayonnaise "roll-ups"
Raspberries (1/2 cup)
Cucumber slices (1/2 cup)
Flavored, calorie-free, sparkling water

Snack

Just the Cheese™ (crunchy) snacks

Dinner

Hot dog
Spaghetti squash with butter and salt (1/4 cup)
Sugar-free flavored Jell-O™ topped with whipped heavy cream

Day 2

Breakfast

Sausage links
Low-carbohydrate yogurt
Water

Lunch

Cheeseburger (no bun)
Cole slaw
Pickle
Heavy whipping cream, water, and unsweetened cocoa powder

Snack

5 macadamia nuts
Mozzarella cheese stick

(continued)

Dinner

Sliced chicken, coated in egg and low carb baking mix then fried in olive oil

Steamed, mashed cauliflower with salt, butter, and pepper (mashed "potatoes")

1/2 cup of strawberries topped with heavy whipping cream

The big similarity between the two diets: *ketosis*. Throughout the book *Dr. Atkins' New Diet Revolution*, there were references to using urine ketone strips to monitor ketosis as a sign of burning fat and of weight loss. In fact, in the "induction phase" of the Atkins diet, limiting carbohydrates to 20 grams/day is advertised as leading to a ketotic state. The high levels of ketosis with the Atkins diet, although surprising to us, turned out to be no surprise to Atkins Nutritionals. When contacted, they were extremely friendly and helpful with information. This heightened our curiosity back in 2003 that the Atkins diet might work for epilepsy.

IS THE MAD DIFFERENT THAN THE KETOGENIC DIET?

Yes. There are many important differences between the MAD and the ketogenic diet. They are listed in Table 14.1. MAD has less fat and more protein and carbohydrates than the ketogenic diet, but is still quite different than a standard diet. The MAD does not restrict protein or calories and can be started without a fast or hospital admission. Certainly some centers do not fast or admit their children for the ketogenic diet, but the MAD can be started quickly in the clinic with limited teaching and dietitian support. It usually takes our center about an hour to teach a family about it. Unlike the ketogenic diet, premade products such as baking mixes, candy bars, and shakes are available in many groceries and restaurants. It allows a child to choose items from a menu at a school cafeteria or restaurant, which is nearly impossible on the ketogenic diet. Families can buy a carbohydrate gram counter (e.g., *CalorieKing* guides) in almost any bookstore or online nowadays and begin the diet at home. Although less restrictive, there is less dietitian support, so families need to be more independent. Side effects such as constipation, acidosis, and weight loss seem to be less common. Lastly, parents can do the Atkins diet themselves, along with their child, and it's probably a healthier way to live. Even your doctor can do it!

TABLE 14.1

Differences Between the Ketogenic Diet and the MAD

	KETOGENIC DIET	MAD
Calories (% RDA)	Measured carefully	Unrestricted
Fluids	Measured, but often ad lib	Unrestricted

(*continued*)

TABLE 14.1

Differences Between the Ketogenic Diet and the MAD (*continued*)

	KETOGENIC DIET	MAD
Fat	80%	60%
Protein	15%	30%
Carbohydrates	5%	10%
Fasting period	Occasionally done	No
Admission to hospital	Usually	No
Meal plans computer-created	Yes	Not required
Foods weighed and measured	Yes	No
Sharing of foods at family meals	No	Yes
Ability to eat foods made in restaurants	No	Yes
"Low-carbohydrate" store-bought products	Not used	Allowed
Intensive education provided	Yes	Less
Used in infants <1 year	Yes	No
Used in adults	Rarely	Yes
Multiple studies over many years proving benefits	Yes	Yes

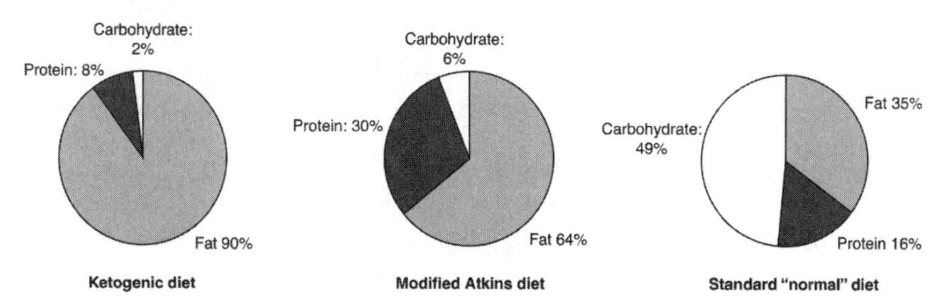

Figure 14.2. Compositions of ketogenic, modified Atkins, and standard diets.

WHY IS THERE A NEED FOR ALTERNATIVES?

Other than perhaps the MCT oil diet and availability of Nutricia KetoCal® and other ketogenic formulas, the ketogenic diet in use today is remarkably similar to that created 80 years ago.

Do we need something new? Maybe.

We have found the MAD to be helpful for children with significant behavioral problems with which the ketogenic diet's restrictiveness would be challenging. Not all epilepsy centers in the world offer the ketogenic diet, as it requires a specially trained dietitian and medical team; the Atkins diet may be a partial solution. Some children have had difficulty with high cholesterol and resultant poor growth; this *may* be less of an issue with a lower ratio (and higher protein) diet like the MAD. Adolescents and adults, commonly discouraged from trying the ketogenic diet (whether this advice is right or wrong!), might be the ideal candidates for the MAD. Lastly, if it is truly easier to start and stick to, maybe the MAD could be used early in the course of seizures, in some cases *before* medications?

FUTURE DIRECTIONS

The MAD is now over a decade old. It works in about half of children (and adults) who start it. Over 450 patients have been recorded in the medical literature, with likely double that number who haven't been published in any trial. The MAD has been shown to work compared to a control group in a study published by Sharma et al. in India in 2013 (just as was done in the United Kingdom and the United States for the ketogenic diet in 2008). The percentage of success stories is strikingly similar to the ketogenic diet. There have been some studies comparing one to the other, but they have been small (and show they are both equivalent). Although a larger, randomized comparison study has been discussed, we are not sure it would sway parents or physicians to use one diet over another no matter what the results were. We see these diets as complementary and not competing.

At Johns Hopkins, we generally advocate the ketogenic diet for most children, but are willing to use the MAD for local patients who need a diet quickly or who clearly do not want to try the ketogenic diet for various reasons. The MAD is typically used for adults nowadays. There are studies looking at it as an option in countries with limited resources. Similarly, it may be a good option for more "benign" epilepsies in which a hospital admission for the ketogenic diet (and all that it entails) is not desired. As doctors are interested in using dietary therapy for conditions other than epilepsy (migraine, autism, Alzheimer's, cancer, etc.), the MAD may be a somewhat more feasible way to provide this treatment. More on this in Section VIII. Also, many patients on the ketogenic diet long term, for more than five years, are being transitioned over to the MAD because of fewer side effects and improved tolerability (especially as they become adults).

As we have reached this unprecedented use of the MAD, we would really like to express here formally our appreciation to Dr. Veronica Atkins, Colette Heimowitz, Dr. Jeff Volek, Dr. Stephen Phinney, and Dr. Eric Westman. Their advice over the past 12 years from the world of obesity research, metabolics, and the vast experience from Atkins Nutritionals has been instrumental in making the MAD more successful for our patients. Thank you!

CHAPTER 15

How Do I Use the Modified Atkins Diet?

So far we've talked about the history of the modified Atkins diet (MAD) and future directions, as well as what the diet basically is. In this chapter, we give you "MAD 101," which is what we teach when we counsel our families. In the next chapter (Chapter 16), we talk about fine-tuning the MAD and switching from the MAD to the ketogenic diet.

THE BASICS OF THE FIRST MONTH

In general, this is meant to be simple. If it's not, something's wrong! Neurologists and dietitians at other centers will ask us for the "MAD protocol" and we'll tell them to read this chapter! It's not meant to be complicated (that's the point!).

Before starting the MAD (or any diet), make sure your child doesn't have a reason *not* to start a diet (see Chapter 5). Also, get a baseline fasting set of blood work, including a CBC, SMA20 (CMP), and fasting lipid profile. Appendix G lists many of these labs and they're the same for the MAD as for the classic ketogenic diet.

We start by telling families that "net" carbohydrates (subtracting fiber) need to be reduced to 10 grams per day (20 grams for adults). We start adolescents at 15 grams per day, but if it's too hard after 1 week, we'll go up to 20. For the MAD, it doesn't matter which carbohydrates you use, although 99% of our patients naturally choose the lower glycemic index carbohydrates because you get "more bang for your buck" in terms of carbohydrates. It is also important not to go *lower* than 10 grams per day: There will be no additional benefit, and it will just make the diet tougher. Food records show that most parents are already within 5 grams of the 10 grams/day of carbohydrate limit when we check—you will do a good job so don't stress that you're giving too many carbs!

Carbohydrate-counting guides are important to show you the macronutrient contents of most foods out there. There are many including *CalorieKing*, but one we like to use nowadays is *Dana Carpender's New Carb & Calorie Counter*. There are also carbohydrate-content lists of common foods available on the Internet. Apps are also easily available nowadays. We list some basic foods from the Atkins books in Appendix F. After a while, you'll get familiar with the carbohydrate contents of most foods your child likes, and you won't need to refer to these guides often.

Second, it is important to remember that this is a high-fat diet. We often tell families that foods should "shine" from the flash of a photograph if you take one! The meals should look similar to those on the ketogenic diet. In fact, we give recipes of ketogenic diet foods. KetoDietCalculator can be used; just calculate a 2:1 ratio to be safe, and double check the number of carbohydrates per day. However, this is usually not needed as meals are flexible and calories are not restricted. Eat typical ketogenic diet foods such as heavy whipping cream, oils, butter, mayonnaise, and soft cheese. On the MAD, these foods are not only ad lib in regard to amounts, but encouraged (one major distinction from the standard Atkins diet). Fats lead to ketosis and are super important. The most common "mistake" patients make is by eating a high-protein/low-carb diet (not a high fat one).

The key aspects of the MAD are: (a) keep carbs to 10 grams per day, (b) eat lots of fats, (c) mix in plenty of protein (but don't forget item b!)

Calories are ad lib. However, just like on the ketogenic diet, we try not to make children gain significant weight. Hunger should *not* be an issue—if your child is hungry at breakfast, give more eggs! If they are hungry at lunch, give more tuna or hamburger meat. Just don't forget the fat, which can be very satisfying, so it's probably better to give more butter and oils. Protein is also ad lib, so good sources like meats, fish, and soy can be given as much as your child wants (but again, don't give them at the expense of fats). Fluids are not only ad lib, but we encourage them! To date we have not seen a kidney stone in a child on the MAD, and that may be due to the extra fluids or less urinary calcium or acid. Drinks such as diet sodas and flavored waters (e.g., Fruit2O®, Aquafina Flavor Splash®, Powerade Zero®, Nestle Pure Life Natural Fruit Flavored Water®, Dasani Natural Flavored Water®, O Clear Water®) are great and really help. Artificial sweeteners are fine. Extra fluids may make the urine seem less ketotic (due to more fluid), but that's okay.

For the first month, check urine ketones as you would on the ketogenic diet using keto sticks. During the first month, they will likely be large. You might even see over-ketosis, described as the "Atkins flu" (see Chapter 24 about the side effects of the diets). However, in some children they can be lower (e.g., moderate) or fluctuate. In our experience, the larger the ketones the first month the better, so give lots of fat if the ketones seem to be dropping. Check them twice a week, and record them on a monthly calendar, along with seizures. In addition, we recommend checking your child's weight weekly. If your child is tired or fatigued the first week, give plenty of fluids and salt.

Start a low-carbohydrate multivitamin and calcium. Any tablet form is fine, as well as the sugar-free chewables but not usually the gummies. This is as important as it is on the ketogenic diet. For the MAD, we do not use other supplements such as carnitine, selenium, or Polycitra K®, unlike the ketogenic diet in which we often do (except in rare cases in patients that already have a history of kidney stones).

During the first month, we have a "tough love" approach. We do not reduce medications, and similar to the ketogenic diet, we switch to carb-free preparations. We also stick to 10 to 15 grams of carbs per day (20 grams for adults). One of our studies surprisingly found that 10 grams of carbs per day (for a child) was better than 20 grams per day for the first 3 months (we didn't test formally switching earlier at 1 month). Try to avoid carbohydrate-free store products the first month, such as those made by Atkins and other companies. In general, they are fine, but only after the first month. Let's see what the MAD can do by itself without any other changes.

THE INTERNET IS YOUR FRIEND

We give families lots of recipes and ideas. However, most of the information we get is from the Internet. Recipes are available at www.atkins.com and www.myketocal.com. We also list some recipes in Chapter 32. It is sometimes easier to tell families what they *can't* eat (e.g., cookies, candies, pasta, rice) than what they *can*. In this way, ideas for foods and recipes can be critical.

Another trick we use is to tell families to go shopping before actually starting the MAD. We often counsel families on Fridays and tell them to fill out a three-day food record from Friday to Sunday of foods their child is eating already. This gives our dietitians a chance to see what the child's normal intake is (especially calories), but it also gives the family the weekend to hit the store and shop. Bring your child and let him or her be part of the shopping.

Plan to spend two to three days reading about recipes online and shopping before actually starting the MAD.

KETOCAL®: A BOOST TO THE MAD

In 2010, we published results from a study in which we tested our theory that a higher fat version of the MAD would work better. By using KetoCal® as a supplement, parents were able to raise the average ketogenic diet ratio of the MAD from 1:1 (historically) to 1.8:1. This improved the chances of the MAD working to a remarkable 80% (from about 50% without KetoCal®). Although certainly giving more natural fat (or MCT oil) might achieve the same goal, we have found that KetoCal® is a potentially easy and palatable way to sneak in the extra fat.

The other part of this study was to see if this was only important for the first month. This also was true. As shown in other studies, after 1 month you can lighten up on the restrictions of any diet, and the KetoCal® could be stopped. About one in five children had slight worsening of seizures, but this is typical for anyone on the diet after the first month. Of course, if your child loves the KetoCal®, it can be continued.

In the study, children were given a case (six cans) of KetoCal® 4:1 powder. This can be purchased from the company and costs about $150. We told families to get in 60 grams per day, which is 2/3 of a cup of the powder. The powder can be used as a milkshake (mixing with either water or Fruit2O®) or can be used to cook with (recipes at www.myketocal.com). The milkshake is made by mixing 2/3 of a cup of KetoCal® with 8 ounces (240 ml) of water to make a 10-ounce shake, which is about 400 calories. Many families reported to us that the milkshakes taste better cold (made the night before) and flavored with either Fruit2O® as the liquid source, carbohydrate-free flavorings (e.g., Bickford®, Starbucks®), or sugar-free Jell-O®. The times to drink it were also up to the family—most children drank the shakes all at once, either for lunch or as an afternoon snack. The carbohydrates in KetoCal® given this way do not need to be counted toward the daily limit.

KetoCal® also comes in a premade liquid form now, in small cartons ("tetrapaks") that look like juice boxes. The premade packs were not tested in our study, but there is no reason to think they won't work as well. We would suggest one pack per day, which is pretty close to 400 calories.

After the first month, if your child doesn't like the KetoCal® (or it's too expensive), it definitely can be stopped without losing seizure control. The decision at this point is up to you. Parents sometimes ask if (a) heavy whipping cream, (b) another company's formula, or (c) extra oil would do the same thing as this study (boost ketosis above the MAD alone). Possibly, but we haven't studied it (yet). It's okay to try and see for yourself with your neurologist and dietitian's involvement. If your ketogenic diet team has a creative way to start the MAD (even theoretically in the hospital with a fasting period), be willing to try if it makes sense to you!

Figure 15.1. KetoCal 4:1 liquid.

READING THE FOOD LABELS

Food labels are critical for any processed or prepared foods. Remember that the carbohydrate content highlighted on the front of the packaging for many low-carb products can be somewhat misleading, as not only fiber but sugar alcohols are excluded (more on this later). Look for the total carbohydrate amount and subtract only fiber. This is the final amount for that product. Remember, portions can be your friend, too: If a candy bar has 10 grams of carbohydrate in it, you can have your child only eat half or 5 grams.

Carbs = Total carbs – fiber

MONTH 2: TIME TO LIGHTEN UP!

Now that you and your child have succeeded in making it to the end of the first month, things can be made less strict if the diet is helping. We do recommend making one change at a time, similar to the ketogenic diet. Each week things can be changed, very carefully, if desired.

The first change that is possible is to increase carbohydrates. Go up by 5 grams of carbohydrate/day each month if desired (e.g., to 15 grams/day for month 2 and 20 grams/day for month 3). For most children and adults, we will not go higher than 25 grams/day. Surprisingly, most children are doing well at 10 grams/day, and this switch is not usually the first one to be made.

The second change is to stop the KetoCal®. As this will lower the ratio slightly by itself, compensate by giving more fat if possible. This is a change to the MAD, so if you plan to stop the KetoCal® (as all families did in our study), count this as a change and do not increase carbs, for example, at the same time.

A third possible change is to reduce medications. We are all in favor of giving this a shot, just do it slowly and leave the MAD unchanged if you're going to do this. If seizures worsen, consider increasing the medications back if medically indicated.

A fourth and final change is to start using low-carbohydrate products. Remember to read the food labels as discussed earlier. At this point we don't count fiber toward the carbohydrate limit, but we do count sugar alcohols (e.g., xylitol, maltitol), which can be in many candy bars and low-carb baking mixes. Many of these candy bars today are now eliminating these sugar alcohols, so it's less of an issue. Another way to think of it is *fiber is free*. If you choose to use these products, and many of our families do, just try one new product per week to make sure it doesn't make seizures worse. Some favorites include the Atkins candy bars, shitake mushroom noodles, low-carb chocolate milk, and baking mixes. Just the Cheese™ snacks are also a great and crunchy snack.

You can also now be less strict about checking ketones. Our studies have shown that it is natural and normal on the MAD to have large ketosis (80–160 mg/dl or dark purple) in the first month but moderate (or trace) ketosis by the sixth month. Most of these children were still doing great, or even better than before. Keep track on the seizure calendar and show your neurologist. We recommend once weekly ketones on the MAD after the first month.

LONG-TERM USE AND MONITORING

After 1 month (or definitely by 3 months) you should be touching base with your neurologist and dietitian. By this point, you should have a good sense if the MAD is helping. If it is, then we recommend filling out a new 3-day food record (now that your child is on the MAD) and rechecking the labs you did before starting the MAD. These results should be compared, especially the total cholesterol and triglycerides. If they are too high, then adjustments to the types of fat may need to be made. Your child should also be seen by the dietitian to check his or her weight and height and answer your questions. Although side effects appear to be less frequent with the MAD compared to the ketogenic diet, they still can occur and need to be looked out for.

> See your diet team every three to six months for (a) height and weight check, (b) labs, and (c) decisions about medications, carbs, and how long to stay on the MAD.

DISCONTINUING THE MAD

In general, we slowly taper the diet until ketones are lost, similar to the ketogenic diet. Go up by 10 grams of carbohydrate per day every 2 weeks until your child reaches 60 grams/day. If seizures worsen, pause and let your neurologist and dietitian know. Once most children reach 60 grams/day they will start to see periods with no ketosis in the urine. Be careful as the MAD may still be working—this is not that different at this point than the low-glycemic index treatment (LGIT). We then tell families to make big substitutions of protein sources for fat (e.g., more tuna than mayonnaise, and more egg than butter/oil as opposed to vice versa).

After two weeks of this, you can start switching daily meals each week, one at a time, for more "regular" meals. For example, for one week, give a lunch with bread, lots of fruit, and not high fat or protein. The next week, give both lunch *and* breakfast this way. The third and final week, your child will be off the diet. Most families will wait to give high-sugar snacks or foods (e.g., cookies, chocolate, pasta) until this point. Some may never give these foods again!

FREQUENTLY ASKED QUESTIONS

1. *Do I need a dietitian or neurologist?*

   Yes. Preferably both, but at least one. This is a medical diet and needs supervision for side effects, efficacy, medication adjustment, weight gain, health, and so forth. We have received many e-mails from families who have started the diet on their own: Some have done well, but many have not. Even the ones who have done well usually have many questions that should be answered by a ketogenic diet team.

2. *Do I have to use KetoCal®?*

   Definitely not. However, it's a nice, convenient way to get the extra fat in during the first month of the MAD. You can use MCT oil, heavy whipping cream, or other sources of fat instead if you want. We understand it can be costly.

3. *What materials do I need to start the MAD?*

   This book is a great start. There's also good information on the Internet, including recipes. Many centers also provide printed materials including recipes, seizure calendars, and blank food records. In addition, a carb-counting guide (e.g., *CalorieKing*) and apps can be very helpful.

4. *How long before I know if it's helping?*

   Similar to the ketogenic diet, the MAD usually works quickly—within 2 to 4 weeks. However, a lot depends upon the seizure frequency when you start. For example, if seizures are every 2 months, you may need 6 to 9 months to know if there has been a true decrease. We usually tell families to give the MAD (or ketogenic diet) 3 to 6 months.

5. *How often should I check labs?*

   Probably at 3 months and 6 months, then every 6 months after that.

6. *Can I use artificial sweeteners?*

   Absolutely. Although there are some families that have noticed problems with seizures when their children eat Splenda™ or Stevia™, these sweeteners are safe and having some sweetness in their diet seems to help children stay compliant.

7. *Can I fine-tune the MAD?*

   Yes! Read the next chapter for more details.

CHAPTER 16

Ways to Fine-Tune the Modified Atkins Diet

Unlike the ketogenic diet, there are fewer specific changes that a dietitian can make to the modified Atkins diet (MAD) if things are either not going well from the start or if seizure control is lost. This can definitely be a disadvantage to the MAD, but there are some changes that can be made that we have found helpful. Many of these are described in the ketogenic diet fine-tuning chapter (Chapter 11), but for the most part these changes include (a) adding more fat, (b) adding supplements, (c) adjusting medications, and/or (d) switching to the classic ketogenic diet. We discuss each in order.

ADDING MORE FAT

Usually the first thing we do is look at the seizure calendar and see if ketones are high and also if they correlate with seizure control and reported compliance. If there is a correlation and ketones are low, we'll look at a 3-day food record and make sure enough fat is being eaten. We might also add extra fat sources such as MCT oil or KetoCal® (assuming the latter has been stopped after the first month by the parent).

This is not easy and we know that. In fact, we decided in 2005 to name the diet the *modified* Atkins diet because most families either doing it on their own or by reading the Atkins diet book were on a high-protein (not fat) diet. Remember to encourage all the foods you've read about in this book, even in the ketogenic diet section: oils, butter, mayonnaise, whipping cream, and so forth. If your child is having a hamburger with vegetables for dinner, that's great . . . but your child should have the fattiest hamburger you can find, grilled in a pan (not on a grill) with oil/butter, and melt some cheese on it! Or you can use mayonnaise as a dip for the burger! This may seem counterintuitive to a family trying to eat healthy, but for a family of a child on the classic ketogenic diet, this is daily practice. If you're not sure your child is getting enough fat, make sure to send a three-day food record to your dietitian for review.

> The most common reason for the MAD not achieving high ketosis is not enough fat and too much protein.

Some children may be eating much smaller portions than before starting the MAD, and we recommend more calories for more fuel, and then more ketones. Surprisingly, others may eat too many calories. We've recommended to families to take the same foods they've been giving and reduce them by a quarter or third (because we don't strictly calculate calories). Just make sure the calories reduced are protein, not fat. This isn't usually overly helpful—in our experience more fat calories are better than less—but you could try it.

SUPPLEMENTS

We sometimes think of the MAD as a "lower dose" of the diet than the classic ketogenic diet. The goal of fine-tuning the MAD is often to "raise the dose" and get closer to the classic ketogenic diet. Besides adding more fat, many families will try other supplements (see Chapter 9). Carnitine has also been helpful for some of our patients (particularly those on valproic acid). Other families have used Omega-3 fatty acids, MCT oil, ketogenic diet formulas (see Chapter 29 for several), and other supplements to boost the fat content and raise ketosis. We have seen success with these supplements and several are in clinical trials (with the MAD).

ADJUSTMENT TO MEDICATIONS

Of course, basic wisdom for all of our ketogenic diet patients applies to children on the MAD. Illness, fever, sleep deprivation, and dehydration can often trigger seizures (and it's not due to the MAD "not working"). Changes in medications or any hidden carbohydrates can also be the culprit, just as they can be with the ketogenic diet. Although there is more flexibility with the MAD, your child still cannot eat brownies, cookies, and cake (it's still a super low-carb diet)—make sure carbohydrates are not creeping up beyond 20 to 30 grams per day. If ketones are high, fat intake is adequate, and no obvious trigger is identified, then the MAD is doing all that it can do to suppress seizures. At this stage we then think about adding a new medication, increasing the dose of a current one, or considering other treatments. As we've said, this does NOT mean the MAD is a failure; it just may need a little bit of help to get seizures under control. After all this fine-tuning and possibly other treatment changes, however, the ultimate question remaining is whether it's worth it to switch to the full ketogenic diet....

SHOULD I SWITCH FROM THE MAD TO THE KETOGENIC DIET?

This is a tough decision. Lots of studies suggest that you can switch your child from the traditional ketogenic diet to the MAD after months or years without loss of seizure control. In fact, this was how we realized this diet worked. Studies show that diets do not need to be so strict after the initial month or two. However, some children can have more seizures with the MAD, similar to those who have more seizures when the ratio is lowered. Just make sure to do this with your neurologist's and dietitian's permission. We usually recommend continuing the multivitamin and calcium but stopping the CytraK or PolycitraK for kidney stone prevention when you switch to the MAD.

What about the *reverse*? Going from the MAD to the ketogenic diet? This is an even tougher decision. Most families come to us for the MAD, as they don't want to weigh and measure foods, be admitted, and be able to order out at restaurants. The ketogenic diet is more work for sure. A recent study from our center in combination with those in Germany, South Korea, and Denmark found that 37% of children who make the switch will have at least a 10% improvement in seizures. Only a few became seizure free, though—interestingly, all with Doose syndrome. Children who didn't improve with the MAD also did not improve when switching to the ketogenic diet, although since this study, we have heard of children improving at other hospitals.

We have not seen a child respond to the ketogenic diet who had absolutely no response to the MAD. They are more alike than different.

Only you and your family can make the decision to switch to the full ketogenic diet. Your neurologist and dietitian have to agree, of course, too and be able to offer the ketogenic diet—some centers may only have the MAD. . . . Some families will try to come off the MAD and if seizures worsen, they'll restart it as proof it was helping. Then they will try the full ketogenic diet to see if they can do even better.

SECTION IV

Adults and Ketogenic Diets

CHAPTER 17

History of Using Ketogenic Diets in Adults

Things are changing quickly in the ketogenic diet world and the use of ketogenic dietary therapy in adults is a primary example. The fourth edition of this book only included two paragraphs discussing diets for adults and the fifth edition addressed the topic in a single four-page chapter. Now, an entire section of the book (Chapters 17–22) is devoted to exploring the role of dietary therapies for adult epilepsy and comments are made throughout the book addressing similarities and differences between ketogenic diets in adults and children.

THE DISCOVERY OF KETOGENIC DIETS FOR ADULTS

As you learned in Chapter 4, fasting was one of the earliest documented treatments for epilepsy (for children and adults) and the ketogenic diet was first introduced into the literature in 1921. The first study published exclusively about adults was by researchers at the Mayo Clinic in Rochester, Minnesota, in 1928. In 1930, they published a follow-up study that is still the largest study to date of 100 adolescents and adults treated with a ketogenic diet and found that 56% benefited from treatment.

EPILEPSY IN ADULTS

RESULTS OF TREATMENT BY KETOGENIC DIET IN ONE HUNDRED CASES *

CLIFFORD J. BARBORKA, M.D.

ROCHESTER, MINN.

Figure 17.1 The largest study to date of the ketogenic diet for adults, published in *Archives of Neurology* in 1930.

With the introduction of new antiepileptic drugs as options for epilepsy treatment, interest in the ketogenic diet for adults waned as it did for children, and research on the ketogenic diet for adults disappeared until the late 1990s.

RENEWED INTEREST IN KETOGENIC DIETS FOR ADULTS

The next study with the terms "ketogenic diet" and "adults" in the title was an article published in 1998 in Hebrew that described the use of a medium chain triglyceride (MCT) ketogenic diet in a 20-year-old man with intractable multifocal epilepsy, resulting in seizure freedom. There were no other studies published in English-language medical journals on the use of the ketogenic diet for adults until 1999 when a paper from Thomas Jefferson University in Philadelphia described treating 11 adults with the ketogenic diet. Their findings were similar to the early Mayo Clinic studies, with results matching the effectiveness in children treated with the ketogenic diet with approximately half of adult patients responding to diet treatment.

The ketogenic diet was not reintroduced as quickly to adults as it was in children in the 1970s, 1980s, and early 1990s, and one possible explanation for this is that there was a general misconception that adults could not follow the diet. Studies in the late 1990s helped address this misconception; however, researchers did note that adults did seem less likely to stay on the ketogenic diet than children, with 36% of patients discontinuing the diet by 8 months as reported in the 1999 paper. Motivated to find ketogenic diets that would be easy for adults to follow, neurologists, dietitians, and nutritionists began investigating other therapeutic diets that began to be used in children in the beginning of this millennium (see also Section VI). These have included the modified Atkins diet (MAD), the low glycemic index treatment (LGIT), and the MCT diet, or combinations of these diets and the ketogenic diet. Typically, carbohydrate limits are slightly higher for adults than those recommended for children, at 40 to 60 grams for the LGIT and 15 to 20 grams of net carbs per day for the MAD. Most studies of these "alternative" or less restrictive diets used by adults have focused on treatment with the MAD. The majority of these studies have included children, adolescents, and young adults but some patients have been older adults and senior citizens (patients age 65 years and over). The percent of patients achieving a 50% or greater seizure reduction with the MAD has been comparable to the classic ketogenic diet and typically ranges from 29% to 55%.

Current studies have shown that patients with certain types of seizures and epilepsy syndromes respond particularly well to ketogenic diets and these have included adult patients that were not tried on ketogenic diets as children. A study published at Johns Hopkins of 71 patients with Lennox-Gastaut syndrome included patients that were 18 years of age and showed that 51% responded to the ketogenic diet. A case series of eight patients with juvenile myoclonic epilepsy with ages ranging from 15 to 44 years treated with the MAD showed a 75% responder rate following the first month of treatment.

Within the past decade, there has also been a recent interest in the use of the ketogenic diet in the intensive care setting for patients with severe (refractory or super-refractory) status epilepticus. Status epilepticus is a seizure lasting for more than 5 minutes or back-to-back seizures without return to normal in between seizures, and is the second most common neurologic emergency worldwide. Status epilepticus is considered refractory when two medications (typically a benzodiazepine and phenytoin) are given and seizures continue. Super-refractory means that status continues even after the patient is placed in a coma with anesthetic medications to stop seizures. Up to 90% of patients with super-refractory status epilepticus have stopped seizing during treatment with a classic ketogenic diet in combination with aggressive antiepileptic drug treatment.

Not surprisingly, side effects in adults on ketogenic diets tend to be comparable to children with the most common including constipation and weight loss (also see Chapter 24). Menstrual cycle irregularities have been reported in many women of childbearing age using ketogenic diets and could not be attributed to weight loss alone. Even in the 1930 study of the classic ketogenic diet, researchers from the Mayo Clinic observed that menses stopped in nearly a quarter of women and increased in one. Total cholesterol and low-density lipoprotein ("bad cholesterol") levels have been shown to rise in adults treated with the MAD but normalize over 1 to 2 years of diet treatment. A recent study of 43 patients with chronic epilepsy (23 on the ketogenic diet and 20 not on any diet therapy) with ages ranging from 19 months to 31 years showed that arterial stiffness increased with prolonged use of the ketogenic diet and that total cholesterol and triglyceride levels were higher compared to controls. These findings indicate that the long-term impact of ketogenic diets on cardiovascular and cerebrovascular health are not yet well appreciated.

THE FUTURE OF KETOGENIC DIETS FOR ADULTS

Today, more adults are researching ketogenic diets and requesting these treatments from their doctors. Pediatric ketogenic diet teams are being asked to continue to follow patients as adults or to start adults on these diets, and several adult centers have opened worldwide to address this need. With the increase in interest in these therapies for adults, we have learned that they are effective when adults are able to tolerate them, that side effects may vary, and that certain patients with certain types of epilepsy particularly benefit. The future challenge is to address the unanswered questions. Some of these questions include:

- Are ketogenic diets safe long-term or life-long? Which one(s)?
- Which diets are best for which adults?
- Can diets be used in adults with chronic epilepsy who want to lower or eliminate medications (as monotherapy)?
- Can diets be used safely in pregnancy?
- When is the right time to consider trying a ketogenic diet as an adult?

Future editions to this book will hopefully include answers to these questions.

CHAPTER 18

The Adult Epilepsy Diet Center at Johns Hopkins

MOTIVATIONS FOR CREATING A DIET CENTER FOR ADULTS

"Why aren't adults offered the ketogenic diet more often?" The current response we hear most often is that the diet is just "too hard" for adults. Diets are perceived as "a severe lifestyle change" with no fast food, alcohol, or high-carb snacks, and so forth. We were motivated to challenge these perceptions by starting an Adult Epilepsy Diet Center (AEDC) at Johns Hopkins in August of 2010 (www.hopkinsmedicine.org/neurology_neurosurgery/centers_clinics/epilepsy/adult/adult-epilepsy-diet-center/) with the generous support of The Carson Harris Foundation (see also Chapter 23). The Center is designed to:

1. Safely transition older children who have been on ketogenic diets into the care of neurolgists and dietitians specializing in adult care;
2. Provide counseling and support to adults who have been started on a ketogenic diet by another doctor, dietitian, and/or nutritionist and are seeking a second opinion or have read about ketogenic diets and have started one themselves; and
3. Start adults with epilepsy on ketogenic diets and provide routine follow-up.

In addition to controlling seizures, motivations for adults to start a ketogenic diet may include avoiding the side effects of additional antiepileptic drugs, reducing antiepileptic drugs, weight loss, and improved cognition. Some patients are eligible for epilepsy surgery but are not yet prepared to move forward with the procedure or are in the process of being evaluated for surgery when they decide to try the diet.

When we opened our center, approximately 90% of our patients had never tried a ketogenic diet before their first visit. Within the past few years, we have found that more and more patients are learning about these diets and trying them before coming to the clinic. We recommend that patients try diet therapies only with the direct support from a physician and nutrition specialist—our goal is to provide that support and access to treatment.

WHICH DIET TO CHOOSE

Adults started on a ketogenic diet at another ketogenic diet center who are tolerating it well with good seizure control are most often kept on the same diet when transitioning to the AEDC with modifications as needed. If they are experiencing difficulty following the diet or intolerable side effects, we may consider transitioning to the modified Atkins diet (MAD). Those who have started a diet without physician or dietitian supervision and those that have never been on diet therapy are most often started on the MAD unless they cannot eat food by mouth. Patients who are tube fed are started on a classic ketogenic diet either at home or with a hospital admission through the Pediatric Ketogenic Diet Center, depending on the age of the patient and other medical conditions.

AEDC CLINIC APPOINTMENTS

A typical clinic day in the AEDC is structured with 1-hour new-patient visits in the morning with the epileptologist (Mackenzie Cervenka, MD) and with the registered dietitian (Bobbie J. Henry, RD). For patients who are starting or transitioning to the MAD and their families or other care providers, these visits are followed by a 1-hour group teaching session on how to follow the MAD. Instructors include the epileptologist, dietitian, and pediatric neurologist (Eric Kossoff, MD), who review the following topics:

- Definitions and history of the ketogenic diet and the MAD
- The Adult Epilepsy Diet Center experience
- The MAD basics
- Potential MAD side effects
- Carbs and food labels
- Fat, fluid, and supplements
- Diet logging and monitoring
- Resources and FAQs

The epileptologist sees follow-up patients for 30 minutes in the afternoon and patients see the dietitian on an as-needed basis (the majority of patients elect to see the dietitian at every visit). Follow-up visits are typically after 1 to 3 months, at 6 months, then annually if the patient is tolerating the diet well.

DIET MONITORING

At the initial visit, patients are asked to keep a daily calendar of the number and type of seizures and are taught to check and record urine ketones. They are asked to record ketones daily until they reach a "moderate" level (40 mg/dl) and then to continue on a biweekly basis. They are also asked to record weights weekly and start and end of their menses if they are women of childbearing age. Routine blood work checking liver and kidney function and cholesterol levels is obtained before starting the diet and additional vitamin and other nutrient levels are checked annually (zinc, selenium, vitamin D, free and total carnitine). Patients also receive a bone density scan every 5 years while on the diet (in some cases, scans are done at the time of the first visit if patients have never had one before and have been on diet and/or antiepileptic medications long term), and more often if there is evidence of osteopenia or osteoporosis. In such cases, patients are also referred to an endocrinologist.

LESSONS LEARNED

We have learned a lot about the use of MAD in adults:

- Initiation is rapid and adults will begin to respond quickly if they are going to respond at all (mean, 5 days).
- Although the amounts of fluids, protein, and calories are unrestricted, it is very important for extra amounts of fat to be eaten daily.
- Adults can start at a slightly higher total carbohydrate allowance than children (20 grams vs. 10 grams) and liberalize up to 25 to 30 grams after several months while maintaining ketosis.
- Two months on MAD is likely a long enough trial on the diet to assess efficacy, as opposed to 3 to 6 months for children on the ketogenic diet; a longer trial is necessary if the patient has infrequent seizures.
- Many adults who started the ketogenic diet as children can continue to do well when they are switched to the MAD.
- Cholesterol increases do occur but tend to return to normal with continued diet use.
- Weight loss can occur—if it's planned, that's great.
- Kidney stones and constipation can occur but risks can be lessened by staying hydrated.
- If adults are not seizure free, they often stop the diet (no matter how tough their seizures have been to control).

We are not the only center interested in the use of diets for adults. Matthew's Friends Clinic opened in London in January 2011 and was followed by registered dietitian, Sue Wood. Dr. Eduard Bercovici started the Toronto Western Hospital Epilepsy Diet Center for adults. Adult patients are being started on ketogenic diets at Rush University Medical Center in Chicago, New York University Comprehensive Epilepsy Center, Thomas Jefferson University, The Queen's Medical Center in Honolulu, University of Virginia, and University of Wisconsin. The Charlie Foundation based in Los Angeles, California, also provides support to adults seeking diet treatment for epilepsy.

Figure 18.1. The Adult Epilepsy Diet Center at Johns Hopkins (from left to right: Joanne Barnett; Mackenzie C. Cervenka, MD; Bobbie J. Henry, RD, LDN; Eric H. Kossoff, MD; Rebecca Fisher, RN).

CHAPTER 19

Evidence for Effectiveness in Adults

EARLY EFFECTIVENESS OF THE KETOGENIC DIET IN ADULTS

Over time, studies have repeatedly shown that ketogenic diets are effective in adults as well as children. The earliest study of the ketogenic diet for the treatment of adult epilepsy, published by researchers at the Mayo Clinic in Rochester, Minnesota, in 1928, described the experience of 49 patients (48 age 18 and over) with idiopathic epilepsy treated with a ketogenic diet. Ketogenic ratios of fat to carbohydrates and protein combined ranged from 1.6:1 to 3.6:1. Over one third of patients (17) stopped the diet before three months of treatment. Seven of these patients became seizure-free on the diet and were on no antiepileptic medications, seven improved but without complete seizure resolution (including one 17-year-old), five improved with a combination of diet and antiepileptic drugs, and 13 saw no benefit. Today, we typically use ketogenic diets and medications in combination, and calculate seizure reduction based on intent-to-treat analyses (including all patients that started the diet). Using these criteria, nearly 40% of adults had reductions in seizures using the ketogenic diet.

In the 100-patient study published two years later by the group at the Mayo Clinic, 81 of the patients were technically adults (age 18 years and over). Of these, 58% derived benefit from the ketogenic diet and 14% were seizure free. Patients were on the ketogenic diet for between 3 months and 5 years. The observation was made that ketosis was achieved and maintained in nearly all patients that became seizure free and half of the patients benefited from the diet. Over half of the patients that did not improve on the ketogenic diet never reached ketosis at any time during treatment, suggesting that compliance with the diet may have been inadequate in these patients.

EFFICACY OF KETOGENIC DIETS FOR ADULTS IN THE CURRENT ERA

As described in Chapter 17, there were no published studies of the ketogenic diet for adults in several decades, likely because of increased interest in the use of new antiepileptic drugs and the perception that the diet was too difficult for adults to follow. The next major study, published at Thomas Jefferson in 1999, evaluated 11 adults ages 19 to 45 years treated with a 4:1 ratio ketogenic diet with fluid restriction. Unlike prior studies, this included only patients with symptomatic epilepsy who were drug resistant. Responders were defined as patients that had a ≥50% seizure reduction. At 8 months, 56% of patients were found to respond to the ketogenic diet. Since then, several other studies using a 3:1 or 4:1 ratio ketogenic diet or MCT diet have shown responder rates ranging from 13% to 54%. Study durations have ranged from 4 months to over 2 years and dropout rates have been between one third and nearly 80% of participants.

Because the majority of studies that investigate the use of ketogenic diets in adult epilepsy present results based on intent-to-treat analyses, and the dropout rates are quite high, reported efficacy rates are overall slightly lower than for children (Table 19.1). Other diets such as the modified Atkins diet (MAD) and the low glycemic index treatment (LGIT) were introduced to address the issue of poor compliance with the goal of providing a less strict and rigid diet plan that adults are able to follow long term.

Several studies have used the MAD for adult epilepsy, the first two of which were published in 2008, and reported on findings in a total of 38 adults treated with the MAD. Both studies were 6 months in duration and approximately 30% of patients had a greater than 50% seizure reduction and over half dropped out before 6 months. Several additional studies investigating the MAD as a treatment for adult epilepsy have shown responder rates ranging from 13% to 56%, with the majority of studies demonstrating a ≥50% seizure reduction in approximately one third of patients over 3 to 12 months. Dropout rates in the largest studies have ranged from 22% to 63%.

TABLE 19.1

Studies of Effectiveness of Ketogenic Diets in Adults

AUTHOR	YEAR	NO. OF ADULTS	DIET	AGE RANGE	SEIZURES	SEIZURE FREE
Barborka	1928	48	KD	18-45	17 (35%)	7 (15%)
Barborka	1930	81	KD	18-56	47 (58%)	11 (14%)
Schiff	1998	1	MCT	20	1 (100%)	1 (100%)
Sirven	1999	11	KD	19-45	7 (88)%	0 (0%)

(continued)

TABLE 19.1

Studies of Effectiveness of Ketogenic Diets in Adults (*continued*)

AUTHOR	YEAR	NO. OF ADULTS	DIET	AGE RANGE	SEIZURES	SEIZURE FREE
Kossoff	2003	3	Atkins	18-52	1 (33%)	0 (0%)
Kossoff	2008	30	MAD	18-53	15 (50%)	1 (3%)
Carrette	2008	8	MAD	30-54	3 (38%)	0 (0%)
Mosek	2009	9	KD	18-45	2[a] (22%)	0 (0%)
Klein	2010	12	KD	25-65	10 (83%)	1 (8%)
Smith	2011	18	MAD	18-55	3 (17%)	0 (0%)
Cervenka	2012	25	MAD	18-66	6 (24%)	1 (4%)
Lambrechts	2012	15	KD	18-40	3 (20%)	0 (0%)
Kossoff	2012	6[b]	MAD	18-44	4 (67%)	1 (17%)
Ramm-Pettersen	2013	2	MAD	18-51	2 (100%)	1 (50%)
Nei	2014	28[c]	KD	18-51	15 (54%)	1 (4%)

[a]All other patients stopped the study before the 12-week endpoint.
[b]Initial study of eight patients included two teenage girls whose results were not included in this table.
[c]Initial study of 29 patients included one 11-year-old girl whose results were not included in this table, following communication with the author.

FUTURE DIRECTIONS

Overall, seizures seem to be better controlled with the ketogenic diet than the MAD (as with children, where the MAD is considered a "lower dose" ketogenic diet) but patients find it more difficult to follow the ketogenic diet. Head-to-head studies directly comparing response to the various ketogenic diets (classic ketogenic, MAD, low glycemic index, and MCT diets) are needed to determine which diets are the most feasible and effective in adults. In addition, studies directly comparing the efficacy of these diets and adjunctive antiepileptic drugs would help further define the role of diet therapies in the algorithm for treating drug-resistant epilepsy.

CHAPTER 20

How to Use the MAD in Adults With Epilepsy

Similar to children, about half of adults with epilepsy benefit from using the modified Atkins diet (MAD). Doctors that take care of children often remind us that children are not just little adults, but when it comes to ketogenic diets, we sometimes do think of adults as big kids! When you read the chapters in this book that are addressed to parents and their children on ketogenic diets, keep in mind that this is equally great advice for adult patients on these diets and their spouses or caregivers as well. In other words, read the whole book, not just the parts about adults. We have found that adults who tried ketogenic diets as children and had improvement in seizures may do well on the MAD. Also, adults with syndromes that began in childhood such as Lennox-Gastaut syndrome, juvenile myoclonic epilepsy, Rett syndrome, and tuberous sclerosis, may do particularly well if they were not tried on these treatments as children. We've also found that adults with just about every type of epilepsy can become seizure free on the MAD.

WHICH ADULTS SHOULD START THE MAD?

Adults who have tried two or more antiepileptic drugs and seizures are not controlled (considered "drug or medically resistant") or adults for whom treatment has been limited by side effects may benefit from the MAD. Epilepsy surgery is more likely to make patients seizure free if they qualify, so that treatment should be considered first if the person is eligible and willing to consider it. The ketogenic diet has been shown to work more effectively with the vagus nerve stimulator (VNS), so adults who have received this device may find particular benefit from the MAD as well.

Adults with epilepsy may have other comorbid conditions for which the MAD may provide benefit. These can include obesity and type 2 diabetes. Like the traditional Atkins diet, patients may lose weight on the MAD, which could potentially treat obstructive sleep apnea and lower the risk of coronary artery disease and stroke. Low-carbohydrate diets are known to be effective in treating type 2 diabetes.

Adults with epilepsy occasionally elect to start the MAD as an alternative to antiepileptic drugs or to lower or eliminate antiepileptic drugs. There is limited evidence to support this practice and patients are typically encouraged to use the MAD as an adjunct to at least a low dose of one antiepileptic drug.

THE MAD PRESCRIPTION FOR ADULTS

The standard prescription that we use for starting the MAD in an adult is to begin with 20 grams of net carbohydrates per day (subtracting fiber), as compared to 10 to 15 grams per day for children. Patients are not prescribed a specific number of fat grams per day but are taught how to check urine ketones and to eat enough fat to reach moderate (40 mg/dl) to large (180 mg/dl) urine ketone levels. To reach ketosis, patients typically need to eat approximately 70% fat calories per day, but this can vary from person to person. Patients should eat enough to feel satisfied and if they do not reach ketosis despite being certain that they have limited carbs to 20 grams, they may have replaced carb intake with protein instead of fat. They should constantly remember that fat has more calories per gram than carbohydrates or protein and that they need to eat less to feel full (more on this in Chapter 22) and to prevent weight gain. They should add fat sources such as butter, olive oil, and cream to increase intake and achieve ketosis.

Patients are encouraged to use fresh produce before incorporating store-bought, low-carbohydrate products in order to become familiar with the carbohydrate content of different fruits and vegetables (e.g., 4.5 grams of net carbs in 25 medium-sized blueberries). Eating at a restaurant is possible if patients plan ahead and review the menu or ask questions. Fast-food restaurants often have meal builder programs online that can be used to plan a high-fat, low-carbohydrate meal before getting to the restaurant.

Patients are prescribed unlimited fluids. They are encouraged to drink at least 64 oz of fluid daily, avoid caffeinated beverages, and drink an additional 8 oz glass of water for every caffeinated beverage consumed. Patients who exercise or work outside in a warm environment are reminded to drink plenty of fluids with electrolytes because sodium is lost when sweating and needs to be replaced as well.

Adults on the MAD, like children, are instructed to begin a multivitamin, vitamin D, and calcium supplement, using the same basic guidelines as children and based on the Recommended Daily Allowances (see also Chapter 9). Many Americans, particularly adults, are vitamin D deficient as a result of inadequate sunlight exposure and some antiepileptic medications. Older drugs such as phenobarbital and phenytoin can also lower vitamin D levels and reduce calcium absorption. Vitamin D levels are routinely checked before beginning the MAD and additional vitamin D can be prescribed if the patient is found to be vitamin D deficient before starting the MAD. We have found that patients do not tend to develop vitamin D deficiencies on the MAD if they take appropriate supplementation daily.

Patients on the MAD track urine ketones at regular intervals (daily to weekly) as well as weight and frequency of seizures and report these to their treating physician and dietitian or nutritionist. The dietitian may request a food record if the patient reports compliance with the diet but is not achieving adequate urine ketone levels or seizure control to determine whether there are "hidden carbohydrates" in their diet, they are eating too much protein, or their fat intake needs to be increased. Most common sources of hidden carbohydrates include foods with sugar alcohols that are not labeled as carbohydrates, medications that contain carbohydrates (particularly gummy vitamins and syrups), and foods that change their ingredients and labeling over time. In general, tablets have fewer carbohydrates than liquids and intravenous liquids and compounds have fewer carbohydrates than syrups. Pharmacists may need to be involved in the process of identifying medications that contain carbohydrates and helping eliminate those from the diet. Some patients who are following the prescribed carbohydrate restriction may benefit from being provided a recommended number of fat grams to eat while on the MAD. If you are prescribed a new medication or plan to take an over-the-counter drug, ask the pharmacist about the carb content and count it toward your 20 grams per day.

MAD CONTRAINDICATIONS IN ADULTS

Contraindications to using the MAD in adults are similar to those in children using ketogenic diets. A history of kidney stones is not an absolute contraindication but may prompt providers to recommend an alkalinizing agent to prevent recurrence when beginning the MAD (see Chapter 9). Baseline elevated fasting cholesterol levels with or without statin therapy is also not an absolute contraindication but may warrant more frequent monitoring of lipid levels in adults. Ketogenic diets are contraindicated in certain rare metabolic disorders that are typically diagnosed in childhood, so screening is not routinely performed in adults interested in starting the MAD at our center. Acute pancreatitis is also an absolute contraindication to starting the MAD as ketogenic diets can exacerbate pancreatitis.

Certain considerations are made for women of childbearing age treated with the MAD including possible changes to their menstrual cycles, use of birth control, pregnancy, and breastfeeding (also see Chapter 21). Regularity of menses has been shown to be impacted in some women by weight loss and by ketogenic diets in ways that are at times unpredictable. The impact on efficacy of oral contraceptives is unknown.

MAD SIDE EFFECTS IN ADULTS

Side effects of the MAD are also similar in children and adults. These most often include weight loss, constipation or other gastrointestinal symptoms, muscle cramping, fainting, and elevated cholesterol levels (also see Chapter 24). Weight loss is a common side effect and is often an intended effect of the diet in adults.

If patients are underweight before starting the diet, they need to increase calorie intake to maintain or improve weight. Constipation is also common and can be prevented with adequate hydration, increased fiber intake, and probiotics. Muscle cramping can be avoided with increased fluid and sodium intake and slowly reintroducing vigorous exercise in patients that were physically active before starting the MAD. Fainting or syncope can be caused by orthostatic hypotension, a condition in which blood pressure drops when standing, resulting in "blacking out" or loss of consciousness. Patients may experience lightheadedness, tunnel vision, or loss of vision on standing before losing consciousness. Again, this can occur in the setting of dehydration and can also be prevented by adequate fluid intake and increased sodium intake. Total cholesterol and LDL cholesterol levels have been shown to increase in children and adults on ketogenic diets including the MAD. Studies have shown that these levels typically rise during the first 3 to 6 months on the MAD then plateau and return to baseline by 1 to 2 years of treatment. Besides weight loss, other positive effects of the MAD that have been reported include reduction in migraine headaches, improved concentration, and improved memory. Recent findings suggest that adults with seizures caused by brain tumors and other cancers may have additional benefit from the low-carbohydrate effects of diets such as the MAD (Chapter 34).

Adults with medically resistant epilepsy may wish to stay on the MAD for life and may need to be monitored for theoretical long-term side effects. These can include certain vitamin and mineral deficiencies such as deficiencies in zinc and selenium that can be avoided by daily multivitamin supplementation. Osteopenia and osteoporosis are known complications of ketogenic diets (Chapter 24) due to vitamin D and calcium deficiency mentioned earlier and are theoretical side effects of the MAD in adults as well, although this has not been reported. In more extreme cases, patients may benefit from referral to an endocrinologist for treatment or changes to antiepileptic drugs.

STOPPING THE MAD IN ADULTS

Children who are seizure free for two years are typically tapered off the ketogenic diet (Chapter 12). In adults, an electroencephalogram (EEG) is obtained and if the study is normal and the patient does not have a known brain lesion or other reason for being at high risk for additional seizures, the subject of tapering the MAD may be discussed. If patients are taking antiepileptic medications, they may consider tapering these first and then stopping the diet if seizures remain controlled. Patients might also elect to stop the diet at any time because of side effects or difficulty with compliance. At the Adult Epilepsy Diet Center (AEDC), we recommend a diet "taper" by increasing net carbohydrates by 5 grams every 3 days until reaching 85 grams per day, then patients return to a "regular" diet. Patients are counseled not to drive during the taper. If seizures return, patients may elect to return to using the MAD or remain on a low-carbohydrate diet while trying a new therapy.

MAD COMPLIANCE

Compliance remains a major limiting factor in adults using ketogenic diets. The MAD is designed to be less restrictive than the classic ketogenic diet by not requiring weighing of foods, fasting, hospital admission, fluid or calorie restriction, and so forth, yet many adults find it difficult to adhere to. This can be true for patients who are providing for dependent children or other family members (elderly parents or grandparents) and need to prepare different meals for a variety of individuals, adults who are "on the go," getting to work and activities, and "picky eaters" who have set food preferences. Patients report that they get "bored" or find themselves "eating the same things all the time." Before they give up on the diet, they are encouraged to reach out to their treating physician, dietitian, or nutritionist for more meal ideas (Chapter 22).

EMERGENCIES

If adults on the MAD for epilepsy are treated in an emergency department or require surgery, they should inform the medical care team that they are on a low-carbohydrate, high-fat diet. Carbohydrate-containing intravenous fluids should be avoided unless there is a concern for hypoglycemia and patients should be kept on their therapeutic diet and antiepileptic drugs in the hospital to avoid an increase in seizures. Pharmacy teams should be informed in case there are medication substitutions that need to be made in the hospital. In patients that cannot take food by mouth in the hospital and require tube feeding, transitioning temporarily to a ketogenic diet is a reasonable option.

CHAPTER 21

Unique Issues That Adults Face With Ketogenic Diets

GOING AWAY TO COLLEGE

Going away to college can be very nerve-wracking for all members of the family. A lot is expected from the student—get good grades, get involved with extracurricular activities, make new friends, manage your epilepsy, and follow a special diet. Things are even more complicated when the adolescent going off to school has not been very involved with his or her diet planning.

We suggest that students involve themselves in planning their diet as early as possible to have the most time to practice meal planning and carbohydrate counting before leaving home. Have them tag along on food shopping trips and practice food label reading. Start cooking simple meals together at home. Have them keep a list of their favorite snacks and ensure that they can prepare them on their own or that they will have a supply at their new location (make sure there is a refrigerator accessible in the dorm). Keep food diaries for a few days so that students can get used to tracking their own intake. Research restaurants that are near campus and help your student identify safe items. Go to a new restaurant and have the student practice menu reading, talking to the wait staff, and ordering meals. Talk to the food service staff at the new school and explain the diet. Share written materials that were provided by the ketogenic diet team. Be sure to explain what you are doing at home to ease the transition, and ask what the school's food service can do to help the student stay on the diet. Some things you may ask of the school's food service:

- Stock favorite items like beef jerky, pork rinds, salami, macadamia nuts, string cheese at the campus store.
- Have a meal tray prepared for lunch and dinner daily.
- Keep plain chicken breasts and thighs and a low-carb vegetable on the buffet line daily for the student to easily put together meals.
- Add net carbs to nutrition facts for all foods served.
- Stock olive oil or the student's favorite dressing at the salad bar.

You may offer to provide recipes and meal ideas to help the food service understand the diet. The food service may even be able to provide salmon and avocado, which are not usually on the menu—the other students will surely be jealous or thankful!

WEIGHT CONTROL

Fat has more calories per gram than carbohydrates and protein, which led to the mistaken belief that fat causes weight gain. By now, after reading the first several chapters of this book, you know that that is not true and, in fact, ketogenic diets are now more than ever being used for weight loss. That's because your body is burning fat as opposed to storing it, as it does on a higher carbohydrate diet.

If losing weight is one of your goals for starting a ketogenic diet, then there are some things that we recommend:

- Commit to the diet, as instructed, for the first 2 months on the diet. Do not stress if your weight hasn't budged, or even if you've gained a few pounds. First, work with your diet team to optimize ketosis to see if the diet can help you reduce or stop seizures. If it doesn't help with your epilepsy, then you can work with a registered dietitian nutritionist to help you with your weight loss journey.
- Ensure that you are not eating too much protein, which can be used for energy instead of ketones or fat. To lose weight, your body needs to use fat, not protein! A good rough estimate for the amount of protein a generally healthy person should have is about 1 to 1.5 grams of protein per kilogram of body weight. Likewise, calculate 0.5 to 0.7 grams of protein per pound of body weight.
- Keep in mind that you may need to adjust your idea of a "portion size." A tablespoon of fat (oil, butter, and mayo) has on average 100 calories; this can very easily replace the calories in the hamburger bun you ditched.
- Eating is such a routine for us. We eat when we are not hungry, but rather when the clock strikes noon or when dinner is ready. If you are just starting a ketogenic diet, eating on a set schedule can help you learn the diet, practice meal planning, learn food and carb counts, and help your body through the process of getting into ketosis. Once fully into ketosis, though, we encourage you to be mindful and become in tune with your hunger and satiety signals. Eat with intention and attention. Eat slowly. Ketones are known to decrease appetite, so let them.
- Sometimes we turn to food when we are bored, stressed, lonely, or just want to relax. If this sounds like you, try keeping a log of the food you eat, how you feel before and after eating, and how hungry you are. Start by noticing the difference between when you're physically hungry and when you want to eat for other reasons. Make a list of things you can do other than eat to help with your feelings, such as calling a friend, cleaning the

house, going for a walk, or reading a book. If you are having very intense feelings or are having difficulty coping without food, many people find it helpful to see a mental health professional.

- It is also possible to lose too much weight! If you feel like your weight loss is out of control be sure to meet with your doctor or dietitian nutritionist.

ALCOHOL USE

Before consuming alcohol, you should consult with your doctor. Alcohol can interact with antiepileptic drugs, in some cases cause seizures (e.g., in patients with juvenile myoclonic epilepsy and other generalized epilepsies), and intoxication can make you forget to take your medications.

We tend to give a few cautions with alcohol, so here they are.

- If you are in ketosis, you'll likely feel the effects of alcohol more quickly. Moderation is key.
- For the most part, alcohol is toxic to your body so it gets metabolized before other fuels, like fat. That means, your body takes a break from using fat as a fuel to using alcohol as a fuel. Again, just use common sense and don't overdo it. It is definitely doable to have a small glass of wine and maintain ketosis.
- Stay hydrated with an extra cup of water after indulging in a small glass of wine.
- Make sure you carb count alcohol. The Atkins website has a "Carb Counter" under their "Free Tools" section. Or just type "carbs in wine" in a search engine for a drop-down list of wine types, most averaging about 4 grams of carbs per 5 fluid ounces. If you aren't a wine drinker, you'll be happy to know that plain spirits contain essentially zero carbs. Avoid regular sodas, flavored syrups, juices, and non-diet tonic. Instead mix spirits with diet drinks, plain or sparkling water. There are a few low-carb beers on the market. It is not impossible to find nutrition info on beer websites, but definitely call the company if you can't locate carb counts. Here are some of the lowest carb beers on the market: carbs per 12 fluid ounces: Miller 64 (2.4 grams), Michelob Ultra (2.4 grams), Bud Select (3.1 grams), Miller Lite (3.2 grams), and Michelob Ultra Amber (3.2 grams).

DRIVING

Driving is a privilege and the driving laws vary from state to state. Universally, the laws state that individuals should not drive within a certain time frame after a seizure or any episode of altered awareness (the length of time varies depending on the state you live in, so you should always find out what the law is in your state), that individuals must report these episodes to the Department of Motor Vehicles, and that individuals must be compliant with their treatment.

The laws do not distinguish between diet treatments and drugs though we consider them the same with regard to compliance. In other words, in order to be fit to drive, you must be consistent and compliant with your diet treatment, just like with antiepileptic drugs. We and other neurologists also recommend not driving when tapering or making changes to your diet because you cannot predict how it will affect your seizures.

PREGNANCY AND BREASTFEEDING

We do not know the effects of ketogenic diets in pregnant women with regard to changes in ketones, antiepileptic drug levels, seizures, and risks of unanticipated side effects. Risk of teratogenicity (adverse effects on the baby) in women on ketogenic diets during pregnancy is also unknown, as with newer antiepileptic drugs. Therefore, the diet is not typically prescribed for women who are pregnant or planning to become pregnant. If a woman becomes pregnant while on a ketogenic diet, the potential risks of continuing the diet may be weighed by her treating team against risks of increased seizures with stopping treatment. Patients who stay on ketogenic diets during pregnancy should be monitored carefully for appropriate weight gain and fetal growth, and should be prescribed prenatal vitamins and appropriate vitamin supplements. Ketone bodies are known to appear in breastmilk in individuals who are in ketosis and breastfeeding and the effect of ketone bodies on a growing infant are also unknown.

CHAPTER 22

Tips, Tricks, and Making It Healthy!

POSSIBLY THE MOST IMPORTANT TIP

If you learn one thing from this chapter, make it this: The modified Atkins diet (MAD) is not a high-protein diet. Don't make the mistake of replacing carbohydrates with protein. Instead, replace the carbohydrates with fat! On a regular diet, most snacks are high in carbohydrates—think pretzels, chips, pieces of fruit. On MAD, snacks tend to be higher in protein and fat—think cheese, nuts, pepperoni slices, pork rinds, and so on (there's more info on snacking later in this chapter). The protein content of your snacks will therefore most likely go up when you start MAD. That's ok! But be careful with your meals. Eating similar amounts of protein (meat, fish, poultry, eggs) at mealtime as you did before starting MAD is a good way to make sure you are not overdoing the protein. Typical meals will include this moderate protein portion, low-carb veggies, and plenty of fat.

GROCERY SHOPPING TIPS

Never underestimate the value of comparison shopping. No, I'm not talking price, but that is an option as well. I'm referring to carbs. While you're shopping, rotate containers to the nutrition facts panel, and then compare net carbs on salad dressings, tomato sauces, pestos, Alfredo sauces, peanut/nut butters, and so forth. Finding the product lowest in net carbs will allow you to save some for later in the day.

You can buy fresh produce; just consult the Atkins Carbohydrate Gram Counter (Appendix F) for the net carbs. If you are new to carb counting or are just in a hurry, shop for prechopped packaged or frozen vegetables to easily locate the nutrition facts panel on the package.

EATING OUT

You may think that you are no longer able eat out after starting the MAD. That is not true at all. I once met a couple who told me that they *only* ate out. I was very nervous for them starting the diet. I thought they would give up or cheat and stop the diet in no time. She is one of my star patients and was able to continue to eat out for about a year, until something happened. The couple got tired of restaurants and started cooking at home! I was very excited to share many simple recipes with them, but they were one step ahead of me. They had been recreating some of their favorite restaurant meals at home and even improving them!

If you are not at that point and would like to eat out occasionally, here are my recommendations:

Check out the menu and nutrition information online for chain restaurants before you go. You'll be prepared and less likely to order impulsively. Some restaurant websites will even allow you to customize your meal online and calculate the nutrition information. This is handy for burger joints where you'd ditch the bun. Just remember to add a few packets of mayo in that case.

Salads are a great way to stay low carb. Just make sure the meat isn't breaded and there aren't too many tomatoes, carrots, or onion that can contribute too many carbs. Get a high-fat dressing like ranch and blue cheese or play it really safe and simply order olive oil on the side. A Cobb salad is an excellent choice! Unbreaded and plain wings are a great meal as well. Ask for extra celery to eat with your high-fat dressing.

Fine dining restaurants may not have nutrition information readily available due to seasonal selections and specials. Be sure to communicate your needs to your wait staff, who may be very equipped, willing, prepared, and eager to accommodate your wishes.

TRACKING YOUR DIET AND MEAL PLANNING

How to Track

Tracking your diet with a food diary, an online program, or phone app will make the diet very manageable and will help to ensure that you are following the guidelines that your clinical team has recommended for you. If you decide to use a paper food diary, you can use a carb counter such as the one in Appendix F to help you figure out the net carb content of your foods and beverages. There are also websites, like www.calorieking.com and www.fatsecret.com, that will show a nutrition facts panel for foods you search, allowing you to keep track of nutrients. An online program or phone app allows you to search for foods easily, log them, and see nutrients all in a few steps.

You can use whichever tracking method you're most comfortable with. But no matter which method you use, entering portion sizes correctly is extremely important. Online programs, apps, and carb counting websites give you nutrition information based on the amount of the food you tell them you ate, so it's very important to put in accurate portions in order to get accurate nutrition information. Use measuring cups, food scales, or specific food units (such as one pork rind or one large egg) to measure your portion sizes. If you don't have a food scale, use this trick: 3 oz of meat is equal to the size of a deck of cards.

And if you're using a carb counting book or food labels, pay attention to the listed serving size. All the information listed is for one serving. If you ate more or less than one serving, do the math to calculate net carbs, and total fat and protein if desired (there's more on which nutrients to track in the next section). Keep a calculator nearby to make it easy.

What to Track

Tracking net carbohydrates is of primary importance while following the MAD. Additionally, tracking total fat and total protein can be useful especially if you are finding it difficult to get into or stay in ketosis. See Chapter 21 for protein recommendations. Many patients have been able to correlate days with lower fat intake with lower ketones, so tracking fat grams can help you find a good range to be in for optimal ketosis.

Meal Planning

Paper food diaries are also great for quick meal planning, especially at the start of diet therapy while you are learning carb counts of foods. You can quickly jot down the next day's meals and approximate carb counts. Re-use the meal plans switching out one meal at a time until you've found a good pattern and learned the foods that you like to eat.

Another suggestion for quick meal planning is to make a list of the foods and net carbs after your grocery shopping trip. This way you can just refer to your list to help you plan meals.

In general, don't over-complicate the diet. Stick to 20 grams of net carbs and replace those ditched carbs with fat. Typical meals look like this: a protein, a low-carb vegetable, and fat. Here are some meal specific tips (see also Chapter 32):

BREAKFAST TIPS

- Breakfast will typically be the lowest carb meal of the day on the MAD diet, and an easy place to add fat.
- There is absolutely NOTHING wrong with eating the same breakfast day in and day out if that is what you like.
- Start your day with hot or cold coffee or tea with 2 to 4 tablespoons of heavy cream. Heavy cream has just under 1 gram of net carb per tablespoon (really, it is 0.8 gram net carb per tablespoon).
- Make a large batch of breakfast quiches or frittata and store in the freezer. You are then just a minute away from a quick, hot, and delicious breakfast on the go.
- Fauxtmeal, the high-fiber MAD version of oatmeal, is a nice break from eggs. Just mix any combination of nuts and seeds (chia, ground flax, hemp

hearts, chopped nuts, and sunflower or pumpkins seeds) with a tablespoon of heavy cream and butter. Sprinkle with cinnamon and sugar substitute to taste. Add water to thin out to your liking. Soak overnight or microwave right before eating. This is great to alleviate constipation.

LUNCH TIPS

- Make extra servings at dinner and take for lunch the next day.
- There are a few brands of low-carb frozen meals (Atkins and Eating Right by Safeway) that make lunch a breeze. Just know that these meals tend to have more protein and lower fat than desired, so be sure to pack a high-fat snack on those days.
- Almost every store has low-carb tortillas or wraps. You can find them for 6 gram net carbs or less! Use them to make lunch wraps, fajitas, quesadillas, nachos or chips, and pizza.

DINNER TIPS

- Batch cooking is a time saver. Cook a whole pan of chicken breasts or thighs or pork chops and keep them in your refrigerator. For meals, just add a low-carb vegetable and a few tablespoons of oil, butter, or mayo.
- Large cuts of meats like beef roasts or pork shoulders are affordable, easily cooked in slow cookers, and can provide meat for lunch and dinner all week. Add a lettuce salad generously doused in olive oil and dry steak seasoning for a fresh touch. This just happens to be my favorite "salad dressing."
- Frozen vegetables are a no brainer! The nutrition facts label makes it easy to count carbs and they are ready in minutes!

SNACK AND DESSERT TIPS

- An avocado a day keeps the dietitian away. Maybe even half an avocado will do. Be sure to sprinkle with salt. Add a dash of cumin, cayenne pepper, or zero-carb sweetener for variation.
- Nuts make a great snack, but be sure to limit portion sized to 1 to 2 oz at a time and count the carbs!
- Pepperoni slices or other cured meats are a great on-the-go snack and can add lots of flavor and fat to recipes.
- Pork rinds will satisfy your desire for crunch. Keep an extra bag handy to bring to potlucks so you can enjoy the quintessential buffalo chicken dip. And for dessert, try them dipped in melted dark chocolate. Yum!

- Berries are the lowest carb fruit. Since you'll be eating them in smaller quantities, I recommend that you buy them frozen. You'll also have the nutrition facts panel readily available.
- Having "Fat Bombs" on hand is a sure way to keep up your fat. Start with 1 cup of any combination of oil, butter, lard, and cream cheese. Mix in flavorings that you like. Portion out in muffin cups or ice cube trays. Keep in the freezer and eat a few for a high-fat treat. Flavor ideas: cocoa powder, mashed berries, bacon, unsweetened shredded coconut, nuts, or even pork rinds. Ask your dietitian for recipes.
- Low-carb baking tips! No need to feel deprived of your favorite foods. Use flax, nut flours, chia seeds, and hemp hearts to make low-carb desserts, breads, and other favorites. Ask your dietitian for recipes, search online, or see Chapter 32.

MAKING IT HEALTHY!

When you're on MAD there are some special things to pay attention to.

Fluid

Staying hydrated by drinking enough fluid throughout the day is very important to alleviate some of the potential side effects of the diet. This is especially true if you are sweating, spending time in the sun, or have an illness. Read more about this in Chapter 24. Options other than plain water include sparkling or seltzer water and milk substitutes like unsweetened almond and coconut milks. Caffeinated coffee, tea, and diet sodas are okay to drink in moderation. Be sure that they are not your sole source of hydration. The same goes for low-calorie drink mixes; drink in moderation to avoid hidden carbohydrates. Low- and zero-carb electrolyte replacement drinks can be found online or at your local sports/athletic store.

Fiber

You may find that your fiber intake takes a nose dive on a ketogenic diet. That's because fiber is a type of carbohydrate. Since you are allowed to subtract fiber grams, though, it can still be easily incorporated into your meal plan. Lettuce greens and cooking greens are great sources, along with nuts and seeds like chia, flax, hemp, and coconut. Incorporating these high-fiber food sources into your diet can regulate bowel movements, which will change whenever you change your diet.

Salt

There is no need to restrict or limit salt on the MAD. In fact, the opposite is true. A body in ketosis actually needs additional salt because the kidneys will get rid of more of it! How much extra? Just give a few extra shakes when you would typically use salt. You can also try sipping broth or cooking with bouillon cubes.

Eat Vegetables

Most of your 20 grams of net carbs should come from the low-carb vegetables! (C'mon, you knew the dietitian would say that!) Vegetables will contribute fiber, volume, and lots of vitamins and minerals to your diet. Oh, and they are delicious smothered in butter!

Vitamin and Mineral Supplementation

Foods manufacturers are legally required to add vitamins and minerals to many of their processed foods due to the lack of nutrient quality. Switching to a low-carbohydrate diet may therefore be lower in micronutrients (vitamins and minerals) compared to a diet full of fortified foods. This is especially true in the first few months of starting MAD when there may be a limited number of foods eaten. With more diet experience there will come more diet variety and more a nutritionally complete diet. However, a good multivitamin and mineral supplement is always recommended to help meet all micronutrients needs. See Chapter 9 for more information regarding supplementation while on dietary therapy.

SECTION V

Life on Ketogenic Diets

CHAPTER 23

Parent Support Groups and the Internet

Over the years we've found that many families first learned about the ketogenic diet, not from their neurologists, but from the Internet. There is a lot of good information out there from reputable sites that deal with epilepsy. Ketogenic diet parent support groups are growing in popularity, and their websites are usually the best places to get information and advice.

However, proceed with caution as there is just as much misinformation available on the Internet. Some websites may be designed with good intentions but share information that might be true for one child on the ketogenic diet, but is not true for most others based on medical literature. In worse cases, these suggestions can be harmful. Web rings and chat rooms have a habit of sharing bad stories as often or even more often than successes. Unfortunately, there are also people out there willing to give miracle cures to desperate parents at a high price, with little medical backing and no perceived responsibility for the risk. Be careful.

In general, the Internet *is* your friend. We advise our families to surf with caution, though, and *never* make any changes to the diet without checking with your keto team first. All neurologists and dietitians are busy, and the rapid replies many parents get from chat rooms and blogs can seem quicker and better. However, always discuss any advice you get with your neurologist and dietitian. They might surprise you and say, "That's a good idea!" They might also tell you that they've heard that advice before from other keto families and it led to disaster.

PARENT SUPPORT GROUPS

The Charlie Foundation (www.charliefoundation.org)

The Charlie Foundation was formed in 1994 at the time of the first edition of this book and was the first dedicated ketogenic diet support group. The Foundation was formed by Jim Abrahams, a movie producer from California, after his son Charlie was treated at Johns Hopkins and became seizure free rapidly on the ketogenic diet (see the foreword to this book). His father was understandably upset at not being told about the ketogenic diet sooner and then later being discouraged from using it. He created the movie *First Do No Harm* with Meryl

Figure 23.1. Courtesy of The Charlie Foundation.

Streep and helped support a 1996 *Dateline NBC* special on the ketogenic diet. The Charlie Foundation has also supported research, such as a multicenter prospective study in 1998 (the first ever). The scientific advisory board of The Charlie Foundation meets annually in December at the American Epilepsy Society meeting and discusses how to continue to move ketogenic diets forward. The Charlie Foundation has also sponsored training sessions for many years for dietitians and neurologists and has been one of the major sponsors of international ketogenic diet conferences, especially those in Phoenix, Chicago, and in 2016 in Banff. Beth Zupec-Kania, RD, has trained many staff at international ketogenic diet centers and runs KetoDietCalculator, used by many families on the ketogenic diet (Chapter 10).

Matthew's Friends (www.matthewsfriends.org)

Figure 23.2. Courtesy of Matthew's Friends.

Matthew's Friends was created in 2004 by Emma Williams, MBE, and is the only foundation dedicated to ketogenic dietary therapies for the entire United Kingdom. It also has registered branches in Canada (www.facebook.com/matthewsfriendscanada) and New Zealand. Emma Williams formed Matthew's Friends after her son Matthew had a similar experience as Charlie Abrahams. Matthew did well on the diet, and his mother created this support group to make the diet available to more children not offered it previously. Similar to The Charlie Foundation, they have sponsored many training sessions and the international ketogenic diet conferences. In addition, Emma has held many parent days for both parents of children on the diet as well as those considering it. The charity has expanded its scope to support adults using ketogenic therapies and those with glucose transporter 1 (GLUT-1) deficiency syndrome and brain cancer. The website is full of useful information and is updated frequently. It also has a scientific advisory board affiliated with the charity, led by Professor J. Helen Cross, OBE.

The Carson Harris Foundation (www.carsonharrisfoundation.org)

Figure 23.3. Courtesy of The Carson Harris Foundation.

This parent support group was created in Baltimore in 2007 by two parents, Gerry and Michael Harris, in response to the successful treatment of their infant daughter Carson at our center. Carson had infantile spasms and was offered the ketogenic diet as an initial treatment in addition to steroids and vigabatrin. The diet worked within days, and Carson was kept on the diet for 6 months total. She is now 10 years old and completely normal. The Harris family created the Foundation and ran a highly successful fundraiser (Carson's FeelGood Fest, with Adam Duritz of the Counting Crows) to fund research related to the ketogenic diet. Gerry Harris also now runs our Johns Hopkins parent support group and, along with about 20 other families, meets with families during their ketogenic diet admission week. Their message of encouraging neurologists to offer the diet much earlier in the course of epilepsy is at the heart of their Foundation (see Chapter 6 for more information) and they have supported the Adult Epilepsy Diet Center (see Chapter 18) since it was created in 2010. Their website offers free on-line webinars you can watch.

The Carley Eissman Foundation (www.carleyeissmanfoundation.org)

Figure 23.4. Courtesy of The Carley Eissman Foundation.

The Carley Eissman Foundation was formed in 2014 to honor their late daughter Carley who was being treated with the modified Atkins diet for juvenile myoclonic epilepsy (JME). They support cooking classes and the University of Southern California ketogenic diet program (Figure 23.4). Their mission is "To provide education and awareness of the efficacy of dietary therapies as an option to ending epileptic seizures. To educate individuals on how a low-carbohydrate diet works to decrease, or eliminate seizures and to teach families how to create recipes that integrate this diet into their daily lives."

KetoKids Club (www.ketokidsclub.com)

Figure 23.5. KetoKids club. Courtesy of Mr. Scott Yucht.

This group was founded in 2015 in New Jersey by three parents to support families using dietary treatments for neurologic disorders. A kick-off event on October 22, 2015 included cooking classes. The primary goal is to provide social communities for patients on ketogenic diets and their families and avoid feelings of isolation by families using dietary therapies. This group also supports the St. Barnabus and New York University ketogenic diet teams.

KETOGENIC DIET SUPPORT AROUND THE WORLD

JAPAN

Figure 23.6. Courtesy of Hiroshi Maruyama.

Mr. Nakasuta, the father of a child with epilepsy who became seizure free on the ketogenic diet, created this group to increase awareness in Japan. Unfortunately, his son died several years ago due to an accident (not related to the diet). He has created a stunning recipe book in Japanese and is trying to increase awareness of the diet in Japan, especially to show that it can be adapted successfully to Asian lifestyles and food preferences.

ISRAEL: Oliver's Magic Diet (www.oliversmagicdiet.com)

Figure 23.7. Courtesy of Talia and Eli Berger.

In 2010, Talia and Eli Berger set up a parent support group in Israel. Their son Oliver has Doose syndrome and has done extremely well on the ketogenic diet. Their goal is to increase awareness and dietitian training in Israel. The website, www.oliversmagicdiet.com, can be translated on Google.com from Hebrew.

AFRICA: The Keilah Foundation (www.keilahfoundation.org)

Figure 23.8. Courtesy of The Keilah Foundation.

This foundation was started to help support dietary therapies in Africa. Keilah is a girl treated with the ketogenic diet for Doose syndrome in South Africa. The foundation hosts events and authors a newsletter.

GREECE: Peter's Friends (www.filoi-tou-petrou.gr/)

Figure 23.9. Courtesy of Peter's Friends Foundation.

This new foundation is based in Greece and also supports ketogenic diet research.

INTERNET SITES

This is a partial list of other websites that we have found helpful. Again, please check anything you read with your ketogenic diet team first before following any advice on your own.

www.epilepsy.com/ketonews

A site run by Eric Kossoff, MD, on epilepsy.com (which has other useful information on epilepsy). It includes a bimonthly newsletter (archived), recipes, lists of ketogenic diet centers worldwide, and links.

www.ilae.org/Commission/medther/keto-index.cfm
The International League Against Epilepsy ketogenic diets site.

www.hopkinsneuro.org
The Johns Hopkins Pediatric Neurology website, with information on the ketogenic diet, Atkins diet, and the adult epilepsy diet center.

www.ketodietcalculator.com
KetoCalculator program

www.facebook.com
Enter the group for Friends of Hopkins Ketogenic Diet Group or "ketogenic."

www.atkins.com
Atkins Nutritionals website, with good tips and recipes.

health.groups.yahoo.com/group/ketogenic
Yahoo.com site

www.myketocal.com
Information on KetoCal™, a ketogenic diet formula supplement.

www.cambrookefoods.com

www.vitaflousa.com

www.ketovolve.com

www.ketobake.com

www.epilepsyfoundation.org
Information from the Epilepsy Foundation

modifiedmom.wordpress.com
This site was created by a mother of a child on the modified Atkins diet.

www.aesnet.org
American Epilepsy Society website

www.atkinsforseizures.com
A useful website created by the family of a child in our first pediatric Atkins study.

www.specialcheese.com/bakedch.htm
Just the Cheese™ snacks

www.dukesmayo.com
High-fat mayonnaise; very useful

www.bickfordflavors.com
No-carbohydrate flavorings

www.tomsofmaine.com
No-carbohydrate toothpaste

www.netrition.com
Useful for buying products, including MCT oil.

www.carbsense.com
Makers of low-carb products with plenty of fiber; well-liked.

www.calorieking.com
Information on *The 2016 Doctor's Pocket Calorie, Fat & Carb Counter,* a helpful resource for modified Atkins diet patients.

www.ketogenicdietindia.org
Information on the diet in India.

www.g1dfoundation.org
GLUT-1 Deficiency Foundation. This condition requires dietary therapy and this website has information about it.

CHAPTER 24

Side Effects of Ketogenic Diets and Handling Illnesses

PART 1: SIDE EFFECTS OF THE KETOGENIC DIET

All therapies—both antiepileptic medications and dietary treatments—have either known or potential side effects. A great deal has been learned over the past few years, and will continue to be learned in the future, about what the unintended consequences of initiating and maintaining the ketogenic diet may be. Now, in 2016, we are sometimes able to prevent side effects before they happen instead of just treating them when they occur. The potential pitfalls and problems fall into four broad categories: prediet evaluation, issues during the initiation of the diet, short-term side effects while on the diet, and the long-term risks.

Of note, this chapter mostly focuses on side effects of the classic ketogenic diet, with lots of information gathered over the years. In addition, what we know we mostly learned from treating children. We do believe that some of the alternative diets (e.g., modified Atkins diet [MAD] and low glycemic index treatment [LGIT]) have slightly lower side effects . . . but not zero. It is important for anyone, child or adult, starting any dietary therapy for epilepsy to be aware of the information in this chapter.

BEFORE EVEN STARTING

In almost every case, one of the physicians on our keto team schedules a face-to-face outpatient clinic visit with the candidate patient and his or her parents/caregivers prior to starting the diet. Nothing can substitute for personally interviewing patients and families, asking additional questions about the history that may not be available from the child's medical records, and examining the patient.

There are exceptions, of course, especially when geographic issues are hard to overcome or the wait for a clinic appointment is much longer than the wait to start the diet. In those cases, we rely heavily on receiving "primary source" records, such as hospital discharge summaries, EEG and MRI data, and laboratory reports. We'll then meet the patient and family for the first time on admission Monday.

There are a few screening tests that must be documented. Most critical is to confirm that the patient is not at significant risk for certain known metabolic conditions. This can be determined by performing studies such as lactate, pyruvate, carnitine, ammonia, plasma amino acids, and urine organic acids, if they are not already documented as normal.

A careful history regarding food allergies and intolerances should be obtained. Because the diet mostly consists of "normal" foods, the likelihood of problems in this area is low but must be screened for. It is possible for a skilled dietitian to design a diet for patients who have food restrictions, and we have done so successfully many times in the past.

Simply stated, the keto team and the patient and parents/caregivers who are considering dietary therapy must communicate clearly and come to an agreement that the "cost/benefit" analysis is favorable enough to proceed. We usually meet as a group a week before admission to discuss each patient individually and how we will be starting the diet for that patient.

PROBLEMS DURING THE START OF THE DIET

Minor problems often arise during diet induction, which is why we initiate the ketogenic diet over the course of a 3-day in-patient hospital stay (Monday through Wednesday). It should be noted that there are some centers that start the diet on an outpatient basis. We believe this can be done in very select patients with *very* careful monitoring (including daily visits to the outpatient clinic during the initiation period). In general, we recommend this only in situations where the risk of the child getting sick from another child in the hospital is too high. We have also occasionally started the diet in children with well-established home nursing care where transport is problematic (e.g., children on ventilators), but even in these situations there is daily contact.

As covered in Chapter 7, there is controversy regarding the need to have children fast prior to starting the diet. Over time, we have modified our protocol from a prediet 48-hour fast to only 24 hours. Exceptions are made for very young infants or children who are medically less stable, whom we do not fast at all. Fasting starts the night before admission so that it is more than half completed by the time the child is on the hospital floor. Fasting clearly accelerates the onset of ketosis, and if carefully monitored in the hospital setting, does not put the child at significant risk. However, studies show that there is no difference in long-term outcomes using fasting versus nonfasting protocols. Remember, even while fasting children can have clear carb-free fluids the entire time.

Hypoglycemia

Fasting may lead to hypoglycemia, or low blood sugar. Blood sugars are monitored about every 6 to 8 hours during the first 1 to 2 days of the diet by checking fingerstick glucoses at the bedside. We know that levels of

40 to 50 mg/dl are not uncommon during diet induction and virtually never require medical intervention. When blood sugar falls below 40 mg/dl, the test is repeated in 1 hour. If the blood sugar level remains low or the child becomes symptomatic—too sleepy or sweaty—30 ml of orange juice may be given and repeated in 30 minutes if necessary. We avoid doing studies that require any type of sedation during this time to avoid possible confusion with hypoglycemia.

Over Ketosis

Hypoglycemia can sometimes lead to over ketosis. Over ketosis is a result of too many ketones building up in the blood, which causes the body to become too acidic, or "acidotic." Signs of too much ketosis include:

- Vomiting
- Irritability
- Increased heart rate
- Facial flushing
- Unusual fatigue or lethargy
- Rapid, panting (Kussmaul) breathing

Over ketosis can also occur during illness. See "Part 2: Caring for a Sick Child on the Ketogenic Diet" at the end of this chapter for more information.

Dehydration

At the onset of ketosis after the fast, many children do not drink fluids at their usual rate. Therefore, we encourage "pushing" oral fluids that are carbohydrate free (water, sugar-free sports drinks, or diluted diet soda or diet ginger ale) during the fast and the entire hospitalization. We no longer measure and restrict fluid intake; there is no evidence of any benefit, and there is a slightly increased risk of dehydration. It is rare for a child to become so dehydrated that he or she requires a bolus of fluid to be given intravenously, but we do that on occasion if a child develops severe vomiting.

Vomiting

After fasting for 24 hours, or even without fasting, the initial food intake, usually given as a "keto shake" or KetoCal®, may cause nausea and vomiting. This does not usually persist for long and can be overcome by having the child take small sips of the shake over a relatively long period of time, as opposed to drinking it rapidly. We find that using the keto shake is better tolerated and less nauseating than progressing straight to ketogenic diet solid foods immediately. In some situations we will give Reglan®, Zofran®, or intravenous fluids. Children with reflux before the diet can have worsened reflux on the diet, so be prepared.

Refusal to Eat

We introduce the total calorie load over 2 days, at a rate of 50% per day divided into three feedings. Thus, the first day, the allotment is one half of calories and the next day it's 100%. Even though most of the children are very hungry after the fast, some respond to being ketotic with hunger suppression. Some of them refuse to eat and need a lot of encouragement. It may require that the keto shake be sipped slowly over several hours, frozen into "ice cream," or microwaved into "scrambled eggs," and eaten slowly. We also do know that most children eat better at home—sometimes the best thing to do is to go home and try there (in your own kitchen!).

SIDE EFFECTS WHILE ON THE DIET

Constipation

This is one of the most common issues encountered by patients on the ketogenic diet, likely caused by reduced bulk and fiber consumption. Fiber is most commonly found in foods such as fruits, vegetables, and whole grains and these foods are consumed in much smaller amounts while on the diet.

It is important to realize that after starting the diet, bowel habits *will* change. This is normal and expected. For example, if your child was previously having a bowel movement every day he or she may only have a bowel movement every 2 to 3 days after starting the diet. This does not mean that your child is constipated. Constipation is diagnosed if the stool is hard and difficult to pass (i.e., if the child is straining), if there is blood on the stool, or if there is abdominal distension as a result of infrequent bowel movements. During the admission week, nearly all children will have decreased bowel movements due to decreased calories for the previous few days.

To help avoid digestive problems we recommend the use of Miralax® (starting with one capful—about 17 grams—daily) and expect parents to make adjustments over time to "keep things moving." Sometimes these products need to be used long term, and that is fine. Parents can also try George's Aloe Vera. If the stool is not easily expelled parents can try a glycerin suppository. Enemas can be used if necessary, but are rarely needed.

If constipation is an ongoing problem, talk to your child's dietitian about adding Group A vegetables to the diet. Group A vegetables increase bulk and fiber. Examples include broccoli, cucumbers, and lettuce. You can also ask your child's dietitian about adding medium chain triglyceride (MCT) oil or incorporating avocados into your child's meal plan. Finally, and perhaps most importantly, be sure to keep your child well-hydrated with sugar-free liquids. We have also found adding salt can be very helpful in preventing constipation.

Do not let your child go more than 3 or 4 days without a bowel movement.

Gastroesophageal Reflux

It is not uncommon for children on the ketogenic diet to have problems with gastroesophageal reflux, or "reflux." Signs and symptoms of reflux include:

- "Heartburn" or a burning feeling in the chest
- Frequent vomiting
- Frequent hiccupping
- Frequent burping
- Abdominal discomfort
- Arching of the torso (in babies and young children)

Most children do not require any treatment but some patients may require a daily acid blocker like Zantac™ or Prevacid™. Many acid-reducing drugs can be found over the counter but be sure to ask your child's pediatrician or keto team about proper dosing. If your child requires a prescription medication then contact your pediatrician or keto team.

Changes in Weight

For average people it takes approximately 3500 calories to gain a pound. If a child has gained a pound in 1 month, then 3500 too many calories have been consumed. Dividing the calories by the number of days (31 in a typical month) reveals that the child has consumed approximately 100 extra calories each day and if the child's calories are decreased by 100 per day, the child should lose 1 pound in a month. Likewise, if a child has lost a pound in 1 month, calculation will reveal that approximately 100 calories should be added to the diet daily. With these additional calories, the child should gain back the lost pound in a month. Changes to the diet should not be made on your own. If you are concerned that your child is gaining or losing too much weight, contact your keto team. Once the child's proper caloric intake is reached, the weight gain or loss will stop. Remember: No two children are identical. Basal metabolic rates differ from child to child, and activity levels can differ markedly. In each case, excessive weight gain or loss indicates that caloric intake must be adjusted.

Hunger

Because the physical quantity of food on the diet (the bulk) is smaller than in a normal diet, many children will feel hungry during the first week or two of the diet until they adjust. This may be especially true of overweight children, who will have their diets calculated to allow for some intentional weight loss. However, ketosis itself decreases appetite, so children are much less likely to be hungry when consistently high levels of ketones are reached, usually within a week of starting the diet.

If a child initially complains of being hungry, try to determine which of the following are true:

- The child is really hungry.
- The child has not yet adapted to the smaller portion sizes.
- The child wants the pleasure and comfort of eating.

Sometimes the child is not hungry at all, but rather it is the parents who feel pity for the child or guilt about the small portions and who project their feelings about the diet onto the child. Other times, in the complex emotional atmosphere of diet initiation, a child's cries of hunger are actually declarations of rebellion against the parents. In any case, most children will lose their feelings of hunger once they adjust to the food they are consuming and achieve consistently high ketosis.

We recommend that parents deal with hunger without trying to add extra calories to the diet, at least for the first few weeks. Tricks to modify hunger without increasing calories include:

- Drinking decaffeinated diet soda or seltzer instead of water for at least part of the liquid allotment
- Freezing drinks, such as diet orange soda mixed with cream, into ice pops
- Eating a leaf of lettuce twice a day with meals
- Making sure that foods, such as vegetables, are patted dry so that water is not part of the weight
- Using smaller plates to make the meals appear larger
- Recalculating the diet plan into four equal meals, or three meals and a snack, while maintaining a constant amount of total daily calories and the proper ketogenic ratio

Vitamin and Mineral Deficiency

The ketogenic diet is deficient in vitamins and sometimes in minerals as well, which can rarely lead to very serious diseases if not replaced. Severe examples are beri beri and optic neuritis due to lack of thiamine. Major minerals such as calcium and trace elements such as selenium are examples of those that are frequently deficient. All ketogenic diet centers prescribe carbohydrate-free multivitamins and mineral supplements, which are readily available. Vitamin D, calcium, zinc, copper, and selenium should always be included in the supplements.

Kidney Stones

Overall, the risk of kidney stones while on the ketogenic diet is increased and without intervention they occur in approximately one in 20 children. However, we now prescribe a daily medication like Polycitra K®, CytraK™, or Bicitra®

as soon as the diet is started for all children. These compounds raise the pH (technically called alkalinization) of the urine, which lowers the likelihood of stone formation by sevenfold.

Kidney stones are generally calcium or uric acid stones, and the first indicator is usually the presence of very small amounts of blood in the urine. Usually the blood cannot be seen with the naked eye. Urine is generally checked every three to six months for blood but can be checked more frequently at home using a Multistix® test strip *if* there is concern for kidney stones. Clinical symptoms of kidney stones may include visible blood in the urine, "gritty" urine, and/or lower back (so-called "flank") pain. Nonspecific symptoms include low-grade fever, abdominal pain, poor appetite, and an increase in number of seizures.

Children whose parents or siblings have a history of kidney stones are more likely to develop kidney stones on the diet than those with no family history. In addition, children taking a medication type called a carbonic anhydrase inhibitor (the common ones are topiramate or Topamax® and zonisamide or Zonegran®) may be at slightly increased risk of kidney stone formation. However, these medications do not have to be discontinued when the ketogenic diet is started or maintained. In fact, some data would suggest the diet is slightly more effective when used in combination with zonisamide! Data are a bit controversial as to whether or not these medications increase the risk over the diet alone.

If kidney stones are suspected, carbohydrate-free fluids should initially be pushed hard to increase urine flow and flush out the urinary tract. If symptoms persist, the primary care physician needs to be consulted so that this possible complication can be differentiated from more common illnesses such as a gastrointestinal virus or flu. The use of diagnostic abdominal ultrasound is recommended in cases where stones cannot be ruled out.

If increasing oral carbohydrate-free liquid intake is not sufficient to flush out the urinary tract, intravenous fluids can be administered. In rare cases, stones must be broken up by lithotripsy (using vibration) or even at times by surgery.

High Cholesterol and Other Lipid Abnormalities

We live in a society very concerned with total cholesterol levels, "good" and "bad" cholesterol levels, and elevated triglycerides. Not surprisingly, when people learn that a child is being given a diet that is in excess of 80% fat, they are both surprised and concerned. Our study of lipid-level changes on the ketogenic diet indicates that in about 30% of children there may be cholesterol and triglyceride levels "that exceed current recommendations for normal children," but in most cases this is a transient finding. As the body (primarily the liver) adjusts to the greatly increased load of fat it must digest when the ketogenic diet is started, the levels begin to stabilize and then return very close to prediet levels after six to twelve months. In cases where children experience exceedingly high lipid levels, there may be a coincident genetic type of familial hyperlipidemia that was exacerbated by the high-fat diet.

One study showed that in children on the diet for longer than six years, most of them had cholesterol levels in the normal range. This is true for adults, too. When the diet is discontinued, and the child returns to a diet with a "normal" fat intake, lipids almost always return to normal. We do not have any evidence that there are long-term effects of a temporary increase in lipids as a child. Recent studies have noticed that the carotid arteries (the arteries in the neck) of children on ketogenic diets seem to be less distensible or flexible while on these therapies. When the diet stops, this goes away. What impact does this have on children? We don't know but in these studies all the children appeared to be fine. However, this absolutely is worth more study.

What if the cholesterol won't come down? Reducing the diet ratio, increasing the percentage of polyunsaturated fats, substituting medium chain triglycerides, and adding carnitine (particularly in patients that are found to be carnitine deficient) are the most common approaches we take. However, a study here showed that although 60% of children have at least a 20% reduction in cholesterol by making some (or all) of these changes, about 40% had their cholesterol decrease by at least 20% with just observation alone. In other words, it may be best to just repeat the labs after one to two months and leave the diet alone.

We have had virtually no child discontinue the diet exclusively for lipid abnormalities, and have never yet treated a child on the diet who has markedly elevated cholesterol with statin medication.

Carnitine Deficiency

Many children on the diet for several months, especially if on valproate (Depakote®) at the same time, will have a decrease in their free carnitine. According to the international consensus statement, these children should then be treated with levocarnitine (Carnitor®). At our center, we usually do that if the levels are low *and* the child is symptomatic (e.g., fatigue, low energy, low ketosis, poor seizure control).

LONG-TERM SIDE EFFECTS

Studies of children on the ketogenic diet for more than 6 years have shown that seizure control and cholesterol are not adversely affected over time. However, the bad news is that bone fractures, kidney stones, and growth retardation *are* more of a problem long term. This doesn't mean the diet has to be stopped, but it does mean that keto teams need to be very aware of this and try to prevent problems before they occur.

There are definitely exceptions. A man in his 30s with tuberous sclerosis who has been on the ketogenic diet for nearly his entire adult life identified himself and presented to our clinic several years ago. He had no history of appetite or growth issues, kidney stones, constipation, or evidence of acidotic episodes. His bone density (DEXA) scan and carotid ultrasound were normal for his age.

Although his height is less than normal, he is happy, healthy, and he remains on the diet, seizure free to this day.

Bone Metabolism

Very debilitated, nonambulatory children who are on the ketogenic diet have a high incidence of bone changes that can be documented on radiologic studies and DEXA scans. We also know that vitamin D levels decrease over time (after initially increasing on the diet due to the added supplements), particularly in patients who are on chronic antiepileptic medications. We supplement 400 to 800 International Units (IU) per day of vitamin D when levels are demonstrably low until they can be normalized and maintained at a lower dose. We do not routinely obtain skeletal x-rays or DEXA scans on our patients in the short term, but if they are on the diet for more than two or three years it is definitely worth considering, especially if the child is still on seizure medications.

Growth Retardation

We expect children to grow normally in height while on the diet, although younger children may have a slight initial drop off of their growth rate. Studies have shown that the problems with height may be related to ketosis itself, so this could happen with the MAD as well, not just the ketogenic diet. Most children grow normally, but if they don't, there is evidence that there is growth "catch up" when the diet is discontinued.

When we see children periodically in follow-up clinic, we measure and chart their weight and height. We want to see weight gain and linear height increase over time, in the context of the child being able to have as much seizure control as possible. If there is a problem, we will sometimes lower the ratio to increase protein, lowering it to a 2:1 or even 1:1 ratio. Some children on the diet in other countries have been started on growth hormone, with early reported good results (no studies yet).

Miscellaneous Complications

Included in this category are bleeding disorders, increased bruising, and hepatitis, which are all liver-related problems; pancreatitis; iron deficiency anemia; prolonged QT intervals (heart related); and alteration in immunoglobulin levels and function (leading to possible increased occurrence of infections). Most of these problems are recognizable with regular clinical and laboratory monitoring and are correctable when diagnosed and treated.

Death

There are rare case reports of deaths occurring that may be attributable to the ketogenic diet. These have been due to cardiomyopathy, selenium deficiency leading to cardiac arrhythmia, or aspiration of fatty food contents (usually liquid formulas) causing lipoid pneumonia. One of our patients died due to recurrence of a cardiomyopathy of unknown cause, which had been identified well before the diet was started. Sadly, some children may die of SUDEP (sudden unexpected death in epilepsy patients), which is more common in those with frequent, generalized tonic–clonic seizures, especially those taking multiple antiepileptic medications.

SUMMARY

The ketogenic diet was not originally intended for long-term use as an epilepsy treatment, but because it has successfully reduced seizure frequency and improved general quality of life for so many patients, its usage has frequently been extended for many consecutive years. It is not free of side effects but, working together, parents/caregivers and the keto team can often prevent or minimize side effects and complications of the ketogenic diet.

PART 2: CARING FOR A SICK CHILD ON THE KETOGENIC DIET

At some point, every child on the ketogenic diet will become ill, as all children do. When this happens the primary focus of the parent should be managing the child's symptoms and preventing complications. Usually this can be done without stopping the diet, but not always. The most important thing is to get the child well again. The diet can be resumed once the child is healthy.

Illness is considered a seizure trigger and breakthrough seizures may occur even in children whose seizures are otherwise well controlled. For children on the ketogenic diet this can occur for several additional reasons. First, sick children often do not feel like eating. They may not finish the entire meal, which can alter the ratio of the meal itself, especially if they eat the carbohydrates but not all of the fat. Their activity level typically decreases and they don't burn as many calories when they are ill. They may also become dehydrated in the setting of a fever, nausea, vomiting, and/or diarrhea. For these and other reasons, many children on the diet experience an increase in their seizures when they are sick.

For the most part, illness symptoms are managed in exactly the same way as they are in children who are not on the ketogenic diet. There are, however, a few important exceptions.

VOMITING OR DIARRHEA

- Give only sugar-free clear liquids. Do not worry about restricting fluids. Offer them as frequently as tolerated.
- If vomiting lasts for more than 24 hours, use unflavored Pedialyte® or Gatorade Zero® to maintain electrolytes. Use for up to 24 hours (but not longer).

- When vomiting stops, you can introduce a one-half strength eggnog meal. Each sip has the proper ketogenic ratio, and it is not necessary for your child to finish the eggnog if he or she does not want to. Increase as tolerated until the child is eating the full diet quantity, then resume regular menus. Your child may be able to go right back to eating regular meals once he or she feels better.
- If your child becomes dehydrated and a visit to the emergency department for intravenous (IV) fluids is required, make sure that the fluids are sugar-free (normal saline, no dextrose). Physicians and nurses in emergency departments are not thinking about the effects that glucose in the IV might have on the diet and on the child's seizures. If blood glucose is below 40 mg/dl, a single bolus of glucose (1 gram per kilogram of body weight) may be given. A word of caution: If the bag of IV fluid in the hospital has a "D" on the bag, be sure to ask the doctor or nurse if the fluid contains sugar, or dextrose. The "D" is an abbreviation for dextrose, which is a type of sugar.
- If your child is using MCT oil with the diet, discontinue it until the illness is resolved. Substitute 1 gram canola or corn oil for each gram of MCT oil. The MCT oil can be resumed when your child is well.

FEVER

- Give a sugar-free, fever-reducing medicine. Smaller children can take Tylenol junior-strength chewable tabs. Older children may be able to use adult strength acetaminophen or ibuprofen tablets, which can be crushed (see Appendix A). **Ask your child's pediatrician what an appropriate dose would be based on your child's weight**. If your child is unable to take tablets, acetaminophen suppositories are an excellent fever reducer that won't interfere with the diet.
- Offer sugar-free liquids without restriction while your child has a fever.
- If an antibiotic is needed, make sure it is sugar free and sorbitol free. Tablets are preferred over liquids.

ANTIBIOTICS AND OTHER MEDICATIONS

- Almost all syrups and elixirs have sugar. Therefore, most liquid medications are NOT "keto friendly." If you are unsure, ask the pharmacist at the drugstore.
- Most tablets and capsules are fine to take on the diet *except for chewable tablets, which DO contain sugar*. If possible, try to give any necessary medications in a nonchewable tablet or capsule form.
- If a medication cannot be given as a tablet or capsule, medications can be compounded into a "keto friendly" liquid by a compounding pharmacy.

HELPFUL TIPS

Identify a compounding pharmacy *before* your child is sick in the event that he or she must take a liquid medication. Make sure that the pharmacy is comfortable making "keto-friendly" medications.

Develop a good relationship with your pharmacist and make sure he or she knows that your child is on the ketogenic diet.

Not all medications that say they are sugar free are keto friendly. Many still have carbohydrates.

TOO MUCH KETOSIS-A POTENTIAL COMPLICATION OF ILLNESS

Just as over-ketosis can be seen during initiation of the diet, it can sometimes develop during the course of an illness.

If you suspect your child may be in too much ketosis, check urine ketones and if they are high, give 2 tablespoons of orange juice. If the symptoms persist 20 minutes after giving the juice, give another 2 tablespoons of orange juice. If the second dose of juice does not improve your child's condition, call your pediatrician and the supervising physician of your child's ketogenic diet immediately.

If you cannot reach the doctors, take your child to the emergency department. The emergency department doctors will check how acidotic your child has become. Intravenous fluids or even a dose of intravenous glucose may be needed to treat the excessive ketosis. In the meantime, ask the emergency department team to continue trying to contact your keto team.

CHAPTER 25

Dealing With the "Nonketo" World

The most important factor contributing to the success of the ketogenic diet is the family's psychological state. This requires everyone in the child's life to "buy in." Committing to the diet requires a great deal of faith. The parents (and grandparents) must believe that the diet can work. If the parents are divorced, they both must be part of the decision to start the diet. The diet is hard and sometimes takes patience. Although seizures often are reduced even during the admission week, that doesn't always happen and the family needs to give it time.

Parents who start out as doubters will focus on the inevitable initial difficulties of the diet instead of focusing on the decrease in seizures and the improved behavior of the child as the diet starts. Without faith, it will be too frustrating when the child accidentally gets an incorrectly prepared meal, when he or she is irritable and demanding, or when the child gets sick and has a seizure 3 weeks into the treatment. It will be too hard on the family if the child cries for afternoon cookies or Sunday night pizza.

If parents start out thinking positively, saying, "We will do whatever is necessary to give this diet a chance to work, the sacrifice is worthwhile if our child has a chance to become seizure free," then they are already halfway there. As stated earlier in this book, more than half of children will have fewer seizures and/or less medicine on the diet. The question will become whether the improvement is sufficient to continue the diet. Families will have a greater chance of success if they think of the opportunity to try the diet as a gift to the child, not as a punishment for having seizures.

Sometimes problems with the diet may not come from the parents or the child. They may come from a "How-will-my-grandchild-know-it's-me-if-I-don't-bring-Hershey's-Kisses?" grandma, or from a jealous "How-come-Peter-gets-all-the-attention?" sister. The optimism and faith that will carry a family through the diet has to come from a team effort, encompassing the whole family, especially the child. If the diet is effective and the seizures are under better control, if the child is functioning better, it becomes much easier to maintain the momentum. At the start it can be very tough. It is the willingness of the parents to meet the challenge that will carry the family through.

It is important to prepare *everyone* in the child's life before starting the diet. This isn't just immediate family members and grandparents; it includes teachers, school nurses, daycare providers, babysitters, and after-school programs. If your child receives special nursing care do not assume that your child's caregiver is familiar with the diet. The caregiver may need education about the diet and what he or she should and should not be doing when caring for a child on the ketogenic diet.

GETTING THE CHILD'S COOPERATION

The diet is likely to go more smoothly if children are enlisted—rather than ordered—to participate. Children do not like having seizures. They do not like being different from their friends. Often, the thing they hate most is taking medications. They want to be cured of their seizures. If possible, explain to a child, in an age-appropriate fashion, how the diet may help fix these problems. If parents communicate their own enthusiasm for the diet as something worth trying, something that really might work, most children will buy in. They will feed on your enthusiasm. Let brothers and sisters participate as well in this—they can be great motivators. We have seen a sister create a coloring book with the story of the diet admission to keep the child with seizures entertained. So don't start the diet if you and your child are not enthusiastic about trying it—without that enthusiasm, it will be too hard.

However, no one should make promises that cannot be kept! Parents cannot guarantee to the child that the seizures will disappear completely or that there will be no more medication. These are goals, but they cannot be promises.

For school-aged children and teens, sticking to the diet will ultimately be the child's responsibility. Parents can help by giving children the psychological and emotional power to handle the tough parts. Role-playing may be useful. Parents can try rehearsing what to say in difficult situations. For instance, a parent might pretend to be a teacher offering a cracker at snack time, and the child might practice saying, "That's not on my diet, thank you!" Or a parent might pretend to be a friend trying to swap a sandwich for the child's cheesecake at lunch and teach the child responses such as, "No, I'm on a magic diet. I have to eat my own food." Children on the diet usually exhibit amazing self-control and willpower. They often handle the diet far better than their parents do—especially when they are doing well.

During the admission week, we also try to have our new parents speak to some parents who have either had their child on the diet for a while (or were on it in the past). This is very helpful in terms of a pep talk, although no medical advice is given. Some families will also communicate with their "roommates" long after the admission week. There's nothing like peer support! Hospital Child Life support can also be super helpful to play with the children and ask them about their thoughts regarding the diet.

GET THE WHOLE FAMILY INVOLVED

When you and your child are making the tremendous effort to stick to the diet in pursuit of an important goal, you need everyone's cooperation and encouragement. You can weigh the food in advance, but if you are not there at dinnertime, someone else—an older sister or brother, a sitter, a grandmother—can put it in the microwave and serve the meal.

A child on the diet and all the child's sisters and brothers, relatives, friends, and teachers should understand that even tiny amounts of cheating can spoil the overall effect of the diet and that their friendship, support, and encouragement are crucial to its success. It helps if family members avoid eating carb-rich foods in large quantities around the child, especially if the child is just starting and adapting to the diet. Low-carb diets are probably healthier than previously thought, so it's not a bad idea for family members to consider a version of it too (with their doctor's approval, of course!).

DIET DON'TS

One mother kept her child out of school for a year and hired an in-home teacher because she did not want the child to be tempted by seeing other children eat. Another family stopped going out entirely—no more McDonald's, no more Sunday dinners at Grandma's—until the child himself finally begged them, explaining that he would enjoy the atmosphere and would not be too tempted by the food. Another mother fed her child earlier and in another room so she "wouldn't feel different" from her siblings. We believe it is better to aim for inclusiveness, for living as normally as possible given the diet's restrictions. In our experience, most children are able to participate in making the diet as much as possible a part of a normal, enjoyable life.

LONG TRIPS

Yes, the family can take vacations. Longer trips by necessity involve more planning than shorter ones. Many families who take long vacations choose to stay in places where they can cook, such as friends' condominiums or motels with kitchenettes, rather than in hotels. They sometimes take eggnog for the road instead of a solid meal. They take their scale and call ahead to make sure that places where they will be staying have heavy cream and a microwave available. With the scale, they can order grilled chicken, steamed vegetables, and mayonnaise and create a quick meal right at the restaurant.

Families take coolers full of prepared ingredients for the first couple of days of a trip, and perhaps staples such as artificial sweetener and mayonnaise. If they are staying in a hotel with no kitchen, they might take a camping stove to cook on. They take a lot of storage containers and the calcium and multivitamin supplements, too, of course—they never forget those.

Apart from the nuisance of planning, the diet should be no obstacle to family fun. There is no reason why a child should not live a rich, full, and healthy life while on the ketogenic diet. There is no reason to deprive yourself or the rest of the family. For more details about travel, see Chapter 26.

CHAPTER 26

Tips for Travel

This chapter was kindly written for us by Mr. Jason Meyers, President of the GLUT-1 Deficiency Foundation. He is an expert on travel while on the ketogenic diet.

TRAVELING

Everyone loves to travel, to see the sites, and to experience other cultures. However, along with the excitement comes the struggles and complexity involved with planning the trip. In addition, traveling with a child or other family member on the ketogenic diet presents its own unique challenges but with some preparation, these challenges can be minimized. Presented in the following are the top five tips for traveling with a loved one on the ketogenic diet.

1. **Be prepared:** Part of the preparation is gathering the tools necessary to carry out the ketogenic diet while away.

   An important concept to become familiar with prior to departure is the ability to recalculate a meal while on the go. In the past, you would have to carry around a computer or some other way to recalculate menus. But with the mobile phones available today, you can be accomplish this task using common apps. A couple of our favorites are DocsToGo and Microsoft Excel. At home, we use our home computer and the Microsoft Excel template from Stanford to calculate meals and have an entire binder filled with different combinations of foods. With just a little effort, this entire workbook can be saved on a phone and manipulated based on the circumstances. These apps also come in handy when a preferred food may be unavailable.

   Another favorite app is PDF Reader. This app allows you to view a PDF version of the Stanford workbook described earlier but does not allow any manipulation. The benefit is the search function; it is much quicker and easier than the others. So, if all that is needed is a quick lookup, this app can accomplish this task quickly.

A second great tool, and very important one at that, is a letter from the treating doctor. This letter should include a detailed explanation as to why you may be traveling with items such as scales, prepared food, and a small ice chest filled with cream and/or some type of oil. In addition to the doctor's name and contact information, this letter should be on facility letterhead and contain enough detail for the reviewer. We have, on occasion, produced this letter for the customs or security agent on duty as additional justification for the materials we were carrying. After a bit of questioning, we were allowed through.

2. **Bring extra scales:** Whenever we travel, we always bring an extra scale or two. They are small, do not take up much space, are relatively inexpensive, and an extra one would be worth its weight in gold in the event the other scale is damaged. As you know, scales with the precision needed for the ketogenic diet must be ordered and are not easily replaced. That's why it is never a good idea to leave an extra scale in a checked bag as it may be damaged during transit and will also be unavailable for use during travel if needed. We always carry our scales in different bags.

   There are a lot of good, reputable suppliers of scales on the Internet. A couple of our favorite sites are Old Will Knott Scales (oldwillknottscales.com) and American Weigh Scales (americanweigh.com). Each of these sites offers a number of small pocket scales with the precision and capacity needed. The Jennings JSR-600 and Fast Weigh TR-600 are a couple of our favorites. Whichever scale you decide to purchase, remember, it should have a precision of 0.1 grams, a capacity greater than 600 grams, and the ability to be recalibrated.

   Traveling aside, in general it is good practice to have more than one scale available at home. We once found one of the scales listed earlier on sale for $5.00 and purchased eight. We kept a few at home and have the remainder strategically placed in our vehicles, siblings' houses, the grandparents' houses, and other locations we frequent. Cheap insurance when you realize you have traveled across town and forgotten the scale at home. Although I often wonder if we were ever questioned about the number of scales we own, we would have a lot of explaining to do!

3. **Have a back-up plan:** It is inevitable; something will not go as planned. Know where extra heavy whipping cream or oil can be obtained. We have spilled our supply a time or two and had to make a dash to the nearest store. Easy near home, but perhaps not so easy in an unfamiliar location. Now we do not travel without extra whipping cream. In fact, Katie brings extra cream to school every day in case of a spill.

   Katie's preferred source of fat is heavy whipping cream. She has been drinking it for so long, it's like milk to her now. For those who do not know, this cream has to be kept very cold or it will quickly thicken then begin to turn sour. While preparing for a camping trip, there was some uncertainty in whether we would have sufficient ice to keep the cream cold enough to prevent spoiling. In anticipation, I brought along some oil which we could substitute as a fat source if the cream spoiled. But the question arose, how much oil do we use to substitute for the cream? For a quick reference, I used Excel to create a table that provided the quantity of oil needed to replace the fat normally received from the cream over a range of increasing quantities of cream. Saved it to my phone and we were ready, just in case.

For a quick snack, Katie will often eat some potato chips followed by some cream. When we first began the diet, the chips of choice were Doritos. Since then, we have discovered that many (not all) varieties of Frito Lay chips have the same nutrition facts and may be used interchangeably. Using the Frito Lay website, I researched the varieties that are acceptable and compiled them into a short list. Now, if we are out and about, we have a quick reference to the chips we can use in her snack. We keep this list (any guesses?) on our phones.

4. **Be aware of special requirements:** Airlines and cruise ships will certainly have special requirements. It is best to call ahead and discuss what may be expected at the airport or port so check-in will go smoothly.

   When flying, as you know, security is tight so a little effort will go a long way. I always place a call to the Transportation Security Administration (TSA) and discuss the items we will be carrying and have generally received the same guidance each time. The TSA states medical foods are allowed to be carried onto the plane, however, at the security check in, you must declare the items to the agent (do not let the agent discover them) and be prepared to spend a little extra time getting these items screened. Be sure to mention if the ice chest will be chilled with ice or frozen gel packs. On one trip we were not allowed to bring the gel packs.

   Prior to our last cruise, I called ahead and discussed what we were planning to bring on the ship. The cruise line was very accommodating and even provided special instructions for check-in. We were able to board the ship with no trouble and with all of our items. Once on board, I was able to speak to the chef and find a couple of items that could be used in preparation of meals.

   By spending a little time upfront, we were able to board a flight, fly across the country, and board a cruise ship with a small ice chest containing 6 pints of heavy whipping cream and very little delay—an amazing feat with present-day security.

5. **Have a list of acceptable chain restaurants:** We have recipes from a few restaurants that have locations throughout the country. When evaluating these places, we look for food choices that are prepared consistently at any restaurant in the chain. For example, a chicken nugget from McDonald's looks the same the regardless of your location. That consistency is what makes McDonald's and Burger King two of our favorite quick-stop locations. We have meals for lunch and breakfast at each of these restaurants. Another fast-food favorite is Popeye's. We have learned that we can order two

chicken thighs, remove the breading, and add a few grams of fries for a quick meal.

For an option at a sit-down restaurant, one of Katie's favorite places is Hooter's. Hooter's signature dish and claim to fame is their buffalo chicken wings. These wings can be ordered either with or without breading and tossed in a hot sauce. Chicken wings are easy to calculate in a menu, but what about the sauce? Not to worry, the main ingredient in the hot sauces is butter. Any sauce on the meat can be considered lagniappe, or extra, and will only increase the ratio slightly.

We try to frequent these places so everyone can eat from the same menu. They also come in handy when everyone is tired and hungry from a day full of sightseeing.

In summary, the key point is that a little preparation goes a long way. For our children (and adults) with GLUT-1 deficiency, the ketogenic diet is the standard of care so it is very important to be able to continue the diet uninterrupted and maintain ketosis. I hope these tips will help make the diet successful both at home and away. With just a little planning, managing the ketogenic diet while on vacation will be a breeze allowing more time to enjoy the trip.

SECTION VI

Other Therapeutic Diets and Modifications

CHAPTER 27

The MCT Ketogenic Diet

This chapter was written by Elizabeth Neal, RD, PhD, who works as a dietitian for Matthews Friends in the United Kingdom and has both clinical and research experience with using the MCT diet.

By the mid-20th century, when the classic ketogenic diet was falling out of favor because of availability of new anticonvulsants and a feeling that large amounts of fat were unpalatable, Dr. Peter Huttenlocher of the University of Chicago set out to invent a new and improved form of the ketogenic diet. He believed that the ketogenic diet was an effective treatment that more families would try—and benefit from—if it were formulated with foods more closely approximating a normal diet. Dr. Huttenlocher and his group replaced some of the long-chain fat in the classic ketogenic diet—that is, fat from foods such as butter, oils, cream, and mayonnaise—with an alternative fat source with a shorter carbon chain length. This medium chain fat, otherwise known as medium chain triglyceride (MCT), is absorbed more efficiently than long chain fat, is carried directly to the liver in the portal blood, and does not require carnitine to facilitate transport into cell mitochondria for oxidation. Because of these metabolic differences, MCT will yield more ketones per kilocalorie of energy than its long-chain counterparts. This increased ketogenic potential means less total fat is needed in the MCT diet. Whereas the classical 4:1 ratio ketogenic diet provides 90% of energy from fat, the MCT ketogenic diet typically provides 70% to 75% of energy from fat (both MCT and long chain), allowing more protein and carbohydrate foods to be included. This increased carbohydrate allowance makes the MCT diet a useful option for individuals who are unable to tolerate the more restricted carbohydrate intake in other ketogenic therapies. Recent evidence from laboratory studies also indicates that MCT may additionally have a direct anticonvulsant action that is specific to medium-chain fatty acids of a particular chain length. Further research into this exciting area is ongoing.

Calculation of the MCT diet is not based on the ketogenic ratio but instead looks at the percentage of dietary energy that is provided by MCT. The original MCT diet provided 60% energy from MCT; the remaining 40% included 10% energy from protein, 15% to 19% energy from carbohydrate, and 11% to 15%

from long-chain fat. However, this amount of MCT caused gastrointestinal discomfort in some children, including abdominal cramps, diarrhea, and vomiting. For this reason, in 1989 Dr. Ruby Schwartz and her colleagues suggested using a modified MCT diet, which reduced the energy from MCT to 30% of total and added an extra 30% of energy from long-chain fat. In many children, this lower amount of MCT may not be enough to ensure adequate ketosis for optimal seizure control, and in practice a starting MCT level of 40% to 50% energy is likely to provide the optimal balance between gastrointestinal tolerance and good ketosis. This can then be increased (or decreased) as necessary during fine-tuning. Christiana Liu and her colleagues in Toronto published a paper in 2013 on their extensive experience of using the MCT ketogenic diet. They report good tolerance of diets with 40% to over 70% energy from MCT, with a generous carbohydrate allowance. However, they highlight the importance of close monitoring of gastrointestinal symptoms, especially during the initiation of the diet where problems can occur if MCT is introduced too quickly.

Schwartz and her group in 1989 also compared the clinical and metabolic effects of the MCT ketogenic diet, both traditional (60% MCT) and modified (30% MCT), with the classic 4:1 ketogenic diet. They found all three diets equally effective in controlling seizures, but compliance and palatability were better with the classic ketogenic diet. However, in this study children were not randomly allocated to one of the diets, leaving it open to possibility of bias. The question of differences in efficacy and tolerability between the classic and MCT ketogenic diets was further examined at Great Ormond Street Hospital in London, in a randomized trial of 145 children with intractable epilepsy, the results of which were reported in 2009. Children were randomized to receive a classic or MCT ketogenic diet and seizure frequency was assessed after 3, 6, and 12 months. Data were available for analysis from 94 children: 45 on the classic diet and 49 on the MCT diet. Table 27.1 shows results for percentage of baseline seizure frequency between the two groups after 3, 6, and 12 months. Although the mean value was lower in the classic group after 6 and 12 months, these differences were not statistically significant at any of the times (the *P* value is greater than .05 at 3, 6, and 12 months). There were also no significant differences in numbers achieving greater than 50% or 90% seizure reduction. Serum ketone levels (acetoacetate and β-hydroxybutyrate) at three and six months were significantly higher in children on the classic diet. There were no significant differences in tolerability except increased reports in the classic diet group's of lack of energy after 3 months and vomiting after 12 months. This study concluded that both the classic and MCT ketogenic diets have their place in the treatment of childhood epilepsy.

So how does the MCT diet work in practice? The MCT is given as a commercially available MCT oil or emulsion. At present there are two emulsions: 50% MCT (Liquigen®, Nutricia) or 20% MCT (Betaquik®, Vitaflo), both of which are available by prescription in the United Kingdom and the United States. The amount of MCT has to be calculated into the diet just as for any other fat and should be divided up over the day and included in all meals and snacks;

TABLE 27.1

Mean Percentage of Baseline Seizure Numbers at 3, 6, and 12 Months in Classic and MCT Diet Groups

TIME (MONTHS)	CLASSIC DIET	MCT DIET	*P* VALUE
3	67% (*n* = 45)	69% (*n* = 49)	0.834
6	49% (*n* = 30)	68% (*n* = 34)	0.165
12	41% (*n* = 22)	53% (*n* = 25)	0.382

Source: From Neal EG, Chaffe HM, Schwartz RH, Lawson M, Edwards N, Fitzsimmons G, Whitney A, Cross JH. The ketogenic diet in the treatment of epilepsy in children: a randomised, controlled trial. *Lancet Neurol.* 2008;7:500–506.

n = number providing seizure data at that time point.

the amount will be specified in the diet prescription provided by the dietician. MCT emulsions can be mixed with milk as a drink (best with skimmed or semi-skimmed milk as full-fat milk causes the mixture to thicken excessively); they can also be added to foods such as soups and mashed potato, or used in recipes, ranging from sugar-free jellies, sauces, and baking. MCT oil also works well in meal preparation and baking. Recipes for meals and snacks are available from Matthew's Friends (www.matthewsfriends.org). *MCT has a low flashpoint, so be cautious when frying, and keep the temperature fairly low!*

As the MCT ketogenic diet allows a wider variety of antiketogenic foods, portions of protein foods are more generous than with the classic diet, as are the allowed amounts of fruits and vegetables. Small amounts of higher carbohydrate foods, such as milk, bread, potatoes, and cereals, can also be calculated into the daily allowance. Sweet and sugary foods are not allowed and low-glycemic index carbohydrate choices are encouraged. As with the classic diet, food must be weighed accurately and energy intake is controlled. Although the prescription can be implemented using exact recipes, many centers will prefer food exchange lists because of the more generous amounts of carbohydrate and protein. The use of separate carbohydrate, protein, and fat exchanges is recommended because this allows an even macronutrient distribution over the meals and snacks. Individual requirements for micronutrients must always be considered with additional vitamin, mineral, and trace element supplementation. The prescribed diet must also meet essential fatty acid requirements.

The MCT diet can be provided as a tube feed if necessary but there is no complete product available as there is for the classic diet, so the prescription and preparation of such a feed will be more complicated; use of a classic ketogenic diet feed product will be preferable.

On commencing the MCT diet, the MCT oil or emulsion needs to be introduced much more slowly than long-chain fat (over about 5–10 days), as it may cause abdominal discomfort, vomiting, or diarrhea if introduced rapidly. During this introduction period the rest of the diet can be given as prescribed, but an extra meal may be needed to make up the energy while using less MCT. Once on the full diet, it must be followed just as strictly as the classic diet. Fine-tuning is usually needed to maximize benefit and tolerance. This is done by increasing or decreasing the MCT dose; the amount of long-chain fat can be adjusted to keep the same total energy from fat in the diet. If a higher level of ketosis is desired and an increased amount of MCT is not tolerated, the amount of carbohydrate in the diet can be reduced and long-chain fat increased to balance overall energy provision.

Discontinuing the MCT diet should be done in a stepwise process. The MCT is slowly reduced and the protein and carbohydrate increased. However if the MCT diet works well, as with other ketogenic therapies, it is usually continued for at least 2 years.

In oil or emulsion form, MCT can also be used as a supplement to the classic ketogenic diet, both to increase ketosis and to help alleviate constipation. Swapping some of the fat allowance for a small dose of MCT can soften the stools and, in limited amounts, is usually well tolerated. In a similar way, MCT is increasingly being used to supplement the modified Atkins diet to boost ketone levels.

CHAPTER 28

The Low Glycemic Index Treatment

This chapter was kindly written by Heidi Pfeifer, RD, from the Massachusetts General Hospital in Boston, where this diet was pioneered.

Throughout time, dietary treatments have been used as an effective treatment for epilepsy, dating back to the use of fasting in biblical times. Over the years, it has become more standardized and regimented with the classic ketogenic diet providing the majority of caloric intake from fat to mimic the fasting state. This high-fat diet is restrictive and can, at times, be unpalatable, which can ultimately decrease compliance. Therefore, over the last few decades more liberalized versions of the diet have been utilized. The low glycemic index treatment (LGIT) for epilepsy was developed in 2002 at the Massachusetts General Hospital by dietitian Heidi Pfeifer and Dr. Elizabeth Thiele as an alternative to the classic ketogenic diet and is now being used worldwide. The efficacy of the LGIT is similar to that of the ketogenic diet with more than half of patients experiencing a reduction in their seizure frequency. The LGIT was shown to be effective when other dietary treatments failed in a recent case study, and a prospective study using the LGIT in children with Angelman syndrome showed a higher efficacy than in the general epilepsy population with subsequent improvements in EEG.

In the 1980s, it was discovered that not all carbohydrates are created equal and that some increase blood sugar more than others. Those that increase blood sugar more were termed high glycemic and those that do not raise blood sugar as high are considered low glycemic. Following this discovery, low glycemic index diets have been used in the treatment of diabetes, heart disease, obesity, and polycystic ovary syndrome. These diets differ slightly from the LGIT for epilepsy, which similarly avoids carbohydrates from high glycemic index sources but also limits total carbohydrates to 40 to 60 grams per day (approximately 10% of daily calories) and promotes higher fat intake with an average of 60% of daily calories from fat. The glycemic index value of a specific food refers to the rise in blood sugar after eating it as compared to a reference food such as table sugar. The LGIT limits intake to foods with a glycemic index of less than 50. A list of some low glycemic index fruits and vegetables is shown in Table 28.1. The glycemic index is affected by different variables such as fiber content and acidity with greater levels of these lowering the glycemic index. The glycemic index can also be manipulated by adding fats or proteins, which slow digestion thereby lowering the glycemic index. For this reason it is recommended to consume a carbohydrate source with a fat and/or a protein to minimize the glycemic effect. Due to the overall limitation in carbohydrate intake, vitamin and mineral supplementation, including at least a multivitamin and calcium with vitamin D, is an integral part of the treatment.

Diet initiation is done as an outpatient during a clinic visit. Patients and families are educated and provided individualized goals for protein, fat, and carbohydrates based on the individual's current intake. These goals are developed based on food records and questionnaires completed by the patient and family prior to the visit. Some families choose to initiate treatment the same day, while other families choose to gradually introduce the new foods, making substitutions for high glycemic index items over time. The method of treatment initiation does not affect the overall efficacy of the treatment.

The LGIT is more lenient in the measurement of the food and relies on portion sizes and household measurement as compared to measuring foods on a digital gram scale to the 10th of a gram, as is required for the classic ketogenic diet. Some families, however, feel more comfortable weighing foods and choose to do so.

TABLE 28.1

Fruits and Vegetables With a Glycemic Index <50

FRUITS	VEGETABLES
Apple	Leafy greens
Grapefruit	Cauliflower
Pears	Broccoli
Strawberry, raspberry, blueberry	Green beans
Kiwi	Asparagus
Orange, lemon, lime	Peppers
Grape	Tomato
Mango	Cabbage
Peach	Cucumber
Cherry	Carrot
Plum	Eggplant

More details can be found on www.glycemicindex.com.

There have been no serious side effects reported with the use of the LGIT with common side effects including weight loss, acidosis, and constipation/GI reflux. Weight loss may occur if the patient's caloric needs are underestimated or if the patient is not meeting the daily goals for fat and protein. Unlike the carbohydrate portion of the diet that is restricted, protein and fat need to consumed to provide the bulk of food intake. Due to the higher carbohydrate intake, acidosis is not as common as with the classic ketogenic diet but electrolytes should be monitored, especially if on concurrent treatment with a carbonic anhydrase inhibitor such as topiramate or zonisamide. If a patient becomes acidotic during treatment, it is recommended that the patient initiate potassium citrate to help buffer the acidosis. In order to avoid constipation, it is recommended that patients consume adequate amounts of fluid daily to maintain good hydration and consume fiber-rich carbohydrates. To monitor for untoward side effects of the LGIT it is recommended that patients follow up 1 month post-diet initiation and then every 3 months thereafter.

If adequate seizure control is not accomplished upon initiation of the LGIT, it can be fine-tuned. Aspects of the diet that may need to be adjusted or addressed over time include the intake of calories, carbohydrates, and fluid, as well as constipation and reflux. The overall calories may need to be titrated up or down so that excess weight gain or loss does not occur. Carbohydrate intake may need to be decreased and meals may need to be adjusted to ensure that carbohydrates are always balanced with a fat and/or a protein, as this also helps to further decrease the glycemic index. Fluid intake goals are not always easy to meet so using creative ways to increase fluids such as ice pops with sugar-/carbohydrate-free sweeteners and flavors can be helpful. Consuming adequate fluids helps to alleviate constipation, but when constipation remains an issue increasing fiber rich foods and providing foods high in medium-chain triglycerides (MCT), such as coconut, can be helpful. MCT oil can also be utilized as a fat source in limited quantities to avoid abdominal distress.

When should the LGIT be chosen over the classic ketogenic diet? Since there are no commercially available LGIT formulas, patients that are strictly G-tube fed are not appropriate candidates. When children are under the age of 2, have a history of infantile spasms, or GLUT-1 or pyruvate dehydrogenase deficiency, it is recommended to start the classic ketogenic diet. The LGIT can be recommended for all others interested in pursuing dietary therapy for whom it is not contraindicated. The list of contraindications is the same as with the classic ketogenic diet (see Chapter 5). If seizure control is not accomplished with dietary adjustments then these patients are transitioned to the classic ketogenic diet if they can tolerate the change.

The therapeutic mechanism of the LGIT, like the classic ketogenic diet, remains unknown. We do know that the diet alters the metabolism to utilize fats as the primary fuel source over carbohydrates. This reduction in glycolytic stress is thought to contribute to the mechanism of action. Fat metabolism results in the production of ketone bodies. In LGIT, ketone bodies may be present in the blood or urine at lower levels than seen with the ketogenic diet and may be undetectable. Additionally, the stabilization of glucose levels may provide a therapeutic effect. Studies have demonstrated a positive correlation between those achieving over 90% seizure control and lower blood glucose levels.

As with the classic ketogenic diet, once seizure freedom is achieved, anticonvulsant medications may gradually be weaned followed by eventual weaning of dietary therapy. This transition is also done gradually by increasing the amount of low glycemic index carbohydrates weekly to the goal of 150 grams per day. Once at this goal, higher glycemic index carbohydrates may also be added back into the diet.

If seizure freedom is not fully achieved after dietary adjustments have occurred, then the benefits and possible risks of remaining on dietary therapy must be discussed among the clinician, patient, and family in order to make a determination whether to continue with dietary therapy.

Sample day of food on the LGIT:

Breakfast: Blueberry almond flour muffin

Snack: Rosemary parmesan chips

Lunch: Turkey, cheese, and avocado in a low-carb wrap

Snack: Hummus and celery

Dinner: Grilled chicken over mixed greens, bacon crumbles with blue cheese dressing

CHAPTER 29

Formula-Only Ketogenic Diets

The ketogenic diet can be calculated for bottle-fed infants, small children making the transition from bottle to soft foods, or children with various feeding problems. The diet can be formulated in any texture—liquid, soft, solid, or a combination—and can be easily used even by children who need to be fed by nasogastric or gastrostomy tube. Multiple studies stress how easy, well-tolerated, and beneficial it can be to use the ketogenic diet as a formula-only treatment.

As discussed previously, seizures or the side effects of anticonvulsant medications may affect a child's ability to eat properly. If the seizures are controlled or medications can be reduced while on the ketogenic diet, the child may be able to work with different therapists to transition from a soft diet to a diet with more textures. The process of calculating the diet and of establishing calorie levels and the grams of fat, protein, and carbohydrate permitted on the ketogenic diet is the same regardless of the consistency of the food.

There are many options for using formula for the ketogenic diet. Based on the formula that the child is on prior to diet initiation, a comparable keto formula is chosen. The formula can consist of many components mixed together with water (called a "modular formula" to equal the correct calories and ratio) or KetoCal®, manufactured by Nutricia North America, which comes as a ready-to-feed liquid or as a powder. The KetoCal® liquid comes in a 4:1 ratio, is nutritionally complete for children over 1 year of age, is vanilla flavored, contains fiber, has no trans fats, and has only 15% saturated fats. KetoCal® powder is formulated in either a 3:1 or 4:1 version and is nutritionally complete for children over 1 year of age. All KetoCal® products are milk based and can be taken orally or via enteral feedings. There is also a new formula called KetoVie® manufactured by Cambrooke Therapeutics, which also comes in a ready-to-feed 4:1 version in chocolate and vanilla flavors.

A modular formula typically consists of three parts:

1. Ross Carbohydrate Free (RCF)® (Abbott)
   - Soy-based protein, avoids symptoms of cow's milk sensitivities
   - Available through Abbott in a concentrated liquid: 13 fluid ounce cans; 12 per case

2. Microlipid® (Nestle)
    - A safflower-oil emulsion that mixes easily in solution
    - Available in 89 ml bottles; 48 bottles per case
3. SolCarb® (Solace Nutrition) or PolyCal® (Nutricia)
    - Source of calories derived solely from carbohydrate
    - Available through Abbott in powder form (350 gram cans); 6 per case

In the case of multiple food allergies or stomach intolerances to intact proteins, there is another formula that can be used in the modular formula instead of RCF®.

4. Complete Amino Acid Mix®
    - Essential and nonessential amino acids
    - Indicated for patients with milk protein allergy
    - Needs complete vitamin supplementation
    - Manufactured by Nutricia

Carbohydrate-free multivitamins and minerals, calcium supplements, and sterile water are added to complete the formula mixture.

Food Values for Liquid Diet Calculation

	QUANTITY	KCALS	PROTEIN	FAT	CARBOHYDRATE
RCF® concentrate	100 ml	81 kcals	4.0 g	7.2 g	–
Microlipid®	100 ml	450 kcals	–	50.0 g	–
Canola oil	100 g	827 kcals	–	93 g	–
SolCarb® powder	100 g	380 kcals	–	–	94.0 g
Complete Amino Acid Mix®	100 g	328 kcals	82 g	–	–

Because it is emulsified, Microlipid® mixes easily with the other ingredients compared to oil. However, Microlipid® can be more expensive than corn oil or canola oil. Vegetable oil (e.g., canola) may be used for larger (older) children or when expense is a factor. MCT oil may also be added to a formula if the dietitian thinks it is needed, for instance, to loosen stools or boost ketosis. (More details on MCT oil were given in Chapter 27.)

TO SET UP A KETOGENIC FORMULA PLAN

Emily was a 13-month-old girl admitted for the ketogenic diet in an attempt to achieve better control of her intractable seizures that had continued despite heavy medications. She had been fed by gastrostomy tube since she was 8 months old. She was started on a 3:1 ratio at 80 calories/kg (decrease calories per kg due to weight/length at the 95th percentile) and protein at 2 g/kg of desirable body weight.

Emily's age: 13 months

Length: 29.7 in. (76 cm), 50th percentile for age

Weight: 26.4 lb (12 kg), 95th percentile for age

Weight/length: 98th percentile

Calories/kg: 80

Protein requirement: 2 grams per kg

Ketogenic ratio: 3:1

Using these numbers in the formula described earlier in this chapter, we calculate the diet order via the following steps (note: numbers are rounded to 0.1 grams).

1. Calories: 80 (kcal/kg) × 12 (kg ideal weight) = 960 calories per day
2. Dietary unit: 960 (kcal/day) / 31 (kcal/dietary unit) = 30.9 units per day
3. Fat allowance: 3 (as in 3:1) × 30.9 (dietary units) = 92.7 grams, fat
4. Protein: 2 (grams per kg ideal weight) × 12 = 24 grams, protein
5. Carbohydrate: 30.9 (protein 1 carbohydrate) – 24 (protein) = 6.9 grams carbohydrate

Emily's daily diet order follows. This will be divided into the number of meals or bottles she regularly gets in a 24-hour period.

Daily: Protein 24 grams, fat 92.7 grams, carbohydrate 6.9 grams, calories 960.

Ketogenic diet for Emily using a *modular formula*:

1. Calculate the amount of RCF® needed to satisfy the child's protein requirement by cross-multiplying.

   Emily is 12 kg. Emily's protein requirement is 2 grams per kilogram of desirable body weight, or 2 × 12 = 24 grams per day. 100 ml of RCF® formula contains 4.0 grams of protein. Emily will need 600 ml RCF® concentrate to meet her 24 grams protein requirement.
2. Calculate the fat in RCF® by cross-multiplying, and calculate enough Microlipid® to make up the difference.

   100 ml RCF® contains 7.2 grams fat. Emily's 600 ml of RCF® contains 43.2 grams. Subtract the 43.2 grams fat from the total 92.7 grams fat needed (92.7 – 43.2 = 49.5 grams). Remaining fat is 49.5 grams.

3. To calculate the Microlipid® needed to make up the remaining 49.5 grams fat in Emily's diet, cross multiply. There are 50 grams of fat in 100 ml Microlipid® = Emily will need 99 ml Microlipid®
4. Calculate an amount of SolCarb® powder sufficient to meet Emily's carbohydrate requirement.
5. The liquid allotment is set at 90 ml per kilogram, giving Emily 1100 ml liquid per day.

Emily's Daily Formula

	QUANTITY	PROTEIN	FAT	CARBOHYDRATE
RCF® concentrate	600 ml	24 g	43.2 g	0.42
Microlipid®	99 ml	–	49.5 g	–
Solcarb® powder	6 g	–	–	6.3 g
Sterile water	400 ml	–	–	–
Total	1100 ml	24 g	92.7 g	6.72 g

Note: In practice this meal would be rounded to the nearest gram for convenience in measuring.

PREPARATION OF KETOGENIC LIQUID FORMULA

1. Measure the RCF® concentrate and Microlipid® separately in a graduated cylinder.
2. Weigh the Polycose® powder on a gram scale and blend with the ingredients as noted in Emily's daily formula table.
3. Add sterile water, reserving 10 to 15 ml per feeding to flush the tube. Shake or stir.
4. Divide into the number of equal feedings the child will receive in a 24-hour period and refrigerate, or refrigerate full amount and divide into individual portions at feeding time.
5. Bring to room temperature or warm slightly before feeding.
6. Remember to supplement this formula with vitamins and minerals.

	QUANTITY	PROTEIN	FAT	CARBOHYDRATE
KetoCal® 4:1	100 g	15 g	72 g	3 g
KetoCal® 3:1	100 g	15.3 g	67.7 g	7.2 g
Ketocal® 4:1 Liquid	100 ml	3.09 g	14.8 g	1.73 g

Weight: 8.1 kg (17.8 pounds) 5th to 10th percentile.
Length: 70 cm (27.5 in.) 20th percentile.
Weight/length: 25%.

Samuel will be started on a 3:1 ratio and using KetoCal® 3:1. His average intake of calories was 600 per day prior to the diet initiation, which provides him with 75 calories per kilogram. The dietitian makes the decision to continue with the same calorie amount.

To prepare this formula using KetoCal 3:1®:

Because Samuel is on a 3:1 ratio, we will use KetoCal® 3:1. There are 699 calories per 100 grams of KetoCal® 3:1. Because Samuel needs 600 calories, divide that number by 6.99.

Samuel's Daily Formula Using KetoCal®

86 gram of KetoCal® 3:1 + 815 ml of water

Parents should continue giving Samuel 4 to 5 oz every 3 to 4 hours. Once Samuel starts to gain some feeding abilities, we will work with speech therapy and feeding therapy to start some baby food and oils.

Ketogenic formulas may be given orally or through a tube. They may be given by continuous feeds or bolus feedings. The tubes may be flushed with sterile water as needed. It may be beneficial to continue the exact same feeding regimen that the child was on prior to initiating the diet.

Children on formulas who do not have a swallowing difficulty, such as growing babies, may be transitioned to soft foods by gradually introducing baby foods mixed with oil at the correct ratio.

Ketogenic formulas are relatively expensive. However, because the ketogenic diet is considered a medical nutrition therapy rather than a food, a family can try and have their insurance or Women, Infants and Children Program (WIC) cover the cost. There is a sample letter at the back of the book that can help you. Work with your case manager or with the formula companies to try and obtain insurance coverage for the ketogenic formulas.

KETOGENIC FORMULAS (AS OF 2016)

KetoCal 3:1® (Nutricia)

A milk-based, nutritionally complete ketogenic formula at a 3:1 ratio (fat: carbohydrate plus protein). Standard dilution, powder plus water, is 1 kcal/ml mixed with water; however, it can be prepared to whatever concentration is needed. This formula is unflavored and can be used "off label" for infants as a sole source of nutrition and meet all their nutritional needs.

www.myketocal.com/product.html

KetoCal 4:1® (Nutricia)

A milk-based, nutritionally complete ketogenic formula at a 4:1 ratio. Standard dilution, powder plus water, is 1 kcal/ml mixed with water; however, it can be prepared to whatever concentration is needed. This formula can be used as a sole source of nutrition either by drinking it or via a gastrostomy tube, or it can be used as supplemental nutrition as a milkshake or calorie booster during the day. This formula is vanilla flavored, aspartame and trans fat free.

KetoCal 4:1 LQ® (Nutricia)

A milk-based, ready-to-feed nutritionally complete ketogenic formula that is available in vanilla and unflavored at a 4:1 ratio. Standard dilution is 1.5 calories per ml, but it can be mixed with water to the desired caloric concentration. It is an easy way to transport formula and can be used as a sole source of nutrition either orally or enterally or as a nutritional supplement.

KetoVie® (Cambrooke Therapeutics)

A milk-based, nutritionally complete, ready to feed formula that is available in either chocolate or vanilla flavor at a 4:1 ratio. Standard dilution is 1.5 calories per ml, but can be mixed with water to the desired caloric concentration. It is an easy way to transport formula and can be used as a sole source of nutrition either orally or enterally or as a nutritional supplement. Twenty-five percent of calories come from medium chain triglycerides (MCT) with no artificial sweeteners.

www.cambrooketherapeutics.com/products/ketogenic

KetoVolve® (Nutr-e-volution)

A milk-based, nutritionally complete, powdered ketogenic formula at a 4:1 ratio. Standard dilution, powder plus water, is 1 kcal/ml mixed with water; however, it can be prepared to whatever concentration is needed. This formula can be used as a sole source of nutrition either by drinking or via a gastrostomy tube or it can be used as supplemental nutrition as a milkshake or calorie booster during the day. It is made up of 100% whey protein and is high in MCT oil with no trans fats and artificial flavors.

www.trademarkia.com/ketovolve-85528217.html

MODULAR FORMULAS

Use different formulas to create a specific ketogenic formula that meets the specific nutrition needs of the patient if the preceding formulas cannot be used.

RCF® (Abbott)

A soy-based formula that is very low in carbohydrates and is used for patients with a milk protein allergy. It is the only formula approved for infants for the dietary management of epilepsy. Mixed with an added fat and protein, it can meet the desired ratio and calories. The vitamin and mineral content has to be evaluated to ensure that it is meeting the needs of the patient.

Microlipid® (Nestle Nutrition)

An emulsified long-chain triglyceride (LCT) fat that mixes very well with other liquids.

Liquigen® (Nutricia)

An emulsified medium chain triglyceride fat that mixes very well with other liquids. Cannot be used as the sole source of fat as it does not contain essential fatty acids

SolCarb® (Solace Nutrition)

A soluble form of powdered carbohydrate in the form of maltodextrin that is used to achieve the desired ratio, it mixes well with liquids or moist foods.
www.solacenutrition.com/products/solcarb/solcarb.php

PolyCal® (Nutricia)

A soluble form of powdered carbohydrate in the form of maltodextrin that is used to achieve the desired ratio, it mixes well with liquids or moist foods.

Betaquik® (Vitaflo)

Medium chain triglyceride oil emulsion. May be used as a drink or mixed into formula, food, or beverages. Cannot be used as the sole source of fat as it does not contain essential fatty acids.
www.vitaflousa.com/

Carbzero® (Vitaflo)

An emulsified LCT fat that mixes very well with other liquids.
www.vitaflousa.com/

Calogen® (Nutricia) (Europe)

Long chain fat oil emulsion. Comes in three flavors; the unflavored is carb-free. Strawberry and banana flavors contain 4.3 grams carbs.
www.nutricia.ie/products/view/calogen

OTHER FORMULAS

Qitong, 4:1 or 2:1® (Liquids) Zenica (China)

A 4:1 soy-based formula and 2:1 formula that contain both casein and soy; both with 30% of total fat from MCT oil.

Ketonia® (Liquid) Namyang (Korea)

A ready-to-feed milk-based formula for oral and tube feedings. Contains olive oil, low lactose.
company.namyangi.com/eng/product/ketonia.asp

KetoKid® (Powder)—British Biologicals (India)

Bonigrasa fat base powder 80% in 4:1 ratio. Vitamins included.
www.britishbiologicals.com/criticare/Epilepsy-Management.php

CHAPTER 30

The Diet for All Cultures, Religions, Food Preferences, and Allergies

My child is on a gluten-free diet. Can the ketogenic diet be done? What about if we are vegetarian? Have allergies? These are all common questions asked by parents prior to starting or inquiring about the ketogenic diet.

The ketogenic diet can be used for all different cultures and food restrictions. It is used in all continents, except Antarctica. In China, Japan, and Korea, it is growing incredibly in popularity. Similarly, in India, it is also becoming widely used.

Many parents would think that it would be impossible to try a diet that already limits many of their child's favorite foods; however, the ketogenic diet can be used for any child who has restrictions due to gastrointestinal issues, allergies, or who follows any diet for religious reasons. Prior to diet initiation, it is important for parents to inform the doctor and dietitian seeing the patient of all the child's allergies, religious food restrictions, and any other food-related restriction.

ALLERGIES

There are many children with food allergies or intolerances. Your child could be allergic to only dairy or have multiple food allergies consisting of milk, soy, eggs, wheat, seafood, and nuts. You might wonder how your child could go on a restrictive diet when you already have to restrict his or her diet.

The trick with allergies is to look at what the child is currently eating, and pair it with a fat that the child can tolerate. There are so many options available now for patients with allergies that working around these food allergies can easily be managed.

Dairy Allergies

Ingredients to avoid:

Butter, butter fat, butter milk	Half and Half
Casein	Lactalbumin
Cheese	Lactalbumin phosphate
Cottage cheese	Lactoglobulin
Curds	Lactose
Cream	Nougat
Custard	Rennet casein
Pudding	Sour cream
Ghee	Sour cream solids
	Yogurt

For high-fat keto replacements:

1. Instead of butter, try margarine or coconut oil
2. Instead of cream, try coconut milk
3. Mayonnaise and oils are dairy free

Egg Allergies

Read the labels and avoid:

Albumin	Egg white
Egg yolk	Dried egg
Egg powder	Egg solids
Egg substitutes	Eggnog
Globulin	Livetin
Mayonnaise	Lysozyme (used in Europe)
Meringue	Ovalbumin
Ovomucin	Ovomucoid
Ovovitellin	Simplesse®

To replace an egg needed for baking, one of the following may be substituted in recipes; however, each ingredient needs to be calculated for each recipe, and they still do not provide enough protein.

- 1 tsp baking powder, 1 tbsp water, 1 tbsp vinegar
- 1 tsp yeast dissolved in 1/4 cup warm water
- 1-1/2 tbsp water, 1-1/2 tbsp oil, 1 tsp baking powder
- 1 packet gelatin, 2 tbsp warm water (do not mix until ready to use)

Soy Allergy

Ingredients to avoid:

Hydrolyzed soy protein	Soy sprouts
Miso	Soy protein concentrate
Shoyo sauce	Soy protein isolate
Soy flour	Soy sauce
Soy grits	Tempeh
Soy nuts	Textured vegetable protein (TVP)
Soy milk	Tofu

And watch these products because they may contain soy:

Flavorings	Natural flavoring
Hydrolyzed plant protein	Vegetable broth
Hydrolyzed vegetable protein	Vegetable gum
	Vegetable starch

Peanuts and Tree Nut Allergies

Peanuts and tree nuts are high in fat and a good source of protein, which is why they are found in a lot of ketogenic recipes; however, they are not an essential part of the ketogenic diet and can be eliminated.

Ingredients to avoid:

Almonds	Chestnuts
Arachis oil	Nut butters
Artificial nuts	Nut oil
Brazil nuts	Nut paste
Cashews	Pecans

(continued)

Hazelnuts (filberts)	Pine nuts (pignolia, pinian)
Gianduja	Pistachios
Hickory nuts	Peanuts
Macadamia nuts	Peanut butter
Marzipan/almond paste	Peanut flour
Nougat	Walnuts
Nu-Nuts®	Cold pressed, expressed, or expelled peanut oil

Wheat Allergies

A wheat allergy is actually very easy to accommodate on the ketogenic diet because most products containing wheat are very high in carbohydrates. However, there are some food products that have wheat in them that you would not expect.

Ingredients to avoid:

Food thickeners	Natural flavoring
Gelatinized starch	Soy sauce
Hydrolyzed vegetable protein	Starch
Meat and crab substitutes	Vegetable gum
Modified food starch	Vegetable starch

Children with any allergy or multiple allergies should have no issue going on the ketogenic diet. However, there must be a long conversation among the doctor, dietitian, and family about the allergies and food intolerances.

Sample Meal Plan for Multiple Food Allergies

Breakfast: coconut pancake (coconut flour, coconut oil, flaxseed, coconut milk, baking powder, gelatin)

Lunch: chicken, avocado, canola oil, coconut milk, and spinach

Dinner: salmon, butternut squash, canola oil, and coconut milk

Snack: bacon, canola oil, McDonald's French fries, coconut milk, and fruit

For children that have multiple food allergies and require a formula, a modular formula needs to be used. If the child is allergic to only milk, then RCF®, SolCarb®, and Microlipid® can be used. If the child has multiple food allergies, then Complete Amino Acid® mix is used instead of RCF®. Complete Amino Acid® mix is just the essential proteins and does not contain any vitamins and minerals.

KOSHER

Keeping kosher is a set of biblical dietary restrictions that many observant Jewish people follow. The word *kosher* is Hebrew and means fit, proper, or correct. The diet consists of restricting certain foods like pork and shellfish, and not mixing certain foods together like milk and meat. Due to these restrictions many foods have certifications from Rabbis to identify that the food is kosher.

One of the restrictions on a kosher diet is not being able to eat meat and dairy mixed together. Since a lot of the classic ketogenic meals have cream added to them, when creating a meal using meat, a substitute for the cream (which is dairy) has to be made. There are many substitutions for either the dairy products or the meat products.

Sample Kosher Meal Plan

BREAKFAST	LUNCH	DINNER
Eggs	Kosher turkey deli	Kosher roasted chicken coated with macadamia nuts
Kosher American cheese	Mayonnaise olive oil (mixed with mayo)	Egg
Butter	Tomato	Oil
Cream	Lettuce	Spinach
Applesauce	Avocado	Margarine or coconut oil

Snacks

Peanut butter and margarine

"Keto yogurt" (sour cream, heavy cream, and fruit)

Currently the only kosher formula on the market is the modular version with RCF® and Microlipid®.

HALAL

Halal is an Arabic word meaning permitted or lawful. Halal is a term that applies to all facets of Muslim life, including food. All foods are considered halal except for pork, alcohol, carnivorous animals, animals that were improperly slaughtered, and any food product containing any of the mentioned products. Starting the ketogenic diet while keeping the laws of halal is not difficult;

all you need to do is obtain the food values for each product, and each product can be added to the computer program to calculate the meals. A meal plan for a child who only eats halal would be very similar to the kosher meal; however, someone who eats only halal can mix milk and meat together and have cream or butter mixed into their foods.

GLUTEN-FREE, CASEIN-FREE

There are many children who follow a gluten-free, casein-free diet for autism or behavioral issues. Gluten is a protein found in wheat, rye, and barley and is the material in flours that acts like a glue and holds the dough together. Maintaining a gluten-free diet on the ketogenic diet is not difficult because gluten is found in foods that are high in carbohydrates. Casein is also a protein found in milk products. Therefore, all cheeses, yogurts, and any product containing milk are avoided.

Before starting the ketogenic diet, children on a gluten-free, casein-free diet will follow a diet similar for those with a milk allergy. All dairy is removed and replaced with nondairy items, such as coconut oils, margarine, ghee, and all other oils. Many of the recipes created by The Charlie Foundation list if they are gluten free or casein free.

VEGETARIAN

There are many different types of vegetarianism, and people choose to follow a vegetarian lifestyle for multiple reasons. The most restricted form of vegetarianism is a vegan diet, which omits all animal products from a diet. While following a vegan diet, the most concerning nutritional issue is protein intake; nevertheless, there are multiple ways to take in adequate protein by eating beans or eating soy proteins while on a regular vegan diet.

The issue with following a vegan diet while on the ketogenic diet is that beans and meat substitutes can be high in carbohydrates as opposed to an animal protein like chicken, which has zero carbohydrates. However, there are protein powders available that could be added to meal plans of cream, fruits or vegetables, and oils and margarine.

If a family chooses to follow another form of vegetarianism, such as lacto ovo or pescetarian, they usually omit animal proteins but will eat fish or dairy and eggs.

ORGANIC

Many families choose to buy only organic foods, both produce and prepared foods. This is a choice made by the family. There are no studies indicating increased seizure reduction while eating an organic diet, however many people believe that the food is better for you. There are no contraindications to following a completely organic diet while on the ketogenic diet.

SUMMARY

It is important for parents and clinicians to realize that the ketogenic diet can be done with all different types of diets. Most important is to look at what the child is eating prior to starting the diet, and figure out a way that fats can be added to what the child currently eats. If the child has an allergy, then look at the foods that he or she is currently eating and figure out how to add in the fat. Can the parents mix oil with mayonnaise? Can they mix coconut oil into baby foods? If these or similar questions can be answered positively, then that child can start the ketogenic diet and will be very successful. It's up to the parents to be enthusiastic about the foods, and it's up to the clinicians to encourage and support the parents and patient while they are evaluating which foods will fit into their lifestyle.

SECTION VII

Ketogenic Cooking

CHAPTER 31

Sample Meal Plans for the Ketogenic Diet

Although quantities are limited and smaller than a child is used to, the variety and appeal of food on the ketogenic diet are limited only by your creativity! Your child can continue to eat the majority of the foods that he or she enjoyed prior to starting the ketogenic diet.

- Filet of beef with a strawberry cream ice pop
- Chicken teriyaki lettuce wraps
- Eggs Benedict
- Cheese omelet with bacon
- Shrimp scampi with pumpkin parfait
- Cheesecake

AS OFTEN AS POSSIBLE, Michael has something that we are having. If I am making pork chops for us, I cook him one. If we are having tuna fish sandwiches, he has tuna fish with mayonnaise wrapped in a leaf of lettuce.

In the beginning, parents should use the basic meal plans for the sake of simplicity and control while learning how to implement the diet and figuring out what works for their child. Once becoming familiar with weighing and measuring foods on the scale, parents can begin to get more creative with new food items and new menu plans.

Herbs and spices, lemon juice, soy sauce, baking chocolate, ketchup, and other flavorings all contain carbohydrates. The overall carbohydrate level in the diet is extremely low so that ketchup calculated into a meal plan may decrease your child's fruit or vegetable allotment. Herbs and spices should be limited to a pinch, and high-carbohydrate flavorings such as ketchup or chocolate should only be used occasionally, if at all. Pure extracts, such as vanilla or strawberry, are allowed up to five drops a meal and can be considered "free." Some children do not even like the taste of the extracts—they are not essential for the diet but are there to add flavoring to some foods.

IT WAS IMPORTANT TO MY SON to feel as though he was getting a dessert. So I always kept a stock of homemade cream ice pops in the freezer, flavored with vanilla or chocolate (which was calculated into his meal plans) and a little bit of Stevia. He got one after every dinner. If he was supposed to have 80 cc of cream and the Tupperware popsicle molds only held 60 cc, he drank the rest of the cream straight.

Think of the recipes included in this chapter in terms of entire meal plans, not as single food items. The ketogenic ratio of food in the diet must balance within a whole meal, so any food calculated into one part of the meal affects what can go into other parts. All the ingredients in the meal can be baked or cooked together, or each item can be eaten separately to equal the correct calories and ratio.

The menus that follow are examples drawn from the experience of various parents and are for a "generic" child. Your own meal plans will take into account your child's calorie level, protein needs, ketogenic ratio, and individual preferences.

TIPS

Following are tips from parents who have experienced the ketogenic diet:

- Kids don't mind eating the same thing over and over. Find several simple menus that you and your child can agree on, and stick with them. Six to eight menus is probably all you'll need. The multivitamin and calcium will take care of the rest.
- Use a salad or dessert plate and bowl so the amount of food appears bigger.
- Fix a few meals in advance and keep them in the refrigerator or freezer in carefully labeled Tupperware containers in case you are not there at mealtimes, or for when your child goes to school or to a friend's house. You will build up a huge Tupperware collection.
- Use the pinch of spices that are allowed (but remember they do contain carbohydrate). A small amount goes a long way toward making the food interesting.
- My son will drink the cream straight down, but I often mix it with sugar-free soda so it will fill him up more.
- Save a couple of favorite meals for extra special times. Use these meals less than once a week so they remain special for times when you are having something your child loves but cannot have, or for times when nothing else sounds good.
- Chopped lettuce with mayonnaise can be a fairly large-looking element of a meal. It really helps fill up the plate, and it helps with bowel movements.
- Find places to hide the fat. Oil hides well in applesauce or ice cream. Butter disappears into peanut butter or cream cheese. Tuna, chicken, or egg salad eats up mayonnaise.
- Select dishes that are familiar and resemble your family's normal meals.
- Don't assume that a zero-calorie powdered drink is okay. Some contain hidden sources of carbohydrates and may say on the label "when prepared this drink will provide 5 calories."

- Don't mix medicine or supplements that have a bad taste with food. Separate medicines from food as much as possible. Sometimes sprinkles of medicines can be mixed in with food as long as your child can't taste it.
- Do not buy diet foods—use real mayonnaise, butter, eggs, and so on. Diet foods tend to have high-water content and extra carbohydrates.
- Counter the small quantity of food with creative shapes and arrangements: Slice meat thinly and fan it out. Pound chicken paper-thin. Cut carrots into carrot chips, cucumbers into shoestring sticks.

BASIC TECHNIQUES

The recipes in this chapter do not have quantities, as these must be calculated for each individual child. Each recipe is for a whole meal, considered as a unit, because foods in one part of the meal affect what can be included in another part while maintaining the prescribed ketogenic ratio. As a rule, ingredients such as ketchup, lemon juice, vinegar, herbs and spices, soy sauce, and baking chocolate are used in very small quantities (such as 2 grams, about 1/8 teaspoon).

Meats should be lean with fat removed. Fish and poultry should be skinless and boneless. This is to ensure that the child's protein allotment will be as close to pure or solid protein as possible.

Cooked foods should be trimmed and weighed on the gram scale after cooking, except in the case of food that is heated only slightly or will not change volume during cooking (such as cheese for melting or eggs). Previously cooked foods do not have to be weighed again after reheating.

The following exchange lists show whether a specific vegetable should be weighed raw or cooked. "What the eye sees, the mind remembers," the old adage goes. But food amounts should not be "guesstimated." You may get used to judging how much 25 grams of chicken or 15 grams of applesauce is, but you should always check with a scale for accuracy. Again, the quantity of each ingredient in these menus varies from child to child, so we have not given exact amounts here. Quantities can be calculated either by hand or by using a computer program in consultation with a doctor or dietitian.

EXCHANGE LISTS

In the hand-calculated ketogenic diet, fruits and vegetables with similar carbohydrate content have been grouped into lists of items that may be substituted for one another interchangeably (Table 31.1). This also assumes to some degree that you're not using a computer program such as KetoDietCalculator. We include this in this edition mostly for your own knowledge and historical purposes. In general, Group A vegetables have half the carbohydrates of Group B, so you are allowed more.

When a menu calls for 21 grams of 10% fruit, you may choose cantaloupe, orange, strawberry, peach, or any other item from the 10% fruit list. Or you may choose to use 14 grams (two thirds the amount prescribed) of a 15% fruit, such as blueberries, pear, or pineapple. Similarly, if a menu calls for 18 grams of a Group B vegetable, you may choose any item or combination of items from the Group B list, including broccoli, mushrooms, or green beans. Or you may choose to use twice that amount, 36 grams, of any Group A vegetable or combination of Group A vegetables, including asparagus, celery, and summer squash.

All the other ingredients in the diet, including meats, fats, and cheeses, should be specified individually in each menu.

Exchange lists allow greater flexibility in using fruits and vegetables. The diet works well with this method, in spite of minor variations in the makeup of each vegetable and fruit. If a child is eating exclusively high-carbohydrate fruits and vegetables such as grapes and carrots, menus should be calculated specifically for these items.

When hand calculation was the norm, meats, fats, and cheeses were also used in generic exchange list form. In spite of significant variations in the content of items on each exchange list, this worked well for some children who could tolerate the resulting fluctuation in diet content. In an effort to provide optimal ketosis for the greatest number of children, and with the more precise computer menu planning now the norm, only fruit and vegetables are now used in generic exchange list form (Table 31.1).

TABLE 31.1

Exchange Lists

Fruit: Fresh or Canned Without Sugar

10% (USE AMOUNT PRESCRIBED)		15% (USE 2/3 AMOUNT PRESCRIBED)	
Applesauce, Mott's	Papaya	Apple	Kiwi
Cantaloupe	Peach	Apricot	Mango
Grapefruit	Strawberries	Blackberries	Nectarine
Grapes, purple	Tangerine	Blueberries	Pear
Honeydew melon	Watermelon	Figs	Pineapple
Orange	Grapes, green	Raspberries	

Vegetables: Fresh, Canned, or Frozen

Measure raw (R) or cooked (C) as specified

GROUP A VEGETABLES (USE TWICE AMOUNT PRESCRIBED)		GROUP B VEGETABLES (USE AMOUNT PRESCRIBED)	
Asparagus/C	Radish/R	Beets/C	Kohlrabi/C
Beet greens/C	Rhubarb/R	Broccoli/C	Mushroom/R
Cabbage/C	Sauerkraut/C	Brussels sprouts/C	Mustard greens/C

(continued)

TABLE 31.1

Exchange Lists (*continued*)

Vegetables: Fresh, Canned, or Frozen Measure raw (R) or cooked (C) as specified			
GROUP A VEGETABLES (USE TWICE AMOUNT PRESCRIBED)		**GROUP B VEGETABLES (USE AMOUNT PRESCRIBED)**	
Celery/C or R	Summer squash/C	Cabbage/R	Okra/C
Chicory/R	Swiss chard/C	Carrots/R or C	Onion/R or C
Cucumbers/R	Tomato/R	Cauliflower/C	Rutabaga/C
Eggplant/C	Tomato juice	Collards/C	Spinach/C
Endive/R	Turnips/C	Dandelion greens/C	Tomato/C
Green pepper/ R or C	Turnip greens/C	Green beans/C	Winter squash/C
Poke/C	Watercress/R	Kale/C	

Fat (Unsaturated fats are recommended)			
Butter	Canola oil	Flaxseed oil	Margarine
Corn oil	Peanut oil	Mayonnaise	Olive oil

Ways to Dress Up Your Cream	
Ice cream ball	• Dust with a speck of cinnamon or nutmeg
	• Flavor with sweetener and vanilla or calculated baking chocolate
	• Whip in canola oil after 1 hour of freezing
	• Flavor with sweetener and vanilla or calculated baking chocolate
Whipped parfait	• Layer with calculated berries
	• Sprinkle with calculated chopped nuts
	• Flavor with a sweetener and vanilla, lemon, maple, almond flavorings
	• Serve on top of calculated sugar-free Jell-O
Cream soda	• Pour cream into fruit-flavored sugar-free soda

DON'T FORGET SUPPLEMENTS. The ketogenic diet must be supplemented with a complete low-carbohydrate multivitamin/mineral and a calcium supplement every day!

Sample Keto Meals

There are no gram amounts listed for the meals and snacks; they are just ideas of meals that patients have enjoyed. Ask your dietitian or use your ketogenic diet program to create one of these meals specifically for your child with the correct calories and ratio. Thank you to three of our keto moms—Kira, Jeanne, and Anja, who are very creative and have worked on and created some of these recipes.

Scrambled Egg Breakfast

Eggs	Cream
Nonstick vegetable oil spray	Mandarin oranges
Butter	

Options (The following must be calculated into the meal plan if desired)

Crisp bacon, ham, or sausage

Grated cheese in omelets

Vegetables, fresh fruit, or applesauce instead of juice

Baking chocolate for cocoa in cream

Beat equal amounts of yolk and white. Cook eggs in a microwave or nonstick pan, which may be sprayed with nonstick vegetable oil.

Transfer to scale and weigh, trimming if necessary. Transfer to plate and add any additional butter. For omelets, the egg should be cooked flat and thin, then put back in pan, filled with calculated cheese or vegetable/butter mixture, heated slightly, and scraped thoroughly onto a plate with a small rubber spatula. Garnish plate with calculated crisp bacon and/or grated cheese sprinkles.

Dilute cream with water or ice to make it more like milk, or make hot chocolate by melting baking chocolate shavings in cream with sweetener.

Your child must consume all the butter on the plate. Drink orange juice or eat fruit last for dessert. If you choose to include bacon or cheese, less egg will be allowed in the meal plan because the protein allotment will be shared.

Keto Yogurt (Variations)

Cream

Fruit (see exchange list in Table 31.1)

Sour cream

Variations: canned pumpkin, watermelon, blueberries, raspberries, cantaloupe

Sweeten with Stevia

Tuna Salad Plate

Tuna	Sugar-free Jell-O
Celery	Sugar-free sweetener
Mayonnaise	Cream
Sour cream	Vanilla
Parmesan cheese	Baking chocolate
Lettuce	
Cucumber	
Tomatoes	

Mix mayonnaise, celery, and tuna; arrange in center of plate. Stir together sour cream and parmesan; mix with chopped lettuce and arrange around tuna. Garnish plate with cucumbers and tomatoes.

For dessert: Sugar-free Jell-O topped with sweetened vanilla whipped cream, sprinkled with baking chocolate shavings.

Options: Hard-boiled egg, cubed chicken or turkey, or baby shrimps may be substituted for the tuna. These salads are easy to prepare in advance, making them ideal travel or school meals.

Hot Dog and Ketchup

Hebrew National hot dog	Baking chocolate
Zucchini or asparagus	Sugar-free Jell-O
Ketchup (Walden Farms®)	Vanilla, sugar-free sweetener
Mayonnaise	Cream
Lettuce	

Boil or grill the hot dog, drain, weigh. Mix ketchup with mayonnaise to make special sauce. Cut into thin slices; dab sauce on each slice. Arrange on a small plate. Steam vegetables; pat dry.

For dessert (make in advance): Add a few drops of baking chocolate for flavoring, a little sweetener, and cream to the sugar-free Jell-O. Allow to set. Or make Keto Sherbet: Whip cream into sweetened Jell-O and freeze in the bowl of an ice cream scoop.

With commercial products such as hot dogs, the brand must always be specified. Brands of hot dog other than Hebrew National may be used in this recipe if calculations are based on accurate information about the specified brand. Jell-O desserts are often calculated into hot dog meals to raise the protein.

"Spaghetti"

- Spaghetti squash
- Parmesan cheese
- Lettuce
- Hunt's tomato sauce
- Ground beef or ground turkey
- Butter
- Mayonnaise
- Cream
- Zero-calorie flavored soda

Boil squash (raw squash may be frozen in individual portions in advance). Drain well and weigh. Cook and weigh ground meat, and sprinkle on squash. Melt butter with tomato sauce and some or all of the cream. Pour on top. Sprinkle grated cheese plus a speck of pepper and oregano if desired. Mix chopped lettuce with mayonnaise for a salad.

For dessert: Pour any remaining cream in a zero-calorie flavored soda and whip lightly.

EVEN THE SMALLEST SPRINKLE of parmesan cheese has to be calculated into the diet. Meatballs can be frozen for later use.

Broiled Steak With Broccoli

- Steak
- Broccoli
- Butter
- Mayonnaise
- Cream
- Orange flavored zero-calorie soda

Broil steak to medium rare. Weigh. Steam broccoli. Melt butter, blend with mayonnaise, pour over broccoli.

Serve with cream poured into orange flavored zero-calorie soda.

Chef's Salad With Maple Walnut Whip

Lettuce	Cream
Mushrooms	Pure maple extract
Carrots	Sugar-free sweetener
Tomato	Crushed walnuts
Cucumber	
Olive	
American cheese	
Ham and/or turkey	
Olive oil	
Vinegar	
Salt, pepper, oregano	
(Mayonnaise is optional)	
Dried parsley	

Combine chopped lettuce, sliced mushrooms, and carrots in a bowl. Arrange tomato and cucumber slices, olive, and strips of cheese, ham, and/or turkey on top. Shake or beat with a fork the oil and vinegar, a speck of salt and pepper, and a few flakes of oregano in a jar with a tight lid (mayonnaise may be substituted for some of the oil for thicker consistency). Pour over salad. Sprinkle a few parsley flakes and a dash of Accent® over all.

For dessert: Whip cream until thick. Add three or four drops of pure maple extract and a few drops of sweetener, and continue whipping until stiff. (Several grams of vegetable oil may also be whipped into the cream if there is too much oil for the salad.) Heap into a parfait dish. Sprinkle with crushed walnuts and serve.

Optional: To make Butterscotch Fluff instead of Maple Walnut Whip, substitute butterscotch extract instead of maple extract and chopped pecans instead of chopped walnuts.

Spinach Salad

Spinach	Cream
Red onion	Vanilla
Mushroom	Sugar-free sweetener

(continued)

Carrot
Olive oil
Vinegar
Dried mustard
Garlic salt
Pepper
Crisp bacon
Hard-boiled egg

Wash spinach, chop coarsely, place in bowl. Sprinkle with chopped red onion, sliced mushroom, and carrot. Shake oil and vinegar together in a jar with a speck of dried mustard, garlic salt, and pepper. Pour over salad. Sprinkle with crumbled crisp bacon and chopped egg (equal parts white and yolk).

Dessert: Serve with vanilla shake or ice pop.

Chicken Soup and Custard

Diced chicken	Egg
Granulated bouillon	Cream
Carrots, celery, lettuce	Salt (a speck)
Butter, mayonnaise	Saccharin (1/8 grain)

Custard: Scald 3 parts cream to 1 part water. Combine with 2 parts beaten egg, salt, saccharin, and vanilla. Pour into a cup and bake in a shallow pan of water 25 minutes at 350°F or until done (knife inserted in center will come out clean).

Soup: Dissolve bouillon cube in 1/2 cup hot water. Add enough chicken to make up the protein left over from the egg (if any) and carrots and celery to fill the carbohydrate allotment. Melt a little butter into the soup, and spread the rest of the fat as mayonnaise on lettuce. Drink any leftover cream as beverage.

Burger With "Potato Salad"

Ground beef	Vanilla, sweetener
Zucchini	Sugar-free Jell-O
Ketchup (Walden Farms®)	
Mayonnaise, oil	
Salt, pepper	
Oregano	
Lettuce	

Flatten the ground beef into a 1/4-in. thick burger. Heat a nonstick skillet with a few drops of the allotted oil or cooking spray. Sauté the burger 1 to 1-1/2 minutes on each side. Weigh the sautéed burger and trim. Meanwhile, measure the ketchup and beat in an equal amount of oil. Steam zucchini. Weigh and cut into 1/2-in. cubes. Mix the zucchini with mayonnaise, oregano, and a pinch of salt and pepper. Arrange the beef on a lettuce leaf. Spread ketchup mixture on steak.

For dessert: Top sugar-free Jell-O with whipped sweetened vanilla cream

Thai Noodles

Cream, 36%
Soy sauce, Kikkoman Naturally Brewed
Onions–green, tops only
Pepper, jalapeno–raw
Noodles, Tofu Shirataki spaghetti-shaped noodle
Peanut butter, creamy–Natural Skippy
Beef, ground 80% lean–cooked
Butter, Kerrygold Pure Irish Butter
Oil, canola
Nuts, cashews

Crumble and cook beef in a pan. Measure portion. Mix with canola oil. Cook noodles according to package. Drain and measure. Mix noodles with beef and oil. In a separate pan, cook chopped jalapenos in butter until tender. Add soy and peanut butter and cook on low heat until melted and smooth. Pour onto noodles and mix or leave sauce on top. Top with crushed cashews and thinly sliced green onions. Serve with cream on the side. OPTIONAL: Serve on top of a bed of free iceberg lettuce.

Tortilla Chips, Salsa, and Guacamole

Cream, 36%
Onions, raw
Tomato, raw
Cilantro–fresh, raw
Lime juice
Tortilla, Mission Carb Balance
Pepper, jalapeno, raw
Oil, canola
Sour cream–cultured, not low fat
Butter
Avocado, California or Mexico (Hass)

Add oil to pan and fry tortilla until brown on both sides (you want it crispy). Meanwhile, chop and measure onion, tomato, cilantro, and tomato and add to bowl. Add fresh lime juice and mix with veggies. Add a pinch of salt. Mash avocado with sour cream in a separate bowl. Cut crispy tortilla into triangle pieces, like chips! Melt butter and add to cream and serve or mix butter with guacamole.

"Pizza"

Egg	Cream
Tomato puree	Vanilla, sweetener
Lettuce	
Olive oil	
Mozzarella cheese	
Pepperoni or ground beef	
Speck of oregano	

Beat egg with cream. Pour into heated nonstick pan. Spread thinly. Turn heat to low and let sit until hardened. Mix olive oil with tomato sauce; spread on egg crust. Sprinkle with a speck of oregano. Cover with grated cheese. Top with pepperoni or ground beef. Broil until melted.

Serve with diluted cream shake. *Note:* A thin slice of eggplant, broiled, can serve as crust for alternative recipe.

Salmon With Tartar Sauce

Salmon	Sugar-free Jell-O
Lettuce	Cream
Tartar sauce	
Butternut squash	
Butter, mayonnaise	
Accent, pepper	

Broil the fish about five minutes or until flaky. Season with a speck of Accent and pepper. Spread with measured tartar sauce. Bake butternut squash or cook frozen; puree. Melt butter into squash puree. Arrange salmon on a small plate with squash and chopped lettuce with mayonnaise.

Dessert: Serve sugar-free Jell-O topped with whipped cream.

Chicken Fingers and Cole Slaw

Oil	Cream
Chicken breast	Vanilla, sweetener
Butter	
Dash of mustard, tarragon, and garlic salt	
Cabbage	
Carrot	
Scallion	
Lettuce	
Mayonnaise	
Vinegar	

Heat a few drops oil in a nonstick skillet. Sauté chicken breast at medium-high heat for about 3 minutes per side or until lightly browned. Remove chicken from heat; weigh and trim. Turn heat off. Add butter (1/3 of fat allotment) to skillet. Add a dash of mustard, tarragon, and garlic salt. Stir until butter is melted. Remove skillet from heat. Cut chicken breast into thin strips or very thin slices and fan out on a small plate. Pour butter sauce over chicken. Meanwhile, chop cabbage (red or green) with a little grated carrot, thinly sliced scallion, and a leaf of lettuce. Mix mayonnaise (2/3 of fat allotment) with a couple of grams of vinegar. Stir in cabbage mixture. Sprinkle with salt and pepper.

Dessert: Serve with frozen vanilla-flavored cream ball.

Chinese Chicken and Avocado

Cream, 36%

Soy sauce, Kikkoman Naturally Brewed

Flour, Bob's Red Mill Almond Flour

Chicken broth, Free Range Trader Joe's

Chicken breast–raw (no skin)

Egg (raw, mixed well)

Oil, sesame

Butter, Kerrygold Unsalted

Avocado, California or Mexico (Hass)

Oil, coconut–unrefined (regular or organic)

Dip chicken in egg and dredge in almond flour. Mix oils and butter and fry chicken. Combine broth, soy sauce, and residual oils. Pour over chicken and bake at 325°F for 15 to 30 minutes (you want the sauce to be soaked up into the chicken). Serve with cream and sliced avocados.

Bacon-Wrapped Avocado

Cream, 36%
Bacon, Nature's Promise
Mayonnaise–Duke's
Avocado, California or Mexico (Hass)
Sour cream–cultured (not low-fat)

Measure and slice avocado into strips. Cook bacon as directed and measure. Wrap avocado slices with bacon. Mix sour cream and mayo together and serve as a dip. Cream on the side.

Shepherd's Pie

Cream, 36%
Carrots, cooked
Onions–raw
Tomato paste–canned
Bouillon, organic chicken base–Better Than Bouillon®
Beef, ground 85% lean, raw
Oil, canola
Butter

Add canola oil to pan. Sauté onion until translucent. Add beef, breaking into small pieces, and cook thoroughly. Add bouillon, tomato paste, and a little water to make a "gravy." Meanwhile, boil carrots until very tender and mash with a fork. Add a few grams of cream and the butter to the carrots; should be creamy. Add beef mixture to small, oven-proof dish. Spread mashed carrots over the top and bake at 350°F for 10 minutes or broil for 3 minutes. OPTIONAL: Add a pinch of salt to carrots. Can use cauliflower instead of carrots; calculate accordingly.

Beef Stew

Roast beef
Pearl onions
Cabbage
Cherry tomatoes
Turnips
Cream
Baking chocolate
Sugar-free sweetener

Steam cabbage, turnip, and onions until tender. Place them in a small, nonstick pot (such as a 1-cup Pyrex) with the roast beef and 1/4 cup water. Add butter and sprinkle with a speck of salt and pepper. Simmer 15 minutes. For thicker sauce, mash some turnip into the liquid. Place cherry tomato halves around a small plate and spoon stew in center.

Dessert: Serve with chocolate ice cream made from baking chocolate, cream, and sweetener.

"Tacos"

Ground beef	Cream
Speck of chili powder	Orange diet soda
Lettuce	

Cook beef in nonstick pan. Weigh. Dust beef with a speck of chili powder. Roll beef, tomato, and cheese or sour cream in lettuce leaf.

Dessert drink: Pour cream into up to 120 grams of orange diet soda.

Keto Waffle With "Syrup"

Egg yolk	Butter
Egg white	Carbohydrate-free pure maple flavoring
Cream	
Sweetener	
Nonstick vegetable oil spray	

Mix egg yolk, whipped egg whites, and whipped cream together with a few drops of sweetener. Pour into the center of a heated waffle iron sprayed with nonstick cooking spray. Melt butter with maple flavoring for syrup.

Keto Donut

Egg whites	Cream, whipped
Macadamia nuts, finely chopped	Butter
Peanut butter	

Spray mini bundt pans with nonstick cooking spray. Mix egg whites, whipped cream, and nuts, set aside. Melt butter and peanut butter together, stir well, and pour into the egg mixture. Pour into mini bundt pans and bake at 350°F for about 30 minutes.

Peanut Butter Pancakes

- Cream, 36%
- Baking powder
- Skippy Natural Creamy Peanut Butter
- Egg (raw, mixed well)
- Butter, Kerrygold Unsalted
- Flaxseed meal, Bob's Red Mill whole ground
- Bacon, Nature's Promise

Mix cream, baking powder, peanut butter, egg, and flaxseed. Fry in butter and pour remaining butter on top of pancakes. Can serve with Walden Farms Pancake Syrup. Serve with bacon.

Jell-O Mold

- Sugar-free Jell-O
- Cream
- Cream cheese
- Sour cream
- Butter
- Saccharin (optional)

Make Jell-O ahead of time and start to cool in the refrigerator. Meanwhile, whip cream. Whip in softened cream cheese, sour cream, and butter. Add 1/4 grain saccharin if desired. Stir into cool liquid Jell-O and let harden. Note: This menu is helpful for children who do not chew well. Every bite is ketogenic, which means it can also be used for children during illness.

Because cream contains so much fat, the more cream you use the less oil, mayonnaise, and butter you will have to fit into the rest of the menu. But if your child doesn't mind eating a lot of mayonnaise or butter, you can use less cream and fill out the carbohydrate allotment with more vegetables or fruit.

Carbquik® Biscuit

- Cream, 36%,
- Carbquik®
- Bacon, Boars Head–cooked crisp
- Butter
- Water

Measure Carbquik and, using two knives, cut 10 grams of butter into the Carbquik until butter resembles coarse crumbs. Measure 8 grams of cream and add to Carbquik along with the water. Mix until the dough comes together. Form into biscuit shape. Cook at 425°F for 8 minutes or until lightly browned. Melt remaining butter and pour over biscuit. Serve with bacon and remaining cream.

Cheesecake

Egg	Butter
Cottage cheese	Cream
Sour cream	Vanilla sweetener
Cream cheese	Fruit slices

Mix together all ingredients except fruit. Add vanilla to taste and 1/2 grain of saccharin dissolved in 1/2 teaspoon of warm water or liquid sweetener to taste. Bake in small, greased Pyrex dish at 350°F for 25 minutes or until light golden brown on top. Cool. Arrange fruit slices on top—sliced strawberries, pineapple, or peach. Makes a whole meal! Save a bit of cream to whip and pile on top for extra excitement.

A cheesecake meal is easy to carry to school in its container for special occasions, such as when other kids are eating cake to celebrate a birthday. Cheesecake also provides a ketogenic ratio in every bite, so it is useful for children who cannot eat a full meal (e.g., when recovering from an illness).

SNACKS AND TREATS

Peanut Butter Balls

Skippy Creamy Peanut Butter
Butter

Mix peanut butter and butter together. Roll out into little balls and place in the fridge for a quick snack.

Keto Yogurt

Cream	Sour cream
Fruit	
Sugar-free sweetener (optional)	

Mix all of the ingredients together in the blender. Or mix the cream and sour cream together and place chopped up fruit in the mixture. You can add a sweetener as well.

Jell-O and Whipped Cream

Cream (whipped)

Sugar-free Jell-O

Mix or whip together; you can place it in the freezer for a frozen snack.

Custard (Baked or Frozen) or Eggnog Snack

Eggs–whole (raw)

Cream

Saccharin drops to sweeten

Pure extract: vanilla, almond, or chocolate and so forth

Whip the eggs, add the rest of the ingredients, and bake.

Turkey or Ham Rollup

Turkey breast or ham

Mayonnaise

Iceberg lettuce

Avocado (optional)

Spread mayonnaise on a lettuce leaf and roll turkey or ham in it. For variations you can add avocado into the wrap.

Peanut Butter Muffins With Keto Icing[a]

Egg yolk

Egg white

PAM® nonstick vegetable oil spray

Butter

Skippy Creamy Peanut Butter

Vanilla extract

Saccharin drops to sweeten

[a]**Recipe makes three servings.**

Spray a miniature muffin/tart pan with PAM® nonstick vegetable oil. Separate the yolk from the white of the egg. Whip the egg white until it is fluffy and measure allotted amount. Fold in allotted egg yolk. Melt butter with the peanut butter. Blend the melted butter and peanut butter with the egg mixture. Spoon it into the pan to make nine little mini muffins. Bake at 350°F for 10 to 15 minutes. Take them out and let them stand until the butter gets absorbed into the muffins. One serving equals three muffins.

Keto-Icing: For a variation you could try setting aside a little butter from the recipe and mixing it with vanilla extract and a few drops of saccharin; spread it on top of the muffins.

Butter Lollipops

Soften butter. Add a tiny drop of vanilla and carbohydrate-free sweetener. Press into candy molds. Add lollipop sticks and freeze 1 hour or overnight. Calculate weight not including the sticks and serve with meals or snacks.

Meringue Cookies

2 egg whites

1/2 tsp cream of tartar

1/2 package Sugar-free Jell-O

Beat egg whites until stiff. Add cream of tartar and dry Jell-O. Drop on aluminum foil sprayed lightly with nonstick cooking spray. Bake at 325° for 6 to 8 minutes, until brown. Cool before eating. Makes 20 cookies. One serving of two cookies contains 1.0 gram protein, 0 grams fat, and 0.1 gram carbohydrate.

Macadamia Buttercrunch

Chopped macadamia nuts

Butter

Macadamia nuts are naturally in a 3:1 ratio. Add enough butter to bring them to a 4:1 ratio. This snack is good for school kids and is easy to bring along on trips.

QUESTIONS ABOUT PREPARING THE DIET

Q: *Is it good to use high-fat meats to increase the fat content of the diet?*

A: Protein is very important for your child's growth. The protein portion of the diet should therefore be close to pure. Meat should be lean and trimmed of fat. Chicken and fish should be without skin. Cooked fat may be trimmed off and measured separately as part of the fat allotment for the meal. High-fat processed meats such as sausage and bologna should be calculated in the menu according to the manufacturer's contents.

Q: *What if some of the food sticks to the pan?*

A: Use nonstick pans and nonstick spray, and scrape out as much as possible with a small rubber spatula. Cook at low temperatures to avoid burning. Better yet, prepare food using nonstick methods: bake or broil meats, microwave eggs, steam vegetables. Remember that the allotted weights are for cooked food unless otherwise indicated, so until you are experienced with the difference between raw and cooked weights, your meats and vegetables or fruits should be prepared and cooked separately and then assembled with fats at the end.

Q: *What if my child refuses to eat the food I make?*

A: It is almost unheard of for a child to go hungry on the ketogenic diet. Remember that you are in charge, not the child! If your child has a tantrum and refuses to eat the food, give it 20 to 30 minutes, then remove the meal and you finish the family meal. Odds are, by the next meal, your child will not be so willing to test your limits and will eat the food.

If meal battles persist, allow the child some say in choosing the food (popular choices such as hot dogs, tuna fish, etc.). Another great trick is to have your child help in the actual meal preparation (e.g., mixing mayonnaise in with tuna, counting out pieces of vegetables). Try to make the child an actual participant in the diet, not just a recipient!

Q: *Should I try to use margarine instead of butter?*

A: We recommend that you use as many unsaturated fats as possible, such as canola, safflower, flaxseed, or olive oil, or margarine made from canola oil. However, no research exists on the effect of a diet comprised of 90% fat, whether saturated or unsaturated. No data indicate that the ketogenic diet, despite its high-fat content, leads to heart disease or atherosclerosis later in life.

Q: *My child is too disabled to care much what she eats, so I just want the simplest menu to prepare. What is easiest?*

A: The simplest ketogenic menu planning involves using the four main food groups of the diet without embellishment:

- Protein (meat, fish, chicken, cheese, egg)
- Carbohydrate (fruit or vegetable)
- Fat (butter, margarine, mayonnaise, oil)
- Cream

It takes very little time to broil a bit of meat or chicken, steam a piece of broccoli or cut up a tomato, put butter on the chicken or mayonnaise on the broccoli, and serve with a cup of cream diluted with ice and water. For a softer consistency, try fruit-topped cheesecake or custard with bacon and cooked vegetables.

Q: *What if the family has to travel or I don't have time to prepare a meal?*

A: The eggnog recipe or a formula recipe that you receive from your dietitian is a very good emergency or convenience food on the ketogenic diet. When traveling, make up to 2 days' meals ahead of time and take them along in a portable cooler. Ask restaurants to microwave them for you if appropriate. Tuna salad with sliced vegetables such as celery, cucumbers, or carrots is especially mobile. Refer to the chapter on tips for travel for further details.

Q: *Can I decrease the amount of cream and use more fat in a given menu?*

A: Cream is an easy, palatable way to get a lot of fat into the diet. If desired, however, the diet can be calculated with little or no cream. The challenge will be to find ways to make a large quantity of fats or oils palatable.

Q: *My child only wants to eat bacon and hot dogs; is that okay?*

A: As long as she is taking her vitamins and minerals it is okay for her to eat the same foods every day. There are no set meals for breakfast or dinner; each meal plan is interchangeable and can be eaten for any meal.

Q: *What if my child only ate the strawberries and then refused to eat the rest of the meal?*

A: Your child could be refusing to eat for many reasons. If it's out of pure control and refusal, then follow the guidelines we gave earlier and discard the meal. However, in the future you should try and give the fats first and then save the fruit as a dessert for the end of the meal; this way you don't have to worry about fighting with your child to get the required fat in. Some meals have all the ingredients mixed in together, and if your child, at times, might not finish a complete meal, it might be best to prepare those types of meals for her. This way you know that she had the entire ratio but just didn't finish all of her calories for that meal.

CHAPTER 32

Modified Atkins Diet Meal Plans and Recipes

MODIFIED ATKINS DIET (MAD)–WEEK 1 ≤ 20 G NET CARBS AND HIGH FAT TWO-WEEK MEAL PLAN WITH SHOPPING LIST, INSTRUCTION, AND RECIPES					
	Breakfast	Lunch	Dinner	Snacks	Dessert
Drinks	Coffee/tea Heavy cream	At least 8 cups of water daily. "Diet" drinks in moderation.			
	1.5				
Monday 18 g	Buttery fried eggs, breakfast meat, avocado with salt	Meat, cheese, and lettuce wraps with mayo	Chicken, broccoli, olive oil	Red pepper and mayo	85%/90% dark chocolate
	3.5	8	3	<2	<2
Tuesday 20 g	MAD oatmeal	Chicken salad tostada	Taco dinner bowl	Avocado with salt	MAD sweet drink
	<5.5	5	<6.5	<2	1.5
Wednesday 19 g	Frittata with butter, cherry tomatoes, cheese	Taco salad (leftovers)	Ham steak Zucchini with butter	Red pepper with ranch dressing	MAD chocolate candies
	5.5	6	4	<3	<0.5
Thursday 18 g	Muffin in a mug, avocado with salt	Cobb salad (leftovers)	Creamy fish with greens and mushrooms	Celery stalk, almond butter	Strawberry sweet drink
	<4	5	4.5	<2	3
Friday 18 g	Buttery fried eggs, fresh salsa, cheese	Tuna in olive oil, greens and mushrooms	Italian sausage with onions, avocado mash	Cucumber, cream cheese	Chocolate PB fat bomb
	4	4	5.5	2.5	<2
Saturday 20 g	Lox and cream cheese on cucumber	Shredded pork with spicy slaw	Steak, cheesy cauliflower, simple salad	Flaxseed crackers, guacamole	Spice muffin with butter
	6.5	<4	4	3.5	<2
Sunday 16 g	Low-carb pancakes with butter	Shredded pork on flax bun	Salmon fillet, green beans almondine	Tomatoes and cheese	MAD merengue cookies
	5	1.5	7	<2	<0.5

TWO-WEEK SHOPPING LIST

PRODUCE:

- ☐ Avocados, 2 or 3
- ☐ Broccoli, 1 bunch or frozen bag
- ☐ Red peppers, green pepper
- ☐ Iceberg and Romaine lettuce (chopped or whole)
- ☐ Celery
- ☐ Cherry tomatoes, 1 pint
- ☐ Zucchini
- ☐ Leafy greens (spinach/ Swiss chard/kale)
- ☐ Bok choy
- ☐ Mushrooms, white or baby bella, 8 oz
- ☐ Cucumbers
- ☐ Onions, small
- ☐ Cabbage (whole head or preshredded)
- ☐ Cauliflower
- ☐ Guacamole (100 calorie snack packs)
- ☐ Green beans
- ☐ Spaghetti squash
- ☐ Baby carrots
- ☐ Cauliflower
- ☐ 2 Portobello mushrooms
- ☐ Asparagus
- ☐ Garlic

MEAT/DELI:

- ☐ Bacon
- ☐ Breakfast sausage
- ☐ Sausage roll for frittata
- ☐ Chicken thighs (with/ without bone/skin)
- ☐ Ham steaks
- ☐ Ground beef
- ☐ Pork butt/picnic/shoulder
- ☐ Salmon fillet
- ☐ Cod fillet
- ☐ Shrimp
- ☐ Steak
- ☐ Gourmet sausages
- ☐ Deli meat
- ☐ Lox
- ☐ Genoa salami
- ☐ Pepperoni
- ☐ Hot dogs
- ☐ Steak Umms®
- ☐ Fiorucci paninos

DAIRY:

- ☐ Heavy cream
- ☐ Eggs
- ☐ Butter
- ☐ Cheddar cheese, block
- ☐ Almond milk, unsweetened
- ☐ Sour cream
- ☐ Feta cheese, crumbled
- ☐ Cream cheese
- ☐ Parmesan cheese, finely grated
- ☐ String cheese
- ☐ Blue cheese
- ☐ Reddi-Whip® (Extra Creamy)

FROZEN:

- ☐ Frozen chopped spinach, 10 oz box
- ☐ Frozen strawberries
- ☐ Tilapia or Swai fish or other white fish
- ☐ Atkins meals

CONDIMENTS AND DRY GOODS:

- ☐ Mayonnaise, regular fat
- ☐ Olive oil
- ☐ Coconut oil
- ☐ Chia seeds
- ☐ Black olives
- ☐ Sugar-free flavored syrups (like DaVinci®)
- ☐ Taco seasoning packet (or make your own)
- ☐ Fresh salsa like Pico de Gallo
- ☐ Salad dressings (look for 0–2 g NC/serving)
- ☐ Mustard, any type
- ☐ Sour relish
- ☐ Almond butter
- ☐ Canned tuna in olive oil
- ☐ Canned chicken
- ☐ Flackers (flaxseed crackers)
- ☐ Capers
- ☐ Alfredo sauce
- ☐ Sugar-free Jell-O cups
- ☐ Atkins shakes

BAKING:

- ☐ Dark chocolate, 85% or 90%
- ☐ Baking chocolate
- ☐ Shredded coconut, unsweetened
- ☐ Walnuts
- ☐ Macadamia nuts
- ☐ Almonds

(continued)

- ☐ Coconut flour
- ☐ Pumpkin seeds, out of the shell
- ☐ Cocoa powder, unsweetened
- ☐ Flaxseed, ground and/or whole
- ☐ Sweeteners (Stevia, Sucralose, etc.)
- ☐ Cream of tartar, for the merengue
- ☐ Almond extract, for the merengue

BREAD/CARB SUBSTITUTES:

- ☐ Low-carb wrap (≤6 g NC for large wraps)
- ☐ Miracle Noodles

OTHER:

- ☐ ____________________
- ☐ ____________________

MEAL PLAN SPECIFICS

This menu is meant to give you lots of ideas about what to eat on the modified Atkins diet (MAD). The menu has three meals, a snack, and a dessert each day. Although the days of the week are listed and a shopping list is provided, you do not have to eat exactly what the menu says. You may find that you can eat leftovers much more frequently. Or, if you have a big family or your spouse is also eating a low-carb diet, you may need to buy more food. This meal plan is excellent for the average-sized, low-active woman. A man, a larger person, or a more active person may benefit from adding an additional snack. Overall, please use this meal plan as an example of 35 meal and snack ideas that you can prepare and eat yourself, but do not tie yourself to it. Feel free to adapt it to your individual needs and family situation.

Abbreviations

NC = net carbs = total carbs minus fiber
tb = tablespoon (the big one)
ts = teaspoon (the little one)

MONDAY

Daily Totals: 18 g net carbs (NC), 141 g fat, 77 g protein, 1680 calories

Eggs, Bacon or Sausage, Avocado With Salt

2 eggs (1 g NC per 2 eggs) cooked in 2 tb butter, oil, or bacon grease; 2 bacon strips (0 g NC) OR 2 sausage patties (varies by brand, but usually 0–2 g NC per 2 patties); 1/2 avocado with salt (like most produce, avocados can vary in size and therefore can have NC ranging from 1.25 g per half to 2.5 g; use 2 g NC per half avocado to make it simpler).

Lunch Wrap

Throw your meat, cheese, and veggie sandwich fillings into a low-carb wrap! Here's one idea: 2 oz deli turkey meat (1 g NC), 1 oz cheddar cheese (0.5 g NC), 1 large iceberg lettuce leaf (0.2 g NC), 1 tb mayo (0.2 g NC), on a low carb tortilla/wrap (6 g NC) = 8 g net carbs for a very hearty and filling lunch!

Baked Chicken Thighs

Chicken thighs with skin can be fairly inexpensive, and you can cook them in large batches in the oven. They can be used throughout the week for different recipes, such as chicken salad wrap, or on top of a salad. Bake chicken thighs with rosemary, salt, and pepper at 350°F until the internal temp reaches 165°F (20–30 minutes) and then broil to crisp skin. Watch them so they don't burn!

Broccoli

Fresh or frozen broccoli can be steamed or sautéed in minutes. You can coat the broccoli in olive oil if you sauté it and, either way, finish with a generous dose of olive oil. Dry steak seasoning mixed with olive oil is a great addition to broccoli or any cooked vegetable! Half a cup of chopped broccoli has 3 g NC.

Red Pepper

Red peppers are very nutritious and are a great source of vitamin C, which can be lacking on low-carb diets. One third of a red pepper has just under 2 g of NC so a whole pepper can serve you three times! Since they are so sweet, they can substitute for dessert on occasion.

Dark Chocolate

85% to 90% dark chocolate is a perfect treat to finish the day. Be sure to read the carbs on the label since ingredients can vary brand to brand. You should be able to find a 90% dark chocolate for 1.75 g NC per piece.

TUESDAY

Daily Totals: 20 g net carbs, 143 g fat, 60 g protein, 1626 calories.

MAD Oatmeal

Mix together a variety of nuts and seeds (almonds, walnuts, sunflower seeds, chia seeds, hemp seeds, flax, etc.) with heavy cream or unsweetened almond milk. Heat in microwave in 30 second to 1 minute intervals adding liquid and sweetener for desired taste and consistency. This could be as simple as 1/4 cup of ground flax with 1/4 cup of heavy cream and water. You will never get bored with this simple recipe! If you follow the recipe exactly, it contains 4.6 g NC per serving.

Chicken Salad Tostada/Wrap

Take the meat from a leftover chicken thigh (0 g), chop up with 1 medium stalk of celery (1/2 g NC) and 1/4 finely chopped red pepper (1 g NC), and mix in 1–2 tb mayo and 1–2 ts mustard. Spoon on top of small, toasted, low-carb tortilla (3 g NC) with lettuce or simply serve over chopped lettuce. 5.3 g NC with small wrap.

Taco Bowl

Make ground beef with taco seasoning according to packet directions or make your own seasoning mix. For dinner, have 1/3 cup taco meat, 2 tb sour cream

(1/2 g NC), 1 tb salsa (1 g NC), and 2 tb shredded cheese of your choice. Serve on top of crunchy iceberg lettuce (1 g NC/cup).

Sweet Drink

Blend 1/2 cup unsweetened almond milk, 2 tb heavy cream, 1–2 tb sugar-free flavored syrup (like DaVinci Gourmet®, Torani®, or Starbucks® brands) and 1 tb light flavored oil (olive, coconut, safflower, avocado, etc.). Pour over ice or drink hot.

WEDNESDAY

Daily Totals: 19 g net carbs, 143 g fat, 74 g protein, 1672 calories.

Frittata

Search for Sausage, Spinach, and Feta Frittata on www.ibreatheimhungry.com. Makes 12 squares for 1.4 g NC each or 18 "muffins" with 1 g NC each. The nutrient daily totals here account for two servings of the frittata squares. Three cherry tomatoes have about 1.4 g NC. There are many other frittata recipes to try. See which one you like! Smother with 2 tb of salty, creamy butter.

Taco Bowl Leftovers

Don't forget to make extra the night before!

Sautéed Ham Steak

Sauté ham steak with butter, mustard, and garlic over medium heat. Since ham steaks are sold in packages of one or more, share with the family or eat for lunch the next day. These freeze really well, so buy extra. You can cook chopped zucchini in another pan with butter or steam it and add butter or olive oil and season well. One cup of chopped and cooked zucchini has 3.5 g NC.

Red Pepper and Ranch Dressing

A third of a red pepper and some ranch or blue cheese dressing makes a satisfying and quick snack. Be picky about your salad dressings as carbohydrate content can vary greatly!

MAD Chocolate Candies

Gently melt together 1/4 cup each unsalted butter and coconut oil. Add 1 tb unsweetened cocoa powder, 1/2-1 teaspoon vanilla extract, and about 10 drops of plain liquid Stevia. Mix very well and adjust sweetener to taste. Carefully pour into candy molds, ice cube trays, or silicone baking cups. Freeze for about an hour. Pop out of trays and keep in storage container in freezer. These do not keep outside of the freezer for very long, so enjoy straight from the freezer. *You may add more cocoa powder; count 2 g net carb per TB, but check with the nutrition facts panel to be sure. This recipe has endless variations – add 2 tb almond butter, nuts, flavored extracts, or fruits to the mix.

THURSDAY

Daily Totals: 18 g net carbs, 147 g fat, 65 g protein, 1680 calories

Muffin in a Mug

Find this recipe on www.charliefoundation.org. Each muffin has 1.7 g NC. Spread with Stevia sweetened butter for additional fat and have half an avocado on the side to keep you full for a long time!

Cobb Salad

Mix 1 cup of chopped iceberg lettuce with 1/4 cup shredded cheddar cheese, 3 cherry tomatoes, 1 hard-boiled egg, and 1 oz of deli-style turkey with 2 tb ranch dressing for a delicious Cobb salad. That should help you use up some of your leftovers!

Tilapia/Swai With Creamy Topping

Swai is a type of fish that is similar in taste to catfish, and is also quite inexpensive. Coat fish with 1 tb mayonnaise mixed with 1 tb any type of shredded cheese. Bake at 350°F for 10–15 minutes, or until fish is flaky.

Greens and Mushrooms

Sauté in a liberal amount of olive oil: 1 pound (weight from store) Swiss chard with 8 oz (package weight) of white or baby bella mushrooms. Season with salt, pepper, onion, and garlic powder. Cook until greens are wilted and mushrooms are done. This should make 4 servings, with 4 g NC per serving.

Celery With Almond Butter

1 medium stalk of celery has 1/2 g NC. Spread on 1 tb almond butter for an additional 1–3 g NC, depending on the brand.

Strawberry Sweet Drink

Follow the directions from Tuesday's dessert, but blend in 2 strawberries instead of using syrup. This has 3 g NC.

FRIDAY

Daily Totals: 18 g net carbs, 143 g fat, 78 g protein, 1682 calories

Eggs, Salsa, Cheese

Most commercial salsas have 2–4 g NC per 2 tablespoon serving. Fresh salsas, like pico de gallo, may have 2 g or less! Always read the nutrition facts to be sure. To save money, buy cheeses in large blocks and shred yourself. Store block tightly wrapped in aluminum foil and plastic bag in fridge to keep it fresh. Store the shredded cheese loosely in a large bag or container. Remember to cook eggs in at least 1 tb of oil, butter, or bacon grease.

Canned Tuna in Olive Oil

This is one of my favorite foods on the MAD. Get the tuna with the pop top lid and it makes a quick, portable, and delicious meal anywhere you go. Bumble Bee® makes tuna in flavored olive oil—Jalapenos, Chipotle, and Sundried Tomatoes. Toss with leftover greens and mushrooms from the night before.

Quick Sausage Dinner

Mash 1/2 an avocado, salt, and 1 tb mayo together to make a quick sauce or side dish. Cook an Italian or Gourmet Sausage in the microwave or on the stove with onions. Easy peasy. Add a side salad with oil if this small but filling meal doesn't do the trick.

Cucumbers and Cream Cheese

This has to be one of the easiest snacks to put together. If your cucumbers aren't organic, I recommend peeling the skin. Otherwise, just chop into slices or spears and pair with 2 tb cream cheese.

Chocolate Peanut Butter Fat Bomb

It doesn't get any better than this. Search for this recipe at www.lowcarbyum.com. If you make 12 servings, each one will be about 1 gram of net carb. Approximately 2 lb of bacon will give you 1 cup of bacon grease. If you cut fudge into 16 pieces, each piece will have about 2 g NC.

SATURDAY

Daily Totals: 20 g net carbs, 134 g fat, 108 g protein, 1790 calories.

Lox, Cream Cheese, and Cucumbers

Cut six slices of a cucumber. Spread 2 tb of cream cheese on the slices and press in the capers so that they don't roll off. Place a slice of red onion on each (watch your onion portion since they are quite high in carbs). Finish off by folding lox on top. Alternatively, you could cut cucumbers into matshsticks and roll up ingredients in the lox. Another idea—make a dip of all ingredients except for the cucumber and use the cucumber slices to eat up!

Shredded Pork With Cabbage

Put a pork butt/shoulder in the slow cooker and season with salt and pepper only. Leave it on low for about 6–8 hours. After it cools, remove the bone, the skin, and most of the liquid. Season again with a low-carb BBQ sauce or a sugar-free dry rub. Continue to cook to let the flavors blend or eat as is if you can't wait. The leftovers can be refrigerated or frozen, and used in various recipes. Serve with a Spicy Slaw at 3.7 g NC (depending on your dressing). Toss together 3/4 cup shredded green cabbage, 2 tb Ranch style, bleu cheese dressing, or mayonnaise, and 1 teaspoon hot sauce of your choice.

Steak

Season and cook up your steak any way you'd like. Limit your cooked portion to a 3–5 oz serving. If you are feeling fancy, you can add a compound butter, like the one found here: www.ibreatheimhungry.com/2014/06/cumin-dusted-strip-steaks-salsa-verde-butter-low-carb.html. Pair with the cheesy cauliflower recipe that follows and a very simple side salad of Romaine lettuce and a low-carb caesar dressing, like Drew's Romano Caesar Dressing.

Cheesy Cauliflower

There are many recipes out there, some with mayonnaise, some with butter; just find which one you like, or experiment with a few. Here is a tasty one: www.ibreatheimhungry.com/2012/01/better-than-potatoes-cheesy-cauliflower.html. This recipe has 3 g NC for 1/4 of the recipe.

Flaxseed Crackers

You can buy Flackers at the store, or make these: lowcarbdiets.about.com/od/snacks/r/flaxcrackers.htm. The entire recipe contains 6 g of NC.

Spice Muffin

Find recipe at lowcarbdiets.about.com/od/breads/r/doughnutmuffins.htm. Each muffin has 2 g NC. These are one of my favorite treats!

SUNDAY

Daily Totals: 16 g net carbs, 137 g fat, 76 g protein, 1640 calories

Pancakes

Search "Lauren's pancakes" on www.yourlighterside.com for this great recipe that doubles as a pizza crust! If you divide the recipe into two servings, each serving has 4 g NC. Add sweetener, cinnamon, or vanilla extract to the pancake batter, as desired. And, of course, pour melted butter over the top before devouring.

Shredded Pork on Flax Bun

Heat-up leftover shredded pork and eat on two of these very versatile flax buns. Add lettuce or leftover slaw if you'd like. Flax bun recipe can be found here, cavemanketo.com/faux-bread-quest-flax-buns/. There are 1.5 g NC for two buns.

Salmon Filet and Green Beans

Remember to portion control with meat/fish and allow only 3–5 oz per meal. Cover salmon in 1 tb olive oil and then bake at 350°F until fish is flaky. In the meantime, sauté 1 cup of fresh green beans in a large helping of butter. Add 2 tb slivered almonds when the beans are cooked to your liking.

Meringue

There are plenty of low-carb meringue recipes out there, so experiment and find one you like. Here is a coconut recipe with 1 g NC for 5 cookies: www.genaw.com/lowcarb/coconut_meringue_cookies.html.

MODIFIED ATKINS DIET (MAD)—WEEK 2: QUICK AND EASY					
	Breakfast	Lunch	Dinner	Snacks	Dessert
Drinks	Coffee/tea Heavy cream	At least 8 cups of water daily. "Diet" drinks in moderation.			
	1.5				
Monday 20 g	Hard-boiled eggs, mayo	Chicken caesar salad	Spaghetti squash with Alfredo sauce	Salami slices Macadamia nuts	Jell-O, whipped cream
	1	5	10	1.5	1
Tuesday 20 g	Scrambled eggs and green pepper	Hot dogs with mayo Carrots	Steak Cauliflower	Chia drink Macadamia nuts	Strawberries with sweet butter
	2.5	8	3	3	2
Wednesday 17 g	Atkins shake 3 Sausage links	Steak salad	Portabello pizza Creamy zucchini	Walnuts and cheese	Avocado with sweetener
	1.5	2	9	2	1
Thursday 20 g	Eggs and bacon	Atkins frozen meal Salad	Steak Umms with spinach and feta	Salami and cheese logs Green peppers	Chocolate drink
	1	10	2	2	3.5
Friday 18.5 g	Breakfast drink	Egg salad wrap	Bunless burger Bok choy	Cucumber salad	Jell-O and whipped cream
	3	7	3	3	1
Saturday 19 g	Vegetable scramble	Cheesy bacon quesadilla	Buttered fish Spinach	Fiorucci Panino Pecans	Chocolate mousse
	3	7	<4	<2	3
Sunday 20 g	Bacon spinach omelet	Chicken salad on wrap	Creamy shrimp with broccoli	Pepperoni slices	2 MAD chocolate candies
	2	8	8	0	0

MONDAY

Daily Totals: 20 g net carbs, 158 g fat, 81 g protein, 1850 calories

Breakfast: 2 hardboiled eggs, 2 tb mayo

Lunch: 3 cups romaine lettuce, 4 oz chicken, 1/2 avocado, 3 tb caesar dressing, 3 tb shredded parmesan cheese

Dinner: 3/4 cup spaghetti squash, 1/3 cup ground beef, 1/4 cup alfredo sauce, 1 tb butter

Snack: 3 slices Genoa salami (approx. 1 oz), 10 macadamia nuts

Dessert: sugar-free Jell-O cup with 2 tb aerosol whipped cream (like Reddi-Whip Extra Creamy)

TUESDAY

Daily Totals: 20 g net carbs, 157 g fat, 73 g protein, 1800 calories

Breakfast: 2 eggs mixed with 2 tb heavy cream and 1/4 medium green pepper scrambled in 1 tb butter

Lunch: 2 hot dogs, 2 tb mayo, 6 baby carrots

Dinner: 5 oz steak covered in 1 oz blue cheese and 1/2 tb butter and buttered cauliflower

Snack: Combine 1 cup unsweetened almond milk and 2 tb chia seeds. Let sit for 5 minutes to thicken and drink.

Dessert: 3 strawberries dipped in 1/2 tb sweetened butter

WEDNESDAY

Daily Totals: 18 g net carbs, 161 g fat, 92 g protein, 1900 calories

Breakfast: Atkins shake with 3 sausage links

Lunch: 3 oz leftover steak over romaine lettuce, 2 tb blue cheese, 3 tb olive oil, 5 black olives

Dinner: 2 baked mushrooms topped with salami, cheese, and seasoning; 1 cup zucchini with caesar dressing

Snack: 5 walnut halves, string cheese

Dessert: Avocado sprinkled with Splenda or other artificial sweetener

THURSDAY

Daily Totals: 20 g net carbs, 169 g fat, 67 g protein, 1900 calories

Breakfast: 3 bacon slices, 2 eggs cooked in bacon grease

Lunch: Atkins frozen Italian Sausage Primavera, 2 cups iceberg lettuce, 2 tb ranch dressing, 2 cherry tomatoes

Dinner: 2 cooked Steak Umms over 1 cup spinach with 2 tb feta cheese, 5 black olives, 2 tb olive oil

Snack: roll up 1 tb cream cheese in 3 salami slices; 1/4 medium green pepper

Dessert: Unsweetened almond milk mixed with 1.5 tb oil, 1 tb cocoa powder, 1 ts vanilla, and sweetener

FRIDAY

Daily Totals: 19 g net carbs, 168 g fat, 71 g protein, 1900 calories

Breakfast: 2 tb heavy cream, 1 cup almond milk, 2 strawberries, 1 tb neutral oil, sweetener

Lunch: 2 boiled eggs, 1 tb mayo, 1 tb chopped celery, 1 ts relish. Serve on low-carb wrap (6 g NC).

Dinner: burger patty, 2 slices cheese, mayo, 1 tomato slice, 1 lettuce leaf; 1 cup sautéed, buttered bok choy

Snack: 1/4 cucumber chopped with 1 oz feta and 2 tb olive oil

Dessert: Jell-O with 2 tb whipped cream

SATURDAY

Daily Totals: 19 g net carbs, 167 g fat, 78 g protein, 1900 calories

Breakfast: 2 eggs, 3 pieces asparagus chopped, 1/8 medium red pepper chopped, 2 tb butter, seasoning

Lunch: 2 slices bacon, 1/4 cup shredded cheese, 1/2 avocado in folded-over low-carb wrap and cooked

Dinner: 4 oz fish cooked and drizzled in butter; spinach sautéed in garlic and olive oil

Snack: 3 slices Fiorucci Panino Salami and 10 pecan halves

Dessert: 1/4 cup heavy cream whipped with 1 tb cocoa powder, sweetener

SUNDAY

Daily Totals: 20 g net carbs, 169 g fat, 76 g protein, 1900 calories

Breakfast: 2 eggs, 2 slices bacon, 1/4 cup sautéed spinach, 1/4 cup cheese, cooked in butter

Lunch: 1/2 cup canned chicken, 2 tb mayo, 2 tb celery, 2 tb red pepper, and lettuce on low-carb wrap

Dinner: Shrimp sautéed with garlic, butter, cream, over Miracle Noodles with 1 cup broccoli, 1 tb oil

Snack: 10 slices pepperoni

Dessert: 2 MAD chocolate candies

CHAPTER 33

Using Diets Around the World

It is literally a brave new world for the use of the ketogenic diet. In the period before the 1990s, only select countries were using diets for epilepsy, mostly the United States, the United Kingdom, Canada, Argentina, France, Australia, and Germany. Other centers certainly existed, but there was very little published from them, and in the pre-Internet era, we didn't know about them. The Charlie Foundation, Matthew's Friends, and the rise of the Internet changed all of that in the 1990s and especially in the 2000s. In 2005, we wrote a paper about the worldwide use of the ketogenic diet and at that time there were 73 centers found in 41 countries. Most of them had started in 1996 and were small, but growing. Now in 2016, we have over 65 countries represented and many of the centers in these countries are large (and publishing their research). The 2014 biennial ketogenic diet symposium in Liverpool saw more representation from outside the United States and the United Kingdom than ever before. In fact, to our knowledge Figure 33.1 is the current map of where the diet is available (countries shown in black). These sites are provided in more detail in Appendix G.

So what should you do if you're a parent (or patient) somewhere in the world and you're reading this book, and want more information for yourself or your ketogenic diet team? Even more critical, what if your country is not currently shown in black in Figure 33.1 and doesn't have a ketogenic diet center? Here are some important tips for you:

1. **Use the Internet**

   There is an incredible wealth of resources available on the Internet about implementing ketogenic diets, including recipes from other countries. Find others, in chat rooms or Facebook groups from your region of the world, and connect. Parent support groups are becoming very active and available worldwide—start with The Charlie Foundation and Matthew's Friends and ask for some local help in terms of resources. More information on parent support groups and the Internet can be found in Chapter 23. Lastly, Eric Kossoff maintains a webpage at www.epilepsy.com devoted to the ketogenic diet called "Keto News" that highlights new information approximately every 2 months. Read it and please send in ideas for articles!

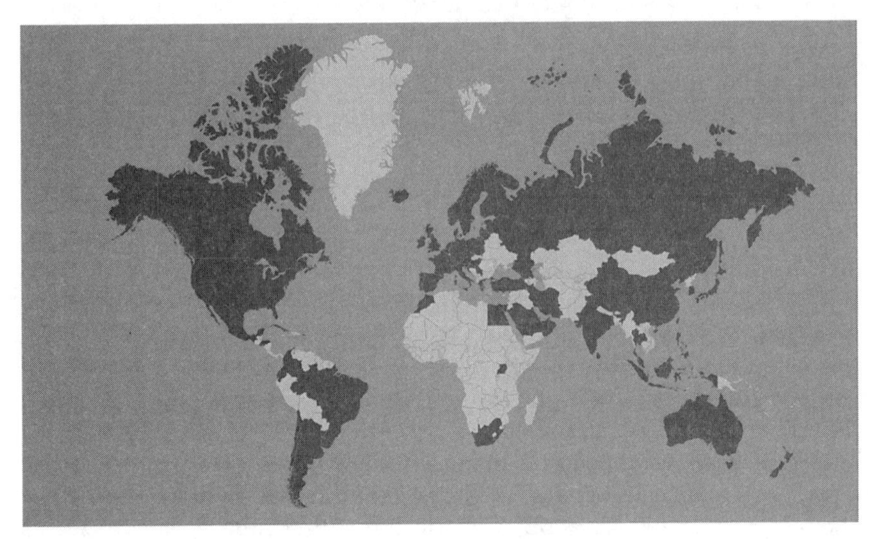

Figure 33.1. Countries offering the ketogenic diet (shown in black).

2. **Use the International League Against Epilepsy Task Force for Dietary Therapy**

In 2013, the International League Against Epilepsy (ILAE) realized that an important need for their member epilepsy specialists around the world was more information on the diet. This was extremely exciting to us and to The Charlie Foundation and Matthew's Friends. The ILAE provided funds to create a 12-member Task Force with the mission of helping bring the ketogenic diet (and other diets) to regions of the world that need them. There was a special interest in regions of the world with limited resources.

The Task Force includes dietitians and neurologists from the United States, the United Kingdom, India, China, South Korea, South Africa, Chile, El Salvador, Oman, and Germany. Authors and contributors to this book from the Task Force include myself (Chair), Mackenzie Cervenka, Beth Zupec-Kania, and Emma Williams. The first project of this Task Force was completed in July 2014, and that was the launch of their webpage. It is housed at the ILAE website, but easy to find (if you search for "ILAE ketogenic"). The website is www.ilae.org/Commission/medther/keto-index.cfm. Many of the pages are available in Spanish thanks to Task Force Members Dr. Ximena Raimann Tampier and Rocio Rivera Claros, RD (from Chile and El Salvador, respectively). This work also could not have been possible without the help of Ms. Deborah Flower from Association Resources who helped create the page.

The website includes exciting news, international recipes, key ketogenic diet articles (that are free for download as PDFs thanks to the generosity of the journals *Epilepsia, Epilepsy and Behavior,* and *Journal of Child Neurology*), information on supplements and products, other websites, and the maintained list of ketogenic diet centers worldwide (see also Appendix G).

At this time the Task Force is working on several other projects, including a slide set of ketogenic diet training materials and lectures that would be available for use in training other new ketogenic diet centers. We have also just published an article detailing the "minimum" requirements for a ketogenic diet center in a region with limited resources, recognizing that the 2008 consensus statement may be the gold standard but may not feasible for some parts of the world.

All members of the Task Force are eager to help you (and your country) succeed on the diet and help make that map of the world completely filled-in with ketogenic diet centers. Feel free to email with questions.

3. **Try to attend the biennial ketogenic diet conferences!**

   These are great meetings to see what is going in the world of dietary therapy and often are Wednesday through Friday, with a Saturday "Family Day" held specifically for parents and patients. The speakers at the main conference often stick around for the Family Day to chat with parents. This is a good chance to get your questions answered, hear the latest research, meet companies making ketogenic diet products, and connect with other parents and parent support groups. Nearly all of the families I meet are so pleased to have attended, despite the occasional expense of travel (www.ketoconnect.org/symposium/index.html).

4. **Be creative with recipes and share them!**

   One of the biggest barriers to getting the diet to areas of the world that need it are the beliefs by physicians and parents in these countries that the diet is very "Western" and not adaptable to their country. We have tried ***hard*** to change that idea. One of the best ways to convince families that it is possible is to show recipes from their country. Some examples are listed at the ILAE Task Force website at www.ilae.org/Commission/medther/keto-recipes.cfm and others can be found in the next chapter. If you have made some great recipes, please share them with us, a parent support group, or other families you've met on your ketogenic diet journey!

5. **Advocate!**

   Many of the amazing parent support groups were started by a parent who wanted to make a difference. There is no reason that can't be you! Speak to your neurologist and dietitian about ways in which you can help bring dietary therapy to the public. Ideas include interviews by the media, posts on the website of the hospital or medical clinic that has helped you start the diet for your child, cooking classes, or group meetings for interested parents at a local hotel or hospital. Jim Abrahams from The Charlie Foundation and Emma Williams from Matthew's Friends are always willing to help a parent do this (having done it themselves in the 1990s!)—you can contact them for tips as well!

Figure 33.2. The Healing Young Hearts ketogenic diet parent support group providing information at a booth at an epilepsy conference in Suzhou, China.

SECTION VIII

Diets for Conditions Other Than Epilepsy

CHAPTER 34

Ketogenic Diets and Brain Tumors

This chapter was written by Roy E. Strowd III, MD, Department of Neurology and Oncology, Johns Hopkins, Baltimore, Maryland, now currently at Wake Forest University, North Carolina.

Brain cancer is one of the most devastating forms of cancer. Of the tumors that originate in the brain, the most common is the glioma, a tumor that arises from the support cells of the brain (i.e., the glia). Most adult gliomas develop during the prime of life (i.e., ages 30–60) and are aggressive, incurable tumors that result in disabling weakness, speech difficulty, seizures, vision changes, or other neurologic problems and lead to death within months to several years. The standard treatments include a combination of surgery, radiation, and chemotherapy. Unfortunately, despite even the most aggressive treatment, the majority of these tumors will recur and progressively worsen. New treatments are needed, and doctors, scientists, and patients are actively seeking new therapies for treating this devastating disease.

For many reasons, brain tumors are perhaps one of the more appealing cancers for investigating the potential utility of ketogenic diets in oncology. Brain tumors appear to have an addiction to sugar. Like all cells in the body, tumors require oxygen, nutrients, adequate blood flow, and glucose (i.e., sugar) to grow. Brain tumors have a particularly high affinity for glucose. In fact, research suggests that brain tumors utilize glucose at three times the rate of normal brain tissue and that withdrawal of glucose may trigger the death of brain tumor cells. Research into the genes involved in brain tumors has further highlighted the importance of the metabolic profile of these tumors. In 2009 the results of The Cancer Genome Atlas (TCGA) Project, an effort to analyze, sequence, and describe all of the genes involved in cancer, highlighted potentially important gene alterations in brain tumors. Genes such as the isocitrate dehydrogenase (e.g., IDH-1 and IDH-2) genes are often altered in brain tumors and contribute to tumor development, growth, and survival. These genes may work by affecting the metabolic pathways of brain tumors.

To date, scientists have explored both nondietary and dietary methods for targeting this metabolic "addiction" to glucose. However, no drugs (i.e., nondietary approaches) are currently available that can be used in the clinic today. For the past decade scientists have studied the role of ketogenic diets in treating brain tumors. Research has been primarily preclinical, meaning that testing has focused on evaluating the effect of ketogenic diets on brain tumor tissues in the laboratory or in animal models. In these studies, scientists have shown that while normal brain cells maintain the ability to use ketone bodies as an alternative source of fuel, brain tumors appear less capable of shifting away from their reliance on glucose. In studies of brain tumors implanted into animals, ketogenic diets have been shown to reduce the rate of tumor growth and prolong the animals' lives. In these studies, calorie restriction (i.e., reducing the total amount of food consumed by these animals) was a particularly critical component and may drive some of the effectiveness of these dietary interventions against brain tumors.

While these findings are exciting, challenges exist in translating this to human patients. It is not clear whether ketogenic diets benefit brain tumor patients in the same way that they affect tissue in the laboratory or an animal. Nevertheless, the importance of glucose in cancer is not new to doctors or patients. For decades doctors have exploited the glucose "addiction" of tumors through the use of an imaging study called the positron emission tomography (PET) scan. This safe and painless imaging procedure is frequently used to diagnose and monitor many different cancers. Patients ingest a glucose substance that is labeled with a radioactive particle called fluoro-deoxyglucose (FDG). FDG lights up tissues in the body that attract glucose and cancer lights up particularly brightly. Brain tumors have a high uptake of FDG; however, the background brain also strongly attracts glucose. As a result, PET scans are not widely used in brain tumor diagnosis and treatment. However, the reliance of cancer cells on glucose as demonstrated in these PET images lends support to the theory of using ketogenic diets in patients with cancerous tumors, including brain tumors.

To date, three published clinical trials have investigated ketogenic diets in patients with cancer. Two studies evaluated diets in patients with advanced cancers and did not include brain tumor patients. In these studies, tolerability varied among patients and the role of ketogenic diets in these patients with very advanced cancer remains unclear. The ERGO trial was published in 2014 and reported on 20 patients with recurrent high-grade brain tumors who were prescribed a 60 grams/day carbohydrate restricted diet. In this study, 85% of patients were able to tolerate the diet for about 5 weeks with 73% achieving measurable ketosis and a small but significant weight loss of 2.2%. The study was not designed to determine the effectiveness of the diet, though all patients did suffer progression of their disease and the investigators concluded that alternatives to their 60 grams/day carbohydrate restricted diet were needed. Whether this result reflects poor activity of ketogenic diets in brain tumors in general, or the need for a more rigorous determination of the ideal dose (i.e., degree of carbohydrate reduction), or the need for incorporating formal calorie restriction (a critical component of these diets in animals) is not clear.

A number of clinical trials are currently being performed to further pursue the role of ketogenic diets in brain tumors (studies can be found at www.clinicaltrials.gov). These studies include a range of ketogenic approaches to brain tumor treatment at various stages of the disease. Two of these trials are investigating the conventional 4:1 ratio ketogenic diet, one a modified Atkins-based diet and others incorporating varying degrees of carbohydrate and calorie restriction. Two studies include intermittent fasting and have incorporated some of the emerging preclinical data on the impact of short periods of significant calorie restriction on cancer growth in animals. Several are also exploring therapeutic combinations by adding the diet to chemotherapy and/or radiation therapy. Eligibility is spread across the varying stages of this disease including newly diagnosed patients as well as at the time of tumor regrowth or as a maintenance strategy after patients have completed their initial treatment. These studies will be .critical for determining the next steps in pursuing ketogenic diets in neuro-oncology. Despite excitement by scientists, clinicians, and patients, there is not currently sufficient evidence to support the safety, tolerability, activity, or effectiveness of these diets in treating brain tumors and thus, these trials are crucial.

Moving forward, existing and future studies will address several important questions regarding the role of ketogenic diets in treating brain tumors. As with the development of any new drug or therapy, two of the most important first steps are determining the dose that is necessary to treat the disease and an initial assessment of safety. To date, the "dose" of diet necessary to treat brain tumors is not clear. The existing studies in brain tumors are incorporating varying degrees of carbohydrate, calorie, protein, and fat restrictions. The classic markers of dietary activity such as urine ketones, which are used in patients with epilepsy, have appeared to be less reliable in treating cancers. Thus, establishing an optimal dose and duration of treatment is a critical first step before this therapy can be further explored in trials and implemented in patients. In addition, important differences exist between brain tumor and epilepsy patients. Brain tumors are quite different from epilepsy with different prior treatments, associated conditions, and need for future surgery, radiation, or chemotherapy. While ketogenic diets have been safe and well tolerated in patients with epilepsy, it is not yet clear that the experience will be the same in brain tumor patients. Bone marrow integrity is critical in cancer populations, and thus it will be important to monitor for these and other potential new side effects that could be experienced in these patients. Clinical trials are an important mechanism for establishing an appropriate dose, defining safety, and ensuring activity against a cancer. Before ketogenic diets can be considered for brain tumor patients, results of these clinical trials are needed.

In conclusion, brain tumors are a new disease for investigating a novel and exciting possible application of the ketogenic diet. There is a long history of safety, tolerability, and effectiveness in treating epilepsy with this therapy. There is also extensive preclinical data that support dietary and nondietary approaches to targeting cancer's "addiction" to glucose. Brain tumors may offer a particularly ideal cancer to initially study. In fact, clinical trials are underway and will seek to define a sufficient dose and duration of treatment, evaluate for markers of whether the diet is working, ensure safety of the diet in this new population, and explore its effectiveness in managing brain tumors.

CHAPTER 35

Diet and Dementia

This chapter was written by Jason Brandt, PhD, Johns Hopkins University School of Medicine, Baltimore, Maryland.

Dementia refers to a loss of previously normal memory and other cognitive (thinking) abilities due to brain dysfunction. Persons with dementia have a normal state of consciousness (in other words, they are alert), but they typically have impairments in language, spatial skills, reasoning, and problem solving, in addition to severe difficulty learning and remembering new things. These cognitive impairments are severe enough to interfere with everyday life. In addition, many patients with dementia experience emotional disorders, personality changes, and problematic behavioral symptoms.

Dementia can be caused by many different conditions (such as severe head trauma, strokes, and degenerative diseases) and can occur at any age. However, it is most common in the elderly, where Alzheimer's disease (AD) is the most frequent cause. Approximately two out of every three cases of dementia in a person over age 65 are due to AD. AD is a progressive brain disease and, while there are symptomatic treatments that are mildly effective, there is no cure for this devastating disorder. It is estimated that there are over 5 million people in the United States with AD or a closely related condition, and over 45 million worldwide.

Physicians and scientists have studied whether diet plays a role in determining who gets AD and whether changes in diet may be useful in treating some of the symptoms. The research done so far has been focused on four major areas: *individual nutrients, specific foods, dietary supplements*, and *special diets*.

INDIVIDUAL NUTRIENTS

The nutrients that have received the greatest interest are compounds that have *antioxidant* properties. Exactly what this means requires a bit of explanation: As a result of normal metabolic processes, the body produces oxygen atoms with unpaired electrons. These are known as oxygen "free radicals" and are highly unstable elements. They are damaging to healthy cells, especially cell membranes. Antioxidants are compounds that act as free radical "scavengers." They neutralize free radicals, and thereby protect tissues.

There is good evidence that damage to brain cells caused by free radicals plays a role in age-related cognitive disorders, including AD. This suggests that eating a diet high in antioxidant compounds would be beneficial. In fact, this appears to be the case.

One of the most potent antioxidants is vitamin E, also known as tocopherol. Several studies have shown that consuming the "alpha" form of tocopherol, either in foods or in supplements, is associated with a lower risk of developing AD. Coenzyme Q10 is a compound that works together with vitamin E to protect cell membranes from attack by free radicals. Vitamin C also has significant antioxidant properties.

Flavonoids are a subset of antioxidant compounds that are plentiful in fruits, vegetables, spices, herbs, red wine, and tea. In general, foods that are high in flavonoids are vibrantly colored: berries, grapes, apples, dark chocolate, parsley, and kale are some prominent examples. Some nutritionists recommend that your dinner plate resemble a painter's palette, with lots of different bright colors!

Another category of nutrient that may be protective against AD is the Omega-3 polyunsaturated fatty acids (PUFAs). These are "good" fats that our bodies need but cannot manufacture. Two are found primarily in fish: docosahexaenoic acid (DHA) and eicosapentaenoic acid (EPA). The third, alpha-linolenic acid (ALA), is found in plant foods, especially nut, seed, and olive oils. Of these, DHA appears to be the most important. It is a primary component of nerve cell membranes, and is most plentiful in the most metabolically active parts of the brain. Laboratory animals fed diets high in Omega-3 fatty acids showed increased levels of important neurotransmitters and growth of neurons in the hippocampus (a region critical for memory). Moreover, they demonstrated improved learning and memory compared to animals fed a conventional diet.

SPECIFIC FOODS

We have already mentioned several specific foods that are high in key nutrients that support brain health. Blueberries, cranberries, blackberries, raspberries, and strawberries are all exceptionally high in antioxidants. Small red beans, kidney beans, and pinto beans are also among the most antioxidant of foods. So, "beans and berries" should be your mantra if you want to eat foods high in antioxidants! Apples and plums are in this category as well.

We have also mentioned fish as a major source of Omega-3 PUFAs. Several studies have shown that dietary intake of fatty fish (especially mackerel, lake trout, sardines, herring, halibut, striped bass, cod, and salmon)—the largest dietary source of DHA—is associated with a lower risk for dementia. Some studies have found that eating oily fish two or more times a week was associated with an approximate 30% reduction in the risk of developing AD.

Olive oil and coconut oil are medium chain triglycerides that are metabolized in the liver to form ketone bodies. These fats are crucial elements of the ketogenic diet and its variations (including the Atkins diet) that are discussed in great detail in other chapters of this book. Their potential role in the treatment of dementia is discussed later in this chapter.

When it comes to drinks that might be protective against dementia, the "adult beverages" are in! We have already mentioned the neuroprotective benefit of red wine; it is high in flavonoid antioxidants and contains resveratrol (found in grape skins), a compound that has been touted for its antiaging properties. However, it is still not clear whether the protective effect of alcohol is limited to just wine or applies equally to all alcoholic beverages. What *is* clear is that, when it comes to alcohol and brain health, *more* is *not* better! Multiple epidemiological studies (surveys of large populations) demonstrate that one standard-size alcoholic drink per day (e.g., 12 oz of beer, 5 oz of wine, or 1.5 oz of liquor) confers some protection against dementia, but more than this is probably harmful. Of course, people with health problems or taking medications that preclude drinking alcohol should abstain entirely.

Coffee and tea are among the most popular beverages in the world, and are often enjoyed for their effects on alertness. Both beverages, but especially coffee, contain caffeine, a compound that blocks binding to the adenosine receptors in the brain. This wards off sleepiness and increases the activity of other neurotransmitters responsible for mental functioning. Several multicenter studies, with thousands of participants, have shown that older adults who consume the equivalent of three or more cups of coffee a day experience less cognitive decline, and have a lower incidence of dementia, than those who abstain from caffeine.

DIETARY SUPPLEMENTS

In general, getting proper nutrition from fresh, wholesome foods is preferred to taking nutritional supplements in pill form. Nonetheless, many Americans take supplements to improve their health or to protect themselves against age-related disorders, including dementia. Among the most popular supplements is fish oil, known to be high in Omega-3 PUFAs. While some research has shown that taking a DHA supplement results in improved learning and memory in normal older adults, studies of patients with established AD find no benefit from fish oil supplements.

Another popular supplement is the antioxidant, vitamin E. The research conducted to date remains inconclusive as to whether taking vitamin E supplements reduces one's risk of developing AD. Once again, among patients with established AD, vitamin E has no effect on rate of progression.

While fish oil and vitamin E are both found in normal diets, *ginkgo biloba* is not. Ginkgo, a compound derived from the leaves of the maidenhair tree, has been used for centuries in traditional Chinese medicine. In the West, it has become very popular as a cognitive enhancer. However, the most scientifically rigorous studies have shown that it is no better than placebo in its effects on learning, memory, attention, concentration, or language skills. Furthermore, the studies published so far provide no support for its protective effect against AD.

SPECIAL DIETS

The most common dietary recommendation for the prevention of AD is to eat a "heart-healthy" diet. This is based on the widely held belief that what is good for the heart (especially the coronary arteries) is good for the brain. As a result, diets that are low in cholesterol and saturated fats have long been recommended. Epidemiological studies have in fact shown that high-cholesterol levels in the blood in midlife are associated with increased risk for developing AD in late life. This has been confirmed in experimental studies as well. In mice that have been genetically modified to accumulate toxic beta-amyloid protein in their brains and develop a syndrome akin to AD, a high-fat and high-cholesterol diet produced greater impairments in learning and memory and more severe death of brain cells.

A widely publicized version of the heart-healthy diet is the so-called "Mediterranean diet." Taking a lead from the traditional diets of Greece, Italy, and surrounding Mediterranean nations, this diet is based largely on fish, fresh fruits and vegetables, legumes, cereals, nuts, and seeds, as well as olive oil and polyunsaturated fats from nut and seed oils. Only very small amounts of meat, saturated fats, and dairy products are allowed. Low to moderate amounts of wine are permitted as well. Many well-conducted epidemiological studies have found that elders whose eating habits conform closely to the Mediterranean diet have a much lower risk of developing "mild cognitive impairment" or frank dementia than those whose diets are least Mediterranean-like. Among patients who already have AD, adhering to a Mediterranean diet resulted in longer survival.

Very recently, the MIND diet (Mediterranean-DASH Intervention for Neurodegenerative Delay) was reported to be associated with reduced incidence of AD. This diet combines features of the dietary approach to stopping hypertension (DASH) diet and the Mediterranean diet. This newly created diet is simple to follow, as it consists solely of eating from 10 "brain-healthy" food groups (green leafy vegetables, other vegetables, nuts, berries, beans, whole grains, fish, poultry, olive oil, and wine) and avoiding five unhealthy food groups (red meats, butter and stick margarine, cheese, pastries and sweets, and fried or fast foods). Berries, in particular blueberries and strawberries, are encouraged for their benefit to brain health. Research has shown that close adherence to either the Mediterranean diet, the DASH diet, or the MIND diet is associated with a reduced risk for AD. However, only the MIND diet appeared to be beneficial if adherence is only moderate.

Note that these uncontrolled population studies reveal only associations; no cause-and-effect relationship can be inferred. For that, randomized, controlled, clinical trials are needed. Such studies of the Mediterranean diet are ongoing.

A distinctly different approach to the dietary prevention and management of AD are diets that are very low in carbohydrates (sugars and starches). It is well established that AD is associated with diabetes and insulin resistance more generally. Therefore, glucose, the basic sugar that typically fuels the cells in our body, is not metabolized normally in this illness. In fact, abnormalities in the brain's use of glucose can be observed with brain PET scanning, even before clinical symptoms of AD are apparent. In patients with established AD dementia, the severity of cognitive impairment is strongly correlated with the decrease in glucose uptake. Ketone bodies, the products of fat metabolism, can serve as a "backup" fuel when glucose is unavailable. Ketone body metabolism appears to bypass the metabolic processes that are abnormal in AD and provide better nourishment for neurons. As a result, ketone body metabolism may slow cognitive decline or even improve cognition in patients with AD. This suggests that low-carb, high-fat diets, such as the Modified Adkins Diet, may be beneficial to delay the onset or progression of AD. Research on this possibility is currently ongoing.

Recently, several "medical foods" for AD have been developed and are being marketed. These include ketogenic agents, such as Axona® (Accera, Inc.) and combinations of cell membrane-supporting nutrients, such as Souvenaid® (Nutricia N.V.). Research on these putatively therapeutic food products is in the early days, but some promising results have been reported. Any supplement should be taken only with doctor supervision.

CONCLUSIONS

Of the 413 clinical trials of new medications for AD that were conducted between 2002 and 2012, 99.6% were failures as reported in one study that reviewed them. Given the growing prevalence of this disease, and the toll it takes on patients, families, and society, the development of alternative approaches to treatment and prevention is essential. The possibility that changes in what we eat and drink might alter risk for this illness or rate of its progression is one that we cannot afford to ignore.

CHAPTER 36

Autism and the Diet

What value does the ketogenic diet have in improvement of some of the more troubling behaviors seen in children with autism? Although this is a relatively new idea (and the first time we've had a chapter specifically on this in this book), the history of the diet and autism goes back several decades. Even in the earliest papers written on the diet in the 1920s and 1930s, patients with intellectual disability were described as "brighter" and "more alert" with the use of the ketogenic diet. This was the case even when seizures were only minimally better! Of course, it's very difficult to determine how much of the improvement in behavior in a child on the diet is from (a) the diet, (b) reducing medication, and (c) seizures decreasing. Even today this is still difficult to decipher.

The first paper to formally look at effects on behavior from the diet was from Dr. Margaret Pulsifer when she was working at Johns Hopkins with our group. In this 2001 paper, 65 children were treated with the ketogenic diet, with about half having seizure reduction. What was really interesting was that there were significant improvements in attention and social skills beyond which could be explained by the reduction in seizures. Other studies, including for Rett syndrome, showed improvements in behavior beyond just the seizure reduction.

Perhaps the true first paper to examine the diet for autism came from Dr. Athanasis Evangeliou from Greece and was published in the *Journal of Child Neurology* in 2003. In this study, Dr. Evangeliou tried the medium-chain triglyceride (MCT) ketogenic diet in 30 children with autism, aged 3 to 10 years, without epilepsy. Interestingly, they used the diet for 6 months but with 2-week periods off the diet (and 4 weeks on)—a great idea to maintain compliance. Eighteen children made it through the 6 months, and of those, two had dramatic improvement (both were boys), eight had modest improvement, and eight had minimal improvement. Interestingly as well, those who had the most improvement started on the milder end of autism. Although preliminary, it showed the diet may have a role for autism.

Since then, there have not been any formal published studies using the ketogenic diet for autism in children. Two papers in 2013 and 2014 have shown improvement in mice that have been made to have features of autism. In the most recent study (by Ahn and others in the journal *Developmental Neuroscience*), problems in mitochondria (the energy producing parts of the cell) in these mice with autism were reversed by using the ketogenic diet.

This is not to say that there isn't definite interest in studying it more for children. A lecture by Dr. Julie Buckley at the 2012 Ketogenic Diet Conference in Chicago was focused on using the diet in autism. Dr. Buckley talked about her own daughter with autism and how incredible the ketogenic diet was in radically improving her behavior when seizures and autistic features were out of control at puberty. Both her IQ and CARS (Childhood Autism Rating Scale) improved, as did her electroencephalogram (EEG). After her lecture, there was a fair amount of discussion among other physicians who had anecdotally seen similar results.

So why would the ketogenic diet help? There are *many* theories. First, perhaps ketones are acting as a neurologic drug, and we know many of our neurologic drugs have beneficial psychiatric effects. The diet has also been proposed as anti-inflammatory, and many people believe that the roots of autism may be in inflammation (or a reaction to some environmental trigger in combination with genetics). Additionally, by its nature, the ketogenic diet is mostly gluten-free, and gluten-free diets continue to be highly used by families of children with autism. Some children with autism have been found to have (possibly) incidental spikes on EEG; maybe the diet would help "quiet" down those spikes and thus improve behaviors. Another possibility is that the inherent nature of the ketogenic diet, with set meals, recipes, and times of day to eat may introduce a strict diet regimen that would appeal to a child with autism who strives for regularity and routine. Would a regular diet, calculated to the gram and given at set times of the day, be similarly successful? Perhaps.

On a practical level, to our knowledge at this time, there are no formal clinical trials studying the use of dietary therapy for autism. We are certainly willing at Johns Hopkins to start the diet in a child with autism and epilepsy, but autism alone is much trickier. The classic ketogenic diet with an admission period would unlikely be approved by insurance without the child having seizures: We have never tried, but predict this would be the case. If you as a parent are thinking about this approach for your child with autism but not epilepsy, it would probably have to be the modified Atkins diet or low glycemic index treatment, and with the help of a dietitian familiar with these treatments. Any supplements, probiotics, oils, or other foods would have to be changed to low carb. We would also strongly advise making sure your child's autism specialist is involved and set goals (perhaps 6 months using a behavioral scale) determined beforehand.

As interest in this idea grows, we expect by the next edition of this book that there will be more research to discuss about how well the diet works and how best to use it for autism. In the meantime, follow this emerging field on the Internet and at ketogenic diet conferences worldwide.

CHAPTER 37

Diet and Migraine: Fact and Fiction

This chapter was written by B. Lee Peterlin, MD, Johns Hopkins University School of Medicine, Department of Neurology, Baltimore, Maryland.

Migraine is a common and largely inherited brain disorder. It affects 10% to 15% of the population around the world. In the United States alone it has been estimated that this equates to 30 million people. Although death is not an immediate consequence, and overall health and survival rates are not meaningfully decreased in those with migraine, there is no doubt migraine can be a very disabling disorder. In the Global Burden of Disease study, the World Health Organization ranked severe migraine as more disabling that angina, rheumatoid arthritis, depression, and even blindness and paraplegia.

If you have trouble believing this, I suspect you have never experienced a severe migraine. Let me describe an attack for you. You wake up and you feel a not unfamiliar pressure in your head and a feeling of dread begins. You have experienced this before and this is not the worst it gets. You get up, ignore the pain, and begin to get ready for the day. However while you are doing this, the pain is increasing—to the point that you feel someone is pounding an anvil from behind your eye. Now the lights hurt as you try to brush your hair on your tender scalp. The nausea begins to swirl in your stomach. You take an Aleve; and go to work as you have an important presentation to give in front of your boss. At work 1 hour later the pounding persists and while you are giving the presentation (the one you have practiced five times before without a hitch), you no longer can remember exactly what you wanted to say. Some words escape you, and you feel like you are in a bit of a haze. You get something out, but you are definitely not doing your best. Somehow you get through it, but then the nausea begins to escalate. You spend the next 20 minutes retching in the bathroom at work. When this is done you are actually grateful, as you feel better. You still feel wiped out, but the pain has started to decrease, and your thinking is improving. Four hours later no one would suspect there was ever a problem. You are back to yourself. Repeat once a month . . . or once a week . . . or worse.

As with epilepsy, while the full cause of migraine is not yet known, the current understanding is that there are changes in the excitability of the brain in those with migraine. These changes in the brain's excitability are associated with changes in the response of blood vessels of the brain as well as in the secretion and production of a variety of inflammatory proteins that are circulating in the blood.

One of the parts of the brain that is involved in migraine is called the hypothalamus. This part of the brain controls circadian rhythms such as when to go to sleep, when to awake, as well as changes in mood, thirst, food cravings, and even the drive to eat or not to eat.

Those with migraine often have certain triggers that can make them more likely to have an attack—such as stress, weather changes, not getting enough sleep, missing a meal. It is also important to realize that migraine triggers are not the cause of migraine, nor are triggers the same for all those with migraine. They simply are things that make someone with the predisposition to having migraine attacks more likely to have an attack. In people without the susceptibility to migraines, they will not trigger a migraine. For example, everyone has stress, but not everyone has a migraine attack that results from stress.

So how can we treat migraine? One important part of treatment is to identify possible triggers and manage (and by "manage" headache doctors generally mean avoid) those triggers that are possible to manage. Long before there were pills to decrease migraine pain, doctors recognized that missing meals and certain foods could trigger a migraine attack. In fact, missing a meal or fasting is a very common migraine trigger. In one study by Dr. Les Kellman, fasting, as a migraine trigger, was second only to stress in men, and was the third most common trigger in women (after stress and their period). Specifically in Dr. Kellman's study, of the 76% of migraine patients with identifiable triggers, stress was a trigger in 80%, menses in 65%, fasting in 57%, sleep changes in 50%, and food triggers in only 27%—a number that is not negligible but also not excessively impressive.

More recently Dana Turner and colleagues looked at eating behaviors in a small group of migraine patients. They found that although eating an early morning breakfast or having a late dinner did not change your risk of having a migraine attack the next day, having a late night snack after your dinner *decreased* the risk of having a migraine the next day by 40% as compared to not eating one.

As a word of caution, if you decide to incorporate a late night snack into your regimen, make healthy food choices. Obesity is associated with an increased risk of both episodic and chronic migraine; and this risk increases with increasing obesity status.

Okay, so what about diets specifically? Physicians have been debating for over a century whether abnormalities in fat or protein metabolism contribute to migraine and whether changing your diet can treat migraines. If you want the short answer—we still aren't 100% sure. For the brave at heart, let's dive into the longer, more complicated answer.

In the mid-1920s some doctors advocated for removal of fats from migraine patients' diets, whereas others believed migraine was an inherited or acquired defect in protein metabolism. In more recent decades, these ideas are still being considered. Low fat, low protein, ketogenic (high protein, high fat, low carbohydrate) diets, and most recently diets that are high in Omega-3 and low in Omega-6 have all been evaluated as possible migraine or headache treatments. Many of these diet studies have been fraught with methodological limitations (unblinded, uncontrolled, presence of confounders) or just not found to be helpful once studied. However, we can glean some important information from these studies when examined together.

In 1928, two manuscripts discussed their experience with the ketogenic diet for migraine patients. These manuscripts were followed by a case series study conducted in 1930 by Clifford Barborka who evaluated the efficacy of the ketogenic diet in a group of women with episodic migraine. In this case series, women with episodic migraine were put on a ketogenic diet for 3 to 36 months. Dr. Barborka noted that the attacks of episodic migraine were controlled or improved in 78% (28% had their migraine controlled [approximately 1 headache per month or resolved], 50% had benefit [attacks less frequent]), whereas 22% had no benefit. He also noted that of those whose migraine was controlled on the ketogenic diet, most maintained constant ketosis. Of those with benefit, their migraines were controlled while in ketosis and when they broke their diet, migraines recurred. Of those who failed to improve, only two patients maintained constant ketosis. Formal statistical analyses were not done, however, and it is not clear what time frame was considered the baseline to the endpoint of the study or how migraine was defined or headache frequency evaluated. Additionally, specifics on the ketogenic diet he utilized were poorly described by today's standards, only noting that the diet was low in carbohydrates and produced ketosis. Additionally weight loss was not reported and it is difficult to determine if the improvements he found were from the diet per se or from weight loss. Nonetheless this was one of the earliest suggestions that a ketogenic diet may be beneficial to women with migraine.

Now let's fast forward to 2016. Recently researchers have reported on a study evaluating 96 overweight women, all with episodic migraine (i.e., headaches 5–6 days per month), who were enrolled in a diet study. One group of women with episodic migraines was put on a 1-month ketogenic diet followed by a 5-month standard low-calorie diet (n = 45). The second group with episodic migraines was given a 6-month standard low-calorie diet (n = 51). The ketogenic group received a 4-week low carbohydrate (~30 grams/day carbohydrates), low fat (15 grams lipids), and normal protein (1–1.4 grams/kg) diet of 800 kcal or less per day. This was followed by gradual reintroduction of carbohydrates in the next 8 weeks and then maintenance on the standard low-calorie diet for the final 3 months. Those on the standard low-calorie diet over the full 6 months received 1200 to 1500 kcal per day with 46% of total energy as carbohydrates, 24% as protein, and 30% as total fat. Those women in the ketogenic diet group had a reduction in headache frequency from five headache days per month at baseline to one headache day per month at the end of the first month while on the ketogenic diet. During this period the participants' body mass index (BMI) also dropped from 28 to 25. When those on the ketogenic diet transitioned to the standard low-calorie diet, the headache frequency went up to three headache days in the second month, but by the end of the entire 6 months (even after transitioning to a standard low-calorie diet) was still decreased at three headache days per month (from five headache days/month). In contrast to those on the ketogenic diet, those on the standard low-calorie diet for the full 6 months did not have a substantial reduction in monthly headache frequency in the first month of the diet; however, they did have a reduction in their headache frequency from 6 headache days per month at baseline to four headache days per month in the second and third months. This was reduced further to three headache days per month at the end of the 6 months. Notably by the end of the 6 month study, the participants' BMI was reduced from 28 to 22 in those with episodic migraines who were placed on the ketogenic diet, and from 28 to 24 in those with episodic migraines who were placed on the standard low-calorie diet. As with the earlier case series reported by Barborka, this study was not blinded and did not use a placebo control group. Although it is not possible to determine if it was the weight loss or the diet per se that resulted in the improvement of the headache frequency in those with episodic migraines, those in the ketogenic diet group had the greatest improvement in headache frequency in the first month when actually on the ketogenic diet.

Only one study to date has evaluated the use of a ketogenic diet in children and adolescents. Dr. Kossoff and colleagues evaluated eight children, 12 to 19 years of age, with refractory chronic daily headache, who were predominantly of normal weight, and placed them on a modified Atkins diet for 3 months. Carbohydrates were restricted to 15 grams/day. After 6 weeks participants were allowed to increase their carbohydrates to 20 grams/day. Weight loss occurred in five children; however, only two lost more than 2.4 pounds. Urinary ketosis was achieved in six of the children. However, none of the children had a reduction in their headache frequency, and only two had improvement in their headache severity.

One study has evaluated the use of a 12-week low-fat diet in a group of adult men and women with predominantly episodic migraine. Dietary fat was restricted to 20 grams/day. Additionally caffeine use was restricted during the study. A significant decrease in weight, along with headache frequency and headache severity, were found at the end of the study. As with other such dietary studies, this study was not blinded and confounded by the restriction of caffeine, which may have contributed to the improvement in headaches over the 12-week trial. Additionally it is difficult to determine if it was the weight loss or the dietary and caffeine restrictions that resulted in the improvements.

One other dietary study is of note. Chronic daily headache participants were randomized to a diet that was high in Omega-3 and low in Omega-6 (e.g., wild salmon, flaxseed) versus a diet low in Omega-6 (e.g., turkey) for 12 weeks as supervised by a nutritionist. All research personnel except for the nutritionist were blinded to the diet. Twenty-eight men and women completed each diet. Both diets showed a reduction in monthly headache frequency from a baseline of 23 headache days per month in both groups, to 15 headache days per month in those on the high Omega-3/low Omega-6 and to 19 headache days per month in those on the low-Omega-6 diet. The reduction was significantly greater in those on the high Omega-3/low-Omega-6 diet as compared to those on the low Omega-6 diet. Although the goal of this dietary intervention was not to lose weight and the results are exciting, BMI and weight were not reported. It is thus difficult to know for sure if weight loss contributed to the improvement in headache frequency or not. In any case, I am confident we will be learning more about the value of diets high in Omega-3 and low in Omega-6 for those with headache in the future.

In summary, as part of a medical community that once believed leeches were state-of-the-art medical therapy, I am very much aware that doctors and science are fallible. Data are subject to interpretation and change. An increasing amount of literature now exists on the impact of when, what, and how much to eat and this association with migraine and headaches. What we believe today may change tomorrow but let me summarize where we stand today in regard to this complex issue of diet and headache.

Triggers are not a cause of migraines. They activate an acute attack in those susceptible to having migraine attacks. Some foods may be migraine triggers but we are not sure which foods exactly are the culprit for everyone. The medical literature has not even established chocolate as a trigger for migraines. Eating chocolate may just be a craving that signals the start of a migraine before the pain begins. However, if you told me chocolate was a trigger for you, I'd still tell you not to eat chocolate for a month. If your headaches were better, then I would suggest you keep chocolate out of your diet as much as possible. Data support that red wine, processed meats with nitrates and nitrites, and perhaps foods with monosodium glutamate are migraine triggers. Many believe aged cheeses can be migraine triggers, although the data are not conclusive. In regard to food triggers, the best advice is: "If it hurts don't do it." Remove one food over a given time, such as 1 month, and reintroduce it later if you see no difference in your headaches.

The best advice in regard to diet and lifestyle for those with migraine is to not skip meals, exercise regularly, and maintain a healthy weight. If you want to consider a specific diet, the current evidence supports, but not does not prove, that a low-fat or ketogenic diet may improve episodic migraine in overweight adults. Additionally for those with chronic daily headache, a diet high in Omega-3 and low in Omega-6 may help. Whether it is the diet or the weight loss that is associated with these improvements remains to be determined.

If you have migraine, whatever you decide to do, talk with your doctor and nutritionist and get their advice. Never give up hope! Several research groups are studying diets for migraine. New information is being learned every year. Stay tuned. With science (as with growing old, at least according to Robert Browning), the best is yet to be.

SECTION IX

Appendices

APPENDIX A

Medications and Vitamins

MEDICATIONS

- Whenever possible, medications should be given in pill or capsule form, or be compounded into a "keto-friendly," carb-free solution.
- Compounding pharmacies can make sugar-free forms of some medications.
- As a general rule, avoid medications in syrup or elixir forms. Chewable (gummies) are also not great to use.
- Carbohydrates are frequently used as fillers and flavor enhancers in medications. Even small amounts of carbohydrate found in medications can sometimes affect seizure control on the diet.
- For the most part, we have stopped keeping a "list" of ideal or preferred medications. Especially for antiseizure drugs, there are so many generic formulations that this becomes impossible to keep up. Therefore, we suggest working closely with a good, small pharmacy where you know and trust the pharmacist and that can give you the medication that your child needs every month without fail.
- Ideally, the total carbohydrate content in medications should be less than 0.1 gram (or 100 mg) for the entire day. Anything higher should be calculated into the meal plan's daily carbohydrate allotment.
- Many over-the-counter and prescription medications are *not* available in sugar-free forms. (Some may be labeled "sugar-free" when they are very low in carbohydrate, but there still may be enough carbs to affect ketosis in your child.)
- If you are unsure about the contents of a medication you should call your pharmacy and explain the situation; they should be able to help.
- Sometimes intravenous forms of medication can be given by mouth. Talk to your doctor and pharmacist.

- As a last resort, if a medication with carbohydrates must be given, you can add a small amount of butter or oil to it to make it ketogenic. Talk to your neurologists or dietician for more information.
- Certain medications, such as antihistamines and antibiotics, can affect seizure control even if they do not contain carbohydrates.

Commonly Used Medications

- Feverall® suppositories (0 carb)—best option for fever, teething, headache, pain. You can buy them over the counter at a local drugstore
- Diastat® suppositories (no carb)
- Tylenol Junior Strength Caplets®—traces of carbohydrate, but less than 1 kcal per caplet, and young children may only need 1/2 of a tablet
- Miralax®—for constipation
- George's Aloe Vera®—for constipation (281-240-2563)
- Benefiber®—for constipation
- Polycitra K® and Bicitra®—for kidney stones
- Saline nose spray
- Vicks® Vapo Rub
- Original Neosporin® first aid ointment
- Desitin® ointment (original—not creamy)
- Genasyme® infant drops—saccharin-based simethecone drops for gas/bloating (like Mylicon® drops); made by Goldline/Ivax (800-327-4114 / 305-575-6000)

VITAMINS AND MINERALS

Frutivits™ (powder)

www.vitaflo.co.uk

Nano VM® 1–3 and 4–8 (powder)

www.solacenutrition.com

Phlexy Vits (powder)

Nutricia

Sugar-Free Bugs Bunny® or Scooby Doo®

www.oneaday.com

Calcium and Vitamin D

Nature Made (500 mgCa/400 IU Vit D)
www.naturemade.com

Nature's Bounty (500 mgCa/400 IU Vit D)
www.naturesbounty.com/

Centrum New Formula®
www.centrum.com

Flintstone Complete Chewable Multivitamin
www.flintstonesvitamins.com
Kirkman®—Childrens Multivitamin/Mineral—hypoallergenic

COMPOUNDING PHARMACIES

Professional Compounding Centers of America, Inc.
To find a compounding pharmacy near you call:
1-800-331-2498
www.pccarx.com
The following are compounding pharmacies that we have used:

H&B Drugs
North Arlington, NJ
Toll free 1-888-383-2010
Fax 201-997-8488
www.hbpharmacy.com/

Professional Arts Pharmacy
Baltimore, MD
1-800-832-9285
Fax 410-788-5686

APPENDIX B

Sample Letter of Medical Necessity for Ketogenic Diet Formulas

TO: ______________________

Case Review Services

Re: Ketogenic Diet Therapy

For: ______________________

DOB: ______________________

Attention Case Manager:

________________________________ is a _____-month-old boy/girl with a diagnosis of __________________________ and an intractable seizure disorder. (His/Her) seizures were occurring _____ times each day despite attempts at seizure control with ________________________________ (name anticonvulsants here).

The ketogenic diet is a high fat, adequate protein, low carbohydrate formula that is individually calculated and prescribed to produce adequate ketosis to suppress the child's seizures. The formula, which is fed by (bottle/gastrostomy tube), comprises __________________. The formula must be supplemented with multivitamins and minerals in order to be nutritionally complete.

We are requesting that, because these components constitute an antiepileptic therapy rather than just a nutritional formula, they be covered under your policies.

Thank you for helping ____________________________ to develop as free of seizures and medications as possible.

Sincerely,

____

APPENDIX C

Sample Letter for Airplanes

DATE:

To the TSA and Whom It May Concern:

_______________ is being treated for intractable seizures with a medically prescribed Ketogenic Diet. The Ketogenic Diet has been used for more then 90 years to treat epilepsy in children whose seizures are unable to be controlled with anticonvulsant medications or who experience ill effects from these medications. It is important that each component of this diet be carried out exactly as prescribed or the health and success of the child on the diet may be jeopardized.

_______________'s family needs to carry all components of the diet with them at all times, including on airplanes and through airports, which includes solid foods, powders, and fluids.

Feel free to contact me with any further questions.

Sincerely,

DOCTOR'S NAME

APPENDIX D

Keto-Friendly Products and Foods

This is a small list of items—always check with your keto team if a product can be used on the diet. Refer to the www.charliefoundation.org website for an updated list of approved products.

SUNSCREENS

Coppertone Sport®
Coppertone Oil Free®

LOTIONS

Johnson's Baby Oil®
Johnson's Soft Lotion®—24-hour moisture
Johnson's Creamy Baby Oil®
Curel® Lotion—original
Lubriderm Seriously Sensitive Lotion®
Nivea Body Original Lotion®

SHAMPOOS AND CONDITIONERS

Pantene Pro V Classic Clean Shampoo®
Pantene Pro V Classic Clean Conditioner®
Pantene Pro V 2 in 1—Shampoo plus Conditioner®
L'Oreal Kids Orange Mango Smoothie Shampoo®
L'Oreal Kids Grape Conditioner®
L'Oreal Kids Extra Gentle 2 in 1 Shampoo®—Burst of Watermelon
Johnson's No More Tangles Spray Detangler®
Baby Magic Gentle Hair and Body Wash®
Baby Magic Gentle Baby Shampoo®

BODY WASH/SOAPS

Dove Sensitive Skin Soap®
Dove Moisturizing Body Bar®
Dove Moisturizing Body Wash®—Sensitive Skin
Baby Magic Gentle Baby Bath®—Original Baby Scent

LIP CARE

Vaseline®
Chapstick® Cherry Lip Balm

TOOTHPASTE

Arm and Hammer Original Paste®—best choice
Arm and Hammer Advance White®—best choice
Tom's of Maine®—peppermint or spearmint paste (trace sorbitol)

BABY SUPPLIES

Baby Orajel Teething Swabs® (no sorbitol)
Desitin Ointment®—(original, not the creamy version)
Johnson's No More Tangles Spray Detangler®
Johnson's Baby Oil®
Johnson's Soft Lotion®—24-Hour Moisture
Johnson's Creamy Baby Oil®
Baby Magic Gentle Hair and Body Wash®
Baby Magic Gentle Baby Shampoo®
Baby Magic Moisturizing Baby Lotion®—powder scent
Baby Magic Gentle Baby Bath®—original baby scent

EXTRACTS

McCormick®—Pure Almond, Pure Lemon, Pure Orange, Pure Peppermint, Pure Anise
Bickford®—This company makes many keto-friendly extracts, including vanilla. Their number is included on your phone number list. When you call them to order, tell them that you are looking for pure extracts with no carbohydrate added.

SWEETENERS

Liquid Sweet'N Low®
Liquid Sweet 10®

Saccharin grains—but you must dissolve them in hot water prior to adding to foods/drinks!
Stevia® Pure Extract (liquid)—can be ordered via the Internet
Don't use large quantities of powder forms of sweeteners, because they contain carbohydrates!

FOODS AND PRODUCTS USED OFTEN

KetoCuisine™

A 5:1 ready to use baking mix
www.ketocuisine.com

Keto Vie Café-Wholesome Bread

3.5:1 individually packaged bread
www.cambrooketherapeutics.com/products/ketogenic/ketovie-cafe/wholesome-bread/

Miracle Noodles®

www.miraclenoodle.com

Konjac Shiratake®

www.konjacfoods.com

Walden Farms

www.waldenfarms.com

Bob's Red Mill

www.bobsredmill.com/

Bickford Laboratories, Inc. (Flavorings)

www.bickfordflavors.com

Canfield Diet Soda® (Diet Chocolate Fudge, Diet Cherry Chocolate, and Diet Swiss Crème)

www.amazon.com

Duke's Mayonnaise®

www.dukesmayo.com

Hawaiian Ice Sno Maker® (Sold at Target)

Just the Cheese™ (Baked Cheese Snacks)

www.specialcheese.com

DaVinci Gourmet: Sugar Free Syrups

www.davincigourmet.com

FORMULAS AND COMPONENTS

KetoCal® 3:1 and 4:1

Nutricia North America
800-365-7354
www.myketocal.com
A consent form is needed from the dietitian prior to ordering.

Keto Vie™ 4:1

Cambrooke Therapeutics
http://www.cambrooketherapeutics.com/products/ketogenic/

KetoVolve

MetaGenes
http://www.metagenes.co/main/product/ketovolve

RCF: Ross Carbohydrate Free®

Abbott Nutrition
http://abbottnutrition.com

Microlipid®

Nestle Nutrition
www.nestle-nutrition.com/products

SolCarb

Solace Nutrition
www.solacenutrition.com

PolyCal

Nutricia North America
www.nutricia.com

Liquigen Emulsified MCT Oil

Nutricia North America
www.nutricia.com

MCT Oil

1. Nestle Nutrition: www.nestle-nutrition.com
2. Sci Fit MCT Oil® (multiple websites)
3. Smart Basics MCT Oil®: http://www.vitacost.com/Smart-Basics-MCT-Oil

SCALES

Ohaus Corporation

1-800-526-0659
www.ohaus.com

American Weigh CD-V2 Compact Digital Scale

www.amazon.com

Smart Weigh ZIP300 Ultra Slim Digital Pocket Scale

www.amazon.com

Pelouze Scale Company

1-800-638-3722
www.healthometer.com

APPENDIX E

Wegmans' List of Foods

LOOKING FOR KETOGENIC DIET FOODS?

Seizures in children with epilepsy may be reduced through a carefully designed food plan called the ketogenic diet. Along with modified Atkins diets, the ketogenic diet has been a medically supervised treatment for seizures that has been in use for decades. Both diets are high in fat and low in carbohydrate, often with some calorie limitations. Balancing kids' food preferences with their growth needs is always a challenge. Any diet for neurological purposes should be done under the strict supervision of a neurologist and registered dietitian.

Typical supermarkets, like Wegmans, have so many products that it can be hard for families to know where to start. Our goal is to point out specific items that can "work" into the meals and snacks of these children.

High-fat foods, including oils, butter, soft cheese, heavy whipping cream, and mayonnaise, for example, help raise the body's ketone levels and likely are responsible for the diet's success. In this guide, we did not distinguish between saturated and unsaturated fats; your dietitian should help you with this topic.

Low-carb foods are typically less than 5 to 10 grams of carbohydrate (not including fiber, but often including sugar alcohols) per listed serving size. These are used occasionally on the ketogenic diet and freely with the modified Atkins diet. Too many carbohydrates can reduce ketosis and occasionally affect seizure control.

This information was developed through collaboration between Wegmans Supermarkets (Jane Andrews, MS, RD, and Hannah Kittrell) and Johns Hopkins Children's Center in Baltimore, Maryland (Eric Kossoff, MD, and Zahava Turner, RD). In addition, this information was reviewed by physicians and dietitians at the University of Rochester, Children's National Medical Center in Washington, DC, Boston Children's Hospital, and several parents in the Baltimore, Maryland, area.

KETOGENIC DIET SHOPPING LIST

		SERVING SIZE	NETCARBS (g): Total Carbs—Fiber	FAT (g)
Bakery				
Dips/Spreads	Rye Dip	2 tbsp (22 g)	<1	11
	Rye Dip with Meat	2 tbsp (22 g)	0	10
Baking	Wegmans Olive Oil, Extra Virgin	1 tbsp	0	14
	Wegmans Canola Oil	1 tbsp	0	14
	Wegmans Vegetable Oil	1 tbsp (14 g)	0	14
	Splenda Sweetener, No Calorie, Granulated	1 tsp	<1	0
	Arrowhead Mills Flax Seeds, Organic	3 tbsp	2	9
	SunSpire Unsweetened Carob Chips	2 tbsp	6	3.5
	Wegmans Food You Feel Good About Grapeseed Oil	1 tbsp (15 ml)	0	14
	Wegmans Food You Feel Good About Organic High Oleic Sunflower Oil	1 tbsp (15 ml)	0	14
	Olivado Oil, Avocado, Extra Virgin	1 tbsp	0	13.8
	Olivado Macadamia Oil	1 tsp	0	4.5
	Rumford Baking Powder, Aluminum-Free	0.125 tsp	0	0
	Wegmans Food You Feel Good About Pecans, Shelled	1/4 cup	1	20
	Pam Cooking Spray, No-Stick, Original	0.25-second spray	0	0
Beverages				
	Wegmans Food You Feel Good About Wonder Water	1 cup (8 fl oz)	0	0
	Nestle Pure Life Water Beverage	1 cup (8 fl oz)	0	0
	Fruit 2O	1 bottle	0	0

(continued)

		SERVING SIZE	NETCARBS (g): Total Carbs–Fiber	FAT (g)
	Wegmans Ginger Ale, Diet	1 cup (240 ml)	0	0
	Sprite Zero Soda, Lemon-Lime, Zero Calories	1 can	0	0
	Propel Zero Water Beverage, Nutrient Enhanced, Zero Calorie	1 cup (8 fl oz)	0	0
Bulk Foods				
	Bulk Hazelnuts	1/4 cup (28 g)	2	18
	Wonderful Pistachios, Roasted and Salted	1/2 cup with shells	5	14
	Sunflower Seeds, Roasted, Unsalted, No Shell	1/4 cup	1	17
	Walnuts, Chopped	1/4 cup	0	20
	Organic Hulled Sesame Seeds	1/4 cup (36 g)	0	20
	Pumpkin Seeds, Raw	1/4 cup	1	14
	Brazil Nuts	6 pieces	1	21
Cheese Shop				
Blue	Blue Stilton	1 oz (28 g)	0	10
	Castello Saga Classic Blue Brie	1 oz (28 g)	0	12
	Cambozola Triple Cream Blue	1 oz (28 g)	0	12
Cheese Spreads	Artichoke Asiago Spread	2 tbsp (30 g)	1	11
	Bacon Chive Cheese Spread	2 tbsp (30 g)	0	11
	Wegmans Buffalo Wing Cheddar Spread	2 tbsp (30 g)	1	11
	Wegmans Garlic and Herb Cheese Spread	2 tbsp (30 g)	1	10
	Leek Cheese Spread	2 tbsp (30 g)	2	9
	Peppadew Cheddar Cheese Spread	2 tbsp (30 g)	2	9
	Pimento Cheese Spread	2 tbsp (30 g)	0	11
	Spicy Garden Vegetable Spread	2 tbsp (30 g)	1	10
Cooked Pressed	Wegmans Medium Gruyere Cheese	1 oz (28 g)	0	9
	Jumi Belper Knolle	2.5 oz (71 g)	3	26

(continued)

		SERVING SIZE	NETCARBS (g): Total Carbs–Fiber	FAT (g)
Feta	Meredith Dairy Cheese, Marinated, Sheep and Goat Blend	1 oz (28 g)	0	14
	Mt. Vikos Barrel Aged Feta	1 oz (28 g)	1	7
	Woolwich Goat Feta	1 oz (28 g)	1	7
Fresh Unripened	Vermont Butter and Cheese Creamery Creme Fraiche	1 oz (28 g)	1	11
	Devon English Cream	1 oz (28 g)	<1	13
	Devon Clotted Cream	1 oz (28 g)	0	13
Goat	The Drunken Goat Semi-Soft Goat Cheese	1 oz (28 g)	<1	10
	Middlefield Goat Cheddar	1 oz (28 g)	0	9
	Vermont Creamery Double Cream Cremont	1 oz (28 g)	1	9
	Woolwich Triple Crème Goat Brie	1 oz (28 g)	1	9
Italian	BelGioioso Manteche Provolone	1 oz (28 g)	0	15
	Galbani Mascarpone	1 oz (28 g)	1	12
	Belgioioso Parmesan	1 oz (28 g)	0	7
Mousse, Terrines, and Pate	D'Artagnan Mousse of Foie Gras	2 oz (56 g)	2	20
	D'Artagnan Mousse Trufee	2 oz (57 g)	4	21
	D'Artagnan Peppercorn Mousse	2 oz (56 g)	3	20
	D'Artagnan Whole Foie Gras Torchon	2 oz (56 g)	1	33
	Trois Petits Cochons Rillettes De Canard	2 oz (56 g)	0	22
	Trois Petits Cochons Mini Mousse Champignon	2 oz (56 g)	2	19
	Trois Petits Cochons Pate Campagne	2 oz (56 g)	1	24
Processed and Fondue	Boursin Red Chili Pepper	2 tbsp (29 g)	1	13
	Boursin with Herb	2 tbsp (28 g)	1	12
	Boursin with Shallot and Chive	2 tbsp (28 g)	1	12

(continued)

		SERVING SIZE	NETCARBS (g): Total Carbs–Fiber	FAT (g)
Soft Ripened and Washed Rind	Brillat Savarin	1 oz (28 g)	1	11
	Old Chatham Hudson Valley Camembert	1 oz (28 g)	0	10
	Wegmans Buttery Coulommiers	1 oz (28 g)	0	6
	Wegmans Buttery Brie, Medium	1 oz (28 g)	1	8
	Wegmans Milky Brie, Mild	1 oz (28 g)	0	9
	Wegmans Earthy Brie, Intense	1 oz (28 g)	1	8
	Wegmans Triple Creme Brie	1 oz (28 g)	1	11
	Champignon with Mushrooms	1 oz (28 g)	0	11
Uncooked Pressed	Kerrygold Skellig Cheddar	1 oz (28 g)	0	32
	Manchego	1 oz (30 g)	0	10
	Plain Havarti	1 oz (28 g)	0	11
	Wegmans Gouda–5 Year	1 oz (28 g)	0	11
	Wegmans Cheddar–Mild	1 oz (28 g)	1	12
Specialty Butter	Kerrygold Butter, Pure Irish	1 tbsp	0	11
Dairy				
	Wegmans Food You Feel Good About Large Eggs, Grade AA	1 egg (50 g)	1	4.5
	Wegmans Food You Feel Good About Sour Cream	2 tbsp (30 g)	1	5
	Wegmans Food You Feel Good About Almond Milk, Organic, Unsweetened	1 cup (340 ml)	1	3
	Wegmans Heavy Cream	1 tbsp (15 ml)	1	5
	Wegmans Original Cream Cheese	2 tbsp (30 g)	2	10
	Wegmans Butter, Sweet Cream, Salted or Unsalted	1 tbsp (14 g)	0	11
	Wegmans Italian Style Pepperoni	16 slices (30 g)	1	13
	So Delicious Coconut Milk, Unsweetened	1 cup	1	4.5

(continued)

	SERVING SIZE	NETCARBS (g): Total Carbs–Fiber	FAT (g)
Dannon Light and Fit Carb and Sugar Control Dairy Snack	1 container	3	3
Wegmans Organic Tofu	1/5 package (79 g)	<2	3
Wegmans Red Hot Dogs	1 link (57 g)	3	14
Wegmans Food You Feel Good About Hummus	2 tbsp (30 g)	4	4
Wegmans Food You Feel Good About Cottage Cheese, 4% Milkfat Minimum	1/2 cup (113 g)	5	5
Earth Balance Buttery Spread	1 tbsp	0	11
Jell-O Gelatin Dessert, Sugar Free	1 snack	0	0
Wegmans Margarine	1 tbsp (14 g)	0	11
Wegmans Food You Feel Good About Soymilk, Unsweetened	1 cup (240 ml)	3	4
Tumaros Low-In-Carb Wraps, Multigrain	1 wrap	4	2
Wegmans Sharp Cheddar Cheese, Shredded	1/4 cup (1 oz/28 g)	1	9
Wegmans Colby Jack Cheese, Shredded	1/4 cup (1 oz/28 g)	1	9
Wegmans Mexican Cheese, Fancy Shredded	1/4 cup (1 oz/28 g)	1	9
Wegmans Mozzarella Cheese, Whole Milk, Shredded	1/4 cup (1 oz/28 g)	1	7
Smart Balance Buttery Spread, Original	1 tbsp	0	9
Wegmans Food You Feel Good About Egg Whites, Liquid	1/4 cup	1	0
So Delicious Coconut Milk, Cultured, Unsweetened	4 oz	2	4
So Delicious Coconut Milk, Cultured, Vanilla, Unsweetened	4 oz	3	3.5

(continued)

		SERVING SIZE	NETCARBS (g): Total Carbs–Fiber	FAT (g)
	Oscar Mayer P3 Portable Protein Pack, Smoked Ham, Sharp Cheddar Cheese, Dry Roasted Almonds	1 package	3	10
	Oscar Mayer P3 Portable Protein Pack, Chicken Breast, Cheddar Cheese, Dry Roasted Peanuts	1 package	3	11
	Oscar Mayer P3 Portable Protein Pack, Turkey Breast, Cheddar Cheese, Dry Roasted Peanuts	1 package	2	11
	Oscar Mayer P3 Portable Protein Pack, Turkey Breast, Marbled Colby, and Monterey Jack Cheeses, Dry Roasted Almonds	1 package	2	11
	Wegmans Cheese, Mild Cheddar	1 inch cube (28 g)	0	9
	Blue Diamond Almond Breeze Almondmilk Coconutmilk Blend, Unsweetened	1 cup	0	3.5
Deli				
Bologna	Hofmann German Bologna	2 oz (56 g)	3	16
	Russer Wunderbar Bologna	2 oz (56 g)	3	14
	Zweigles Beef Bologna	2 oz (56 g)	2	16
Charcuterie	Panino–Jamon and Manchego	4 pieces (85 g)	2	19
	Panino–Prosciutto and Mozzarella	4 pieces (85 g)	2	19
	Panino-Salami and Mozzarella	4 pieces (85 g)	2	25
Chicken and Turkey	Carving Rotisserie Turkey Breast	2 oz (56 g)	0	3
Hots and Pepperoni	Hofmann German Red Hots	1 link (75 g)	1	20
	Hofmann White Hots	1 link (75 g)	6	21
	Margherita Stick Pepperoni	1 oz (28 g)	1	12
Liverwurst	Hatfield Liverwurst	2 oz (56 g)	3	16
	Smith's Braunschweiger	2 oz (56 g)	3	17

(continued)

		SERVING SIZE	NETCARBS (g): Total Carbs—Fiber	FAT (g)
Ham	Hormel Spiced Ham	2 oz (56 g)	1	11
	Hormel Chopped Ham	2 oz (56 g)	3	11
Hartmann's	Hartmann's Apple and Cinnamon Sausage	1 link (112 g)	2	19
	Hartmann's Apricot and Cranberry Sausage	1 link (112 g)	2	19
	Hartmann's Frankfurters	1 link (112 g)	1	21
	Hartmann's Hickory Smoked Bacon	2 oz (56 g)	0	26
	Hartmann's Knackwurst	1 link (112 g)	1	21
	Hartmann's Landjaeger	1 link (57 g)	1	20
	Hartmann's Smoked Hungarian Sausage	1 link (149 g)	0	25
	Hartmann's Bauernwurst	1 link (112 g)	1	21
	Hartmann's Smoked Chorizo Sausage	1 link (112 g)	2	20
	Hartmann's Smoked Kielbasa	1 link (112 g)	1	21
Salami Loaves	Battistoni Thuringer	2 oz (56 g)	1	16
	Hormel AC Thuringer Sausage	2 oz (56 g)	0	15
	Russer Olive Loaf	2 oz (56 g)	5	13
	Wegmans Italian Classics Salami, Genoa	1 oz (28 g)	0	6
Frozen Foods				
Frozen Veggies and Fruits	Wegmans Food You Feel Good About Just Picked Blackberries	1 cup (140 g)	15	0.5
	Wegmans Food You Feel Good About Just Picked Strawberries	1 cup (140 g)	10	0
	Wegmans Food You Feel Good About Just Picked Green Beans, Cut, Steamable	2/3 cup	5	0
	Wegmans Food You Feel Good About Just Picked Broccoli Cuts, Steamable	1 cup	2	0
	Wegmans Food You Feel Good About Just Picked Blueberries	1 cup (140 g)	13	1

(continued)

		SERVING SIZE	NETCARBS (g): Total Carbs–Fiber	FAT (g)
	Dole Cranberries, Whole	1/2 cup	4	0
Frozen Meals	Atkins Day Break Farmhouse-Style Sausage Scramble	1 bowl	5	29
	Atkins Chicken and Broccoli Alfredo	1 tray	5	20
	Atkins Chicken Pot Pie, Crustless	1 bowl	5	22
	Atkins Beef Merlot	1 tray	6	21
	Atkins Meatloaf, with Portobello Mushroom Gravy	1 tray	7	20
	Atkins Pasta Bake, Italian-Style	1 tray	7	21
	Atkins Swedish Meatballs	1 tray	6	25
	Atkins Bacon Scramble	1 bowl	5	28
Grocery				
	Wegmans Mayonnaise, Classic	1 tbsp	0	11
	Hormel Bacon Bits, Real	1 tbsp	0	1.5
	Herr's Pork Rinds, Original	0.5 oz	0	5
	Wegmans Italian Classics Basil Pesto Sauce	1/4 cup (60 g)	5	38
	Wegmans Food You Feel Good About Macadamia Nuts, Salted Dry Roasted	1/4 cup (28 g)	2	21
	Wegmans Food You Feel Good About Almonds, Raw	1/4 cup (28 g)	3	14
	Wegmans Food You Feel Good About Pecans, Shelled	1/4 cup (28 g)	1	20
	Wegmans Food You Feel Good About Peanut Butter, Natural, Organic, Creamy	2 tbsp (30 g)	4	16
	Wegmans Food You Feel Good About Almond Butter, Organic, Unsalted	2 tbsp (30 g)	5	18
	Wegmans Food You Feel Good About Tahini Butter, Organic	2 tbsp (30 g)	0	17
	Wegmans Yellow Mustard	1 tsp (5 g)	<1	0
	Wegmans Tomato Ketchup	1 tbsp	4	0

(continued)

	SERVING SIZE	NETCARBS (g): Total Carbs–Fiber	FAT (g)
Wegmans Italian Classics Capers	1 tsp	0	0
Wegmans Food You Feel Good About Prepared Horseradish	1 tsp	0	0
Bellino Sun Dried Tomatoes, in Pure Olive Oil	1 oz	1	19
Wegmans Kosher Dills, Whole	1 oz (about 3/4 pickle) (28 g)	1	0
Wegmans Kosher Dill Spears, Reduced Sodium	1 oz (about 1 spear) (28 g)	1	0
DeLallo Anchovies	4 pieces	0	2
Bumble Bee Premium Select Chub Mackerel	1/4 cup	0	4
Wegmans Food You Feel Good About Salsa	2 tbsp (31 g)	2	0
Season Sardines, in Pure Olive Oil	1 can drained	<1	17
Bumble Bee Wild Alaska Pink Salmon	2.2 oz	0	5
Wegmans Food You Feel Good About Sauerkraut	2 tbsp (30 g)	0	0
Wegmans Buffalo Style Wing Sauce	2 tbsp (30 g)	1 (<1 g Fiber)	3
Wegmans Dressing, Creamy Ranch	2 tbsp (30 g)	3	14
Wegmans Food You Feel Good About Dressing, Creamy Caesar	2 tbsp (28 g)	0	17
Wegmans Dressing, Blue Cheese	2 tbsp (30 ml)	2	14
Bertolli Sauce, Alfredo, with Aged Parmesan Cheese	1/4 cup	2	10
Wegmans Olives, Stuffed with Red Peppers	2 olives	0	1.5
Wegmans Olives, Stuffed with Garlic	2 olives	1	1.5
Wegmans Olives, Stuffed with Almonds	2 olives	1	2.5

(continued)

	SERVING SIZE	NETCARBS (g): Total Carbs–Fiber	FAT (g)
Wegmans Olives, Stuffed with Blue Cheese	2 olives	0	2.5
Wegmans Olives, Extra Large Ripe, Pitted	3 olives (14 g)	1	2.5
Purity Farms Clarified Butter, Ghee	1 tsp	0	5
Sunbutter Sunflower Seed Spread	2 tbsp (30 g)	3	16
MaraNatha Coconut Almond Butter	2 tbsp (30 g)	3	17
Wegmans Food You Feel Good About Cashew Butter	2 tbsp (30 g)	7	16
Wegmans Chicken Broth, Reduced Sodium	1 cup (236 g)	1	1.5
Matador Beef Jerky, Original	1 oz	6	1.5
Wegmans Triple Fruits Fruit Spread, Sugar Free	1 tbsp (16 g)	2	0
Wegmans Food You Feel Good About Cashews	1/4 cup (28 g)	7	13
Krinos Tahini, Ground Sesame Seeds	2 tbsp	2	23
Dukes Mayonnaise, Real	1 tbsp	0	12
Swiss Miss Hot Cocoa Mix, Diet	1 envelope	3	0
Starkist Tuna, Chunk Light, in Vegetable Oil	1/4 cup	0	4.5
Ortiz Bonito del Norte, in Olive Oil	1/4 cup	0	11
Lindt Excellence Dark Chocolate, Extra Dark, 85% Cocoa	4 squares	9	18
Bumble Bee Tuna, Premium, Solid White Albacore in Oil	1/4 cup	0	3
Hain Mayonnaise, Safflower	1 tbsp	0	11
Hain Safflower Oil	1 tbsp	0	14
Wegmans Food You Feel Good About Organic Greek Vinaigrette	2 tbsp (30 ml)	1	11
Spectrum Naturals Apricot Kernel Oil, Expeller Pressed	1 tbsp	0	14

(continued)

		SERVING SIZE	NETCARBS (g): Total Carbs–Fiber	FAT (g)
	Smart Balance Omega Oil, Natural Blend of Canola, Soy and Olive	1 tbsp	0	14
	Spectrum Oil Blend, Canola and Coconut, Expeller Pressed	1 tbsp	0	14
	Crystal Light Drink Mixes, Sugar Free, All Flavors	0.5 tsp	0	0
	Dole Peaches, Diced, Yellow Cling, No Sugar Added	1 container	6	0
	Bumble Bee Tuna, Albacore with Jalapenos and Olive Oil	2 oz drained	0	9
	Nuco Premium Liquid Coconut Oil, Original	1 tbsp	0	14
	Wegmans Food You Feel Good About Carrots, Sliced, No Salt Added	1/2 cup (120 g)	4	0
	Wegmans Food You Feel Good About Green Beans, Cut, No Salt Added	1/2 cup	2	0
	Hunt's Tomato Sauce	1/4 cup	3	0
	Eden Organic Kidney Beans	1/2 cup	8	0
Health and Wellness				
	Nature Made Calcium Magnesium Zinc Tablets	1 tablet	0	0
	Wegmans Calcium, with Vitamin D	1 tablet	0	0
	Atkins Day Break Bar, Peanut Butter Fudge Crisp	1 bar	6	7
	Atkins Advantage Shakes, Any Flavor	1 shake (11 oz)	2	9
	Centrum Multivitamin Tablets	1 tablet	0	0
	NuNaturals Chocolate NuStevia	approx. 7 drops	0	0
	NuNaturals White Stevia Powder	1/4 tsp	<1	0

(continued)

		SERVING SIZE	NETCARBS (g): Total Carbs—Fiber	FAT (g)
International Foods				
	Kadoya Sesame Oil, Pure	1 tbsp	0	14
	Ortega Green Chiles	2 tbsp	1	0
	La Banderita Tortillas, Soft Taco, Low Carb	1 tortilla	5	2
	Wegmans Asian Classics Soy Sauce, Reduced Sodium	1 tbsp	2	0
Meat				
Beef	Wegmans Ribeye Steak	3 oz cooked (84 g)	0	20
	Wegmans 80% Lean Ground Beef	3 oz cooked (85 g)	0	14
	Wegmans Beef Rib Roast, USDA Choice	3 oz cooked (84 g)	0	21
Lamb	Wegmans Food You Feel Good About Lamb Roundbone Chops	3 oz cooked	0	8
Pork	Wegmans Boneless Center Cut Pork Chops	3 oz cooked	0	6
	Wegmans Bone-In Pork Shoulder Blade Steak	3 oz cooked (84 g)	0	12
	Wegmans Organic Food You Feel Good About Pork Back Rib	3 oz (85 g)	0	20
	Wegmans Breakfast Pork Sausage	2 pan fried links/1 patty (50 g)	<1	10
	Wegmans Bone-In Country Style Pork Ribs	3 oz cooked (84 g)	0	22
	Wegmans Bacon, Center Cut, Thick Slice	3 pan-fried slices	0	5
	Wegmans Food You Feel Good About Applewood Smoked, Uncured Pepper Bacon	2 slices	0	6

(continued)

		SERVING SIZE	NETCARBS (g): Total Carbs–Fiber	FAT (g)
Poultry	Wegmans Bone-In Chicken Thighs, with Skin	3 oz (84 g)	0	13
	Wegmans Chicken Wings, Family Pack	3 oz (84 g)	0	13
	Wegmans Fresh Chicken, Whole Fryer	3 oz cooked (84 g)	0	14
	Wegmans Boneless Chicken Breast Cutlet	3 oz cooked	0	0.5
Ready-to-Cook	Irradiated Jalapeno Cheddar Burger	1 burger, cooked (128 g)	1	23
	Irradiated Bacon Cheddar Burger	1 burger, cooked (113 g)	1	22
	Irradiated Blue Cheese Burger	1 burger, cooked (113 g)	0	21
	Basil Pesto-Panko Lamb Rack	3 oz cooked portion (85 g)	6	21
	Seasoned Strip Steak	1 strip steak, cooked (184 g)	0	32
	Spice Rubbed BBQ Pork Spareribs	1/14 spare-rib, cooked (85 g)	1	26
	Garlic Parmesan Topped Chicken Breast	1 breast, cooked (198 g)	8	28
	Lobster Stuffed Chicken Breast	1/2 stuffed breast, cooked (149 g)	6	28
	Feta and Pepper Stuffed Flank Steak	1 stuffed flank, cooked (198 g)	3	20
	Cheese and Herb Stuffed Flank Steak	1 stuffed flank, cooked (198 g)	1	25
	Artichoke Bruschetta Stuffed Chicken	1 stuffed breast, cooked (255 g)	9	25
	Roasted Italian Whole Fryer (Cook in Bag)	1/8 fryer, cooked (154 g)	1	23
Veal	Wegmans Veal for Stew	3 oz (84 g)	0	8
	Breast	3 oz (84 g)	0	8

(continued)

		SERVING SIZE	NETCARBS (g): Total Carbs–Fiber	FAT (g)
Mediterranean Olive Bar				
Antipasto	Bocconcini	1 each (50 g)	0	6
	Chopped Olive Tapenade	1/4 cup (40 g)	1	16
	Grilled Mushrooms and Red Pepper	1/2 cup (85 g)	3	11
	Green Pepper Shooters with Ham and Mozzarella	1 each (34 g)	2	11
	Provolini Antipasti	1/2 cup (83 g)	5	15
Dips and Spreads	Armanino Basil Pesto	1/4 cup (60 g)	1	19
	Artichoke and Asiago Dip	2 tbsp (30 g)	1	15
	Artichoke Lemon Pesto	1/4 cup (60 g)	3	18
	Baba Ghanouj	1/4 cup (60 g)	4	22
	Smoked Chipotle Lentil Hummus	1/4 cup (60 g)	5	10
	Tomato and Kalamata Bruschetta	1/2 cup (120 g)	6	16
Olives	Anchovy Stuffed Olives	1 olive (15 g)	0	7
	Feta Stuffed Olives	1 olive (17 g)	0	7
	Gorgonzola Stuffed Olives	1 olive (15 g)	0	7
	Greek Feta Salad	1/2 cup (85 g)	2	18
Nature's Marketplace				
	Carrington Farms Coconut Oil, 100% Organic, Extra Virgin	1 tbsp	0	14
	Wegmans Food You Feel Good About Just Tea, Green Jasmine	1 cup (240 ml)	0	0
	Spectrum Organic Coconut Oil, Refined	1 tbsp	0	14
	Spectrum Essentials Organic Flax Oil	1 tbsp	0	14
	Spectrum Naturals Almond Oil	1 tbsp	0	14
	Spectrum Walnut Oil, Expeller Pressed, Refined	1 tbsp	0	14

(continued)

		SERVING SIZE	NETCARBS (g): Total Carbs—Fiber	FAT (g)
	Spectrum Essentials Chia Seed, Omega-3 and Fiber	1 tbsp	0	4
	So Delicious Coconut Milk, Cultured, Unsweetened	4 oz	2	4
	Artisana Pecan Butter, Raw, 100% Organic	1 package	2	20
	Brown Cow Yogurt, Plain, Cream Top	1 container	9	7
	Maple Hill Creamery Yogurt, Creamline, Plain	1 container	8	7
	Bob's Red Mill Coconut Flakes, Unsweetened	1/4 cup	2	10
	Bob's Red Mill Organic Flax Seed Meal, Whole Ground	2 tbsp	0	4.5
	House Foods Tofu, Shirataki, Fettuccine and Spaghetti	4 oz	1	0.5
	Bob's Red Mill Hazelnut Meal/Flour	1/4 cup	2	17
	Bob's Red Mill Soy Flour	1/4 cup	5	6
	Bob's Red Mill Coconut Flour, High Fiber, Organic	2 tbsp	3	2
	Bob's Red Mill Hulled Hemp Seed	2 tbsp	1	6
	Bob's Red Mill Almond Meal/Flour	1/4 cup	3	14
Prepared Foods				
$6, $8, and $10 Meals	Grilled Lemon Garlic Chicken Breast (Homestyle Gravy), $6 Meal Entrée	8.5 oz (251 g)	5	18
	Italian Sausage with Peppers and Onions, $6 Meal Entrée	9.5 oz (263 g)	7	41
	Roasted Cauliflower with Parmigiano Reggiano, $6, $8, $10 Meal Side	4 oz (113 g)	2	9
	Roasted Vegetables, $6, $8, $10 Meal Side	4 oz (113 g)	5	7

(continued)

		SERVING SIZE	NETCARBS (g): Total Carbs–Fiber	FAT (g)
	Seasoned Broccoli, $6, $8, $10 Meal Side	4 oz (113 g)	2	8
	Seasoned Green Beans, $6, $8, $10 Meal Side	4 oz (113 g)	5	9
	Chicken Florentine (Lemon Butter Sauce), $8 Meal Entrée	10 oz (295 g)	7	34
Asian Bar	Szechuan Beef	4 oz (113 g)	6	10
	Chicken Makhani	4 oz (113 g)	3	11
	Lamb Roganjosh	4 oz (113 g)	2	14
	Salt and Pepper Squid	4 oz (113 g)	3	10
	Shrimp in Cream Sauce	4 oz (113 g)	9	34
	Paneer Makhani	4 oz (113 g)	5	27
	Spicy Ma Po Tofu	4 oz (113 g)	3	15
Fruit and Salad Bar	Bacon Bits	1 oz (28 g)	0	10
	Grilled Lemon Garlic Chicken Breast	4 oz (113 g)	1	12
	Guacamole	2 oz (57 g)	2	19
	Raw Cashews	1 oz (28 g)	8	13
	Sunflower Seeds	1 oz (28 g)	4	14
	Tamari Almonds	1 oz (28 g)	3	14
	Walnuts	1 oz (28 g)	2	18
Hot Homestyle Bar	Bronzed Chicken Thighs with Creole Sauce	4 oz (113 g)	2	12
	Bronzed Tilapia in Creole Sauce	1 piece (200 g)	4	14
	French Market Red Bean Sausage	2 oz (57 g)	2	16
	Pan-Seared Italian Sausage with Peppers, Onions, and Seasoned Tomatoes	9.5 oz (268 g)	7	41
	Roasted Chipotle Chicken	12 oz (350 g)	8	17
	Meatballs in Sauce	1 meatball with sauce	6	16

(continued)

		SERVING SIZE	NETCARBS (g): Total Carbs–Fiber	FAT (g)
	Autumn Roasted Vegetables	4 oz (113 g)	7	10
	Garlicky Greens	4 oz (113 g)	8	16
	Rappi with Pan Roasted Garlic	4 oz (113 g)	2	17
Hot Kettle Soup	Escarole, Bean, and Sausage Soup	12 oz (340 g)	9	11
Hot Wing Bar	Marzetti Blue Cheese Side Sauce (for calzones)	1.5 oz (43 g)	2	21
	Garlic Romano Chicken Wings	1 piece (42 g)	0	11
	Plain Chicken Wings	1 piece (33 g)	0	21
	Garlic Romano Chicken Fritters	1 piece (60 g)	8	15
	Mozzarella Sticks	1 stick (44 g)	8	13
Packaged Salads	Chef Salad	1 package, 12 oz (350 g)	6	9
	Sesame Ginger Dressing	2 oz (57 g)	8	13
	Caesar Dressing	2 oz (57 g)	5	10
	Balsamic Dressing	2 oz (57 g)	9	14
	Blue Cheese Yogurt Dressing	2 oz (57 g)	6	12
	Organic Blueberry Pomegranate Vinaigrette	2 oz (57 g)	6	21
	Tarragon Vinaigrette	2 oz (57 g)	4	15
	Curry Yogurt Dressing	2 oz (57 g)	6	12
	Ranch Yogurt Dressing	2 oz (57 g)	6	12
Pizza Dough and Toppings	Wegmans Sliced Pepperoni	1 oz (28 g)	1	12
	Spicy Small Cup Pepperoni	1 oz (28 g)	1	13
Rotisserie	Honey Brined Rotiesserie Chicken	3 oz (85 g)	0	8
	Honey Brined Turkey Breast	3 oz (85 g)	1	5
Service and Grain Salads	Curry Chicken	4 oz (113 g)	8	18
	Greek Feta and Peppers Salad	4 oz (113 g)	6	16
	Grilled Chicken Salad	4 oz (113 g)	2	24
	Homestyle Cole Slaw	4 oz (113 g)	8	25

(continued)

		SERVING SIZE	NETCARBS (g): Total Carbs–Fiber	FAT (g)
	Italian Antipasta Salad	4 oz (113 g)	4	25
	Six Bean Salad	4 oz (113 g)	9	10
Vegetables and Sides	Broccoli with Pesto	4 oz (113 g)	4	12
	Wegmans Egg Salad	4 oz (113 g)	1	28
	Green Bean, Mushroom, and Raw Cashew Salad	4 oz (113 g)	4	10
	Greek Goddess Yogurt Dip	4 oz (113 g)	5	23
	Green Beans Almondine	4 oz (113 g)	6	10
	Herb Baked Tofu	4 oz (113 g)	2	20
	Parmesan Florentine Cake	1 cake (3.5 oz)	3	12
	Shrimp, Asparagus and Walnut Salad	4 oz (113 g)	3	10
	Southwest Roasted Tofu	4 oz (113 g)	1	20
	Wegmans Tuna Salad	4 oz (113 g)	1	19
	Blue Cheese Wedge Salad	173 g	4	18
	Caprese Wedge Salad	177 g	3	16
	Summer Vegetable Crunch Salad	4 oz (113 g)	7	12
Vegetarian Bar–Cold	Caprese Salad	4 oz (113 g)	2	12
	Pesto Tofu	4 oz (113 g)	2	25
	Southwest Tofu and Black Bean Salad	4 oz (113 g)	4	16
Vegetarian Bar–Entrees	Chicken-less French	1 piece with sauce (165 g)	8	22
	Chicken-less Piccata	1 piece with sauce (167 g)	8	22
	Bruschetta Stuffed Portabellas	1 mushroom (168 g)	5	14
Vegetarian Bar–Hot	Indian "Squeaky Cheese" with Tomato Sauce (Paneer Makhani)	4 oz (113 g)	6	12
	Mushroom Flan	4 oz (113 g)	4	26
	Mushrooms Rockefeller	1 each (123 g)	7	20

(continued)

		SERVING SIZE	NETCARBS (g): Total Carbs–Fiber	FAT (g)
	Spinach and Feta Flan	1 each (152 g)	10	30
	Vegetable Samosa	1 each (152 g)	9	16
Produce				
Fruit	Hass Avocados	2 tbsp mashed, 1 ounce (28 g)	1	6
	Driscolls Blackberries	1 cup (144 g)	5	0.5
	Cantaloupe	1/4 medium, raw (4.8 oz)	11	0
	Guava	1 guava	2	0
	Homegrown Strawberries	8 medium, raw (5.3 oz)	1	0
	Wegmans Food You Feel Good About Watermelon Chunks	1 cup (140 g)	10	0
	Blueberries	1/2 cup	8.9	0
	Driscoll's Raspberries	1 cup (123 g)	5	0.7
Vegetables	Wegmans Food You Feel Good About Fresh Baby Spinach	4 cups	Cooked: 1.6 Raw: 1	0
	Seeded Cucumbers	1/3 medium cucumber	Raw: 1.6	0
	Lettuce, Red Leaf	2 cups, shredded	Raw: 1	0
	Large Celery	2 stalks	Cooked: 1.9 Raw: 2	0
	Wegmans Food You Feel Good About Cleaned and Cut Cauliflower Florets	3 oz (85 g)	Cooked: 1.7 Raw: 3	0
	Purple Eggplant	1 cup	Cooked: 5.1 Raw: 2	0.2
	Asparagus	5 spears	Cooked: 1.6 Raw: 2	0
	Beet Greens	1 cup	Cooked: 3.7 Raw: 0	0
	Endive	1 cup, chopped	Raw: 0	0
	Green Pepper	1 medium	Cooked: 5.5 Raw: 4	0

(continued)

	SERVING SIZE	NETCARBS (g): Total Carbs–Fiber	FAT (g)
Radish	3 oz	Raw: 2	0
Rhubarb	1 stalk	Raw: 1.4	0
Swiss Chard	2 cups, chopped	Cooked: 7 Raw: 2	0
Plum (Roma) Tomatoes	1 medium	Raw: 4	0
Turnips	1 cup, cubed	Cooked: 4.8 Raw: 6	0
Watercress	10 sprigs (25 g)	Raw: 0	0
Wegmans Food You Feel Good About Cleaned and Cut Broccoli Florets	3 oz (85 g)	Cooked: 3.3 Raw: 1.9	0.3
Brussel Sprouts	4 sprouts	Cooked: 3.8 Raw: 4	Cooked: 0.4 Raw: 0
Wegmans Food You Feel Good About Baby-Cut Carrots	9 carrots (85 g)	Cooked: 4.4 Raw: 6	0
Dandelion Greens	1-1/2 cup chopped, raw (85 g)	Cooked: 5.5 Raw: 5	Cooked: 0.9 Raw: 1
Green Beans	3/4 cup cut	Cooked: 4.4 Raw: 2	0
Kale	1-1/2 cups chopped	Cooked: 7 Raw: 0	Cooked: 0.8 Raw: 0.5
Wegmans Food You Feel Good About White Mushrooms, Sliced	3 oz (1 cup) (84 g)	Cooked: 4.8 Raw: 2	Cooked: 0.7 Raw: 0
Mustard Greens	1-1/2 cups chopped	Cooked: 0.21 Raw: 2	Cooked: 0.5 Raw: 0
Okra	6 pods (83 g)	Cooked: 1.8 Raw: 5	0
Wegmans Food You Feel Good About Cole Slaw, Cabbage and Carrots	1-1/2 cups (85 g)	3	0

(continued)

		SERVING SIZE	NETCARBS (g): Total Carbs–Fiber	FAT (g)
	Marzetti Dressing, Classic Ranch	2 tbsp	1	17
	Walden Farms Dressing, Any Flavor	2 tbsp	0	0
	Spaghetti Squash	1/2 cup	3	0
	Red Onion	1/2 cup (80 g)	6.1	0
Seafood				
Fresh	Wegmans Salmon, Atlantic, Farm Raised	4 oz (113 g) cooked	0	14
	Wegmans Food You Feel Good About Chilean Sea Bass, Wild Caught	4 oz (113 g) cooked	0	14
	Farm Raised King Salmon Fillet	3 oz cooked	0	10
	King Mackerel Fillet, Store Cut	3 oz cooked	0	15
	Fresh Yellow Fin Tuna Steak	3 oz cooked	0	1
	Wegmans Food You Feel Good About Farm Raised EZ-Peel Shrimp from Belize	3 oz	0	1
Ready-to-Cook	Bacon Wrapped Scallops	4 pieces, cooked (113 g)	2	17
	Bacon Wrapped Shrimp	4 pieces, cooked (113 g)	2	17
	Signature Crab Cake	1 cake, cooked (134 g)	7	29
	Lemon and Garlic Salmon Kabob	1 kabob, cooked (255 g)	5	31
	Salmon with BBQ Rub	1 fillet, cooked (138 g)	2	21
	Salmon with Lemon Pepper Marinade	1 fillet, cooked (150 g)	1	23
	Seasoned Bronzini	1/3 fish, cooked (104 g)	2	24
	Almond Crusted Salmon	1 fillet, cooked (170 g)	4	41
	Pesto Crusted Salmon	1 fillet, cooked (170 g)	2	27

(continued)

		SERVING SIZE	NETCARBS (g): Total Carbs–Fiber	FAT (g)
	Pistachio Crusted Salmon	1 fillet, cooked (170 g)	4	33
	Portabella Bruschetta Salmon	1 fillet, cooked (170 g)	6	28
	Crab Stuffed Salmon	1 stuffed fillet, cooked (227 g)	4	35
	Lobster Stuffed Salmon	1 stuffed fillet, cooked (198 g)	7	30
	Lobster Tail, Warm Water	1 full tail, cooked (170 g)	2	25
	Lobster Tail, Cold Water	1 full tail, cooked (142 g)	1	27
	Crab Dip with Jalapeno and Cheddar Cheese	1/3 cup (107 g)	3	32
	Lobster Dip with Peppers and Mozzarella Cheese	1/3 cup (109 g)	5	21
	Venetian Calamari Salad	1/2 cup (108 g)	3	21
Sushi				
	Wegmans Spicy Kampachi Skinny Roll	161 g	8	3
	Wegmans Rainbow Skinny Roll	123 g	5	8
	Wegmans California Skinny Roll	110 g	8	4.5
	Wegmans Tuna Tataki Sashimi Style	113 g	1	1
	Wegmans Sashimi Selection Large	227 g	1	12
	Wegmans Ahi Tuna Sashimi Style	170 g	0	1.5
	Wegmans Salmon Sashimi Style	170 g	0	22
	Wegmans Seared Tataki Albacore Sashimi	113 g	1	13
	Wegmans Seaweed Salad	85 g	4	4
	Spicy Sauce	57 g	4	30

APPENDIX F

Atkins Carbohydrate Gram Counter

The Atkins Carbohydrate Gram Counter is from *Dr. Atkins' New Diet Revolution 2002,* reproduced with permission of Atkins Nutritionals, Inc.

CARBOHYDRATE GRAM COUNTER

FOOD	CARBOHYDRATE GRAMS
MILK PRODUCTS	
Cream (light, 1 tbsp)	0.6
(sour, 2 tbsp)	1.0
(heavy, 1 tbsp)	0.5
Half and Half (1 tbsp)	0.7
Milk (whole, 1 cup)	11.0
(soy, unsweetened, 1 cup)	13.0
Plain Yogurt (skim, 1 cup)	13.0
(whole, 1 cup)	12.0
CHEESE	
American (1 oz)	0.5
Camembert (1 oz)	0.5
Cheddar (1 oz)	0.6
Cottage (fat-free, 1 cup)	10.0
(whole, 1 cup)	8.0
Cream Cheese (2 tbsp)	1.0
Feta (1 oz)	1.0
Muenster (1 oz)	1.0
Provolone (1 oz)	1.0
Swiss (1 oz)	0.5
NUTS	
Almond Paste (1 oz)	14.5
Almonds (1 oz)	5.5
Brazil (1 oz)	3.1
Cashews (1 oz)	8.3
Coconut (1 oz)	4.3
Hazelnuts (filberts) (1 oz)	4.7
Macadamia (1 oz)	4.5
Peanut Butter (1 tbsp)	3.0
Peanuts (1 oz)	5.4
Pecans (1 oz)	4.1
Pignolia (1 oz)	3.3
Pistachio (1 oz)	5.4
Pumpkin Seeds (1 oz)	4.2
Sesame Seeds (1 tbsp)	1.4
Soybeans (½ cup)	6.0
Sunflower Seeds (1 oz)	5.6
Walnuts (1 oz)	4.2
GRAINS	
Bagel (1)	30.0
Bread (pumpernickel, 1 slice)	17.0
(whole wheat, 1 slice)	11.0
Corn Muffin	20.0
Farina (1 cup)	22.0
Frozen Waffle	29.0
Noodles (1 cup cooked)	37.3
Oatmeal (1 cup cooked)	27.0
Pancake (using dry mix)	17.4
Popcorn (popped, 1 cup)	5.0
Rice (cooked, 1 cup)	49.6
(puffed, 1 cup)	11.5
SOUPS	
Chicken Consommé (1 cup)	1.9
Chicken Gumbo (1 cup)	7.4
Cream of Chicken (1 cup)	14.5
Cream of Mushroom (1 cup)	16.2
Turkey Rice (1 cup)	10.0
HERBS	
Allspice (1 tsp)	1.4
Basil (1 tsp)	0.9
Caraway (1 tsp)	1.1
Celery (1 tsp)	0.6
Cinnamon (1 tsp)	1.8
Coriander Leaf (1 tsp)	0.3
Dill Seed (1 tsp)	1.2
Garlic Clove (1)	0.9
Ginger Root (fresh, 1 oz)	3.6
(ground, 1 tsp)	1.3
Saffron (1 tsp)	0.5
Tarragon (1 tsp)	0.8
Thyme (1 tsp)	0.9
Vanilla (double strength, 1 tsp)	3.0
VEGETABLES	
Asparagus (4 spears)	2.2
Beans, green (boiled, 1 cup)	6.8
Beans, yellow or wax (boiled, 1 cup)	5.8
Broccoli (1 cup)	8.5
Brussels Sprouts (1 cup)	9.9
Cabbage (1 cup)	6.2
Carrot (7 in.)	7.0
Cauliflower (1 cup)	5.1
Celery (1 stalk)	1.6
Coleslaw (1 cup)	8.5
Collards (1 cup)	9.8
Corn (1 ear, 5 in.)	16.2
Cucumber (sliced, 1 cup)	3.6
Dandelion (1 cup)	6.7
Endive (1 cup)	2.1
Kale (1 cup)	6.7
Kohlrabi (1 cup)	8.7
Lettuce (Romaine, 1 cup)	1.9
(Boston, 1 cup)	1.4
(Iceberg, 1 cup)	1.6

FOOD	CARBOHYDRATE GRAMS
Mushrooms (1 cup)	3.1
Mustard Greens (1 cup)	5.6
Okra (1 cup)	9.6
Onion (1 cup)	14.8
Parsley (1 tbsp)	0.3
Parsnips (1 cup)	23.1
Peas (1 cup cooked)	19.4
Peppers (green, 1 cup)	7.2
(red, dried, 1 tsp)	1.4
Potato (baked, 1)	32.8
Potato Salad (1 cup)	33.5
Pumpkin (3½ oz)	7.0
Radish (large, 10)	2.9
Spinach (1 cup)	6.5
Squash (summer, 1 cup)	6.5
(winter, 1 cup)	25.5
Sweet Potato (baked, 1)	37.0
Tomato (raw, 2½ in.)	5.8
(cooked, 1 cup)	13.3
(juice, 1 cup)	10.4
Turnips (cooked, 1 cup)	11.3
(greens, 1 cup)	5.2

PROTEIN (FAT OR LEAN, WITHOUT BREADING)

Fish, Poultry, Meat, or Eggs	0-trace

FATS/OILS

Olive, Canola, Safflower, etc.	0-trace

BEANS

Black-eyed (1 cup)	38.0
Lima (1 cup)	33.7
Navy (1 cup)	40.3
Red Kidney (1 cup)	39.6
Soybeans (1 cup cooked)	19.4
Split Peas (1 cup)	41.6
Tofu/Bean Curd (2-in. cube)	2.9

FRUIT

Apple (1 medium, 2¾ in.)	20.0
Applesauce (unsweetened, 1 cup)	26.4
Apricots (fresh, 3)	13.7
Avocado (California)	13.0
(Florida)	27.0
Banana (1)	26.4
Blackberries (1 cup)	18.6
Blueberries (1 cup)	22.2
Cantaloupe (½ melon, 5 in.)	20.4
Cherries (1 cup)	20.4
Grapefruit (pink, ½)	10.3
Grapes (10)	9.0

FOOD	CARBOHYDRATE GRAMS
Honeydew (1 cup)	13.1
Kiwi (1 medium)	9.0
Lemon	6.0
Lemon Juice (1 cup)	19.5
Mango (1 cup)	27.7
Olive (green, pitted)	2.5
Orange (1 medium)	16.0
Papaya (1 medium)	30.4
Peach (2½ in.)	9.7
Pear (3½ in.)	31.0
Pineapple (1 cup)	21.2
Plum (1 medium)	17.8
Prunes (1)	5.6
Raspberries (1 cup)	21.0
Rhubarb (cooked w/sugar, 1 cup)	97.2
Strawberries (1 cup)	12.5

SAMPLES OF CARBOHYDRATE "FATTENING" ITEMS

Apple Pie (homemade, 1 slice)	61
Apple Turnover	30
Banana Split	91
Bean Burrito	48
Cheeseburger (¼ pounder)	33
Chicken Salad Sandwich	27
Cornbread Stuffing (½ cup)	69
Devil Dog	30
Egg Roll (1)	30
French Toast (2 slices)	34
Graham Crackers (1)	5
(chocolate covered, 1)	8
Hard Candy, Gumdrops, Jelly Beans (1 oz)	25
Honey (1 oz)	34
Hot Dog with Bun (1)	24
Ice Cream Soda (1 cup)	49
Macaroni with Cheese (1 cup)	40
Onion Rings (fast food order)	33
Peanut Brittle (1 oz)	23
Pecan Pie (homemade, 1 slice)	41
Pizza (1 slice)	24
Popsicle	17
Rolled Oats (1 cup cooked)	23
Saltines (1)	2
Shake (medium)	90
Sherbet (lemon, ½ cup)	45
Soda Crackers (1)	4
Tapioca, Cream (½ cup)	22
Toaster Pastry (frosted, blueberry)	34
Waffles (plain, homemade, 1)	28
Whaler	64
White Sugar (1 oz)	28

Courtesy of Atkins Nutritionals, Inc.

APPENDIX G

Physicians Providing the Ketogenic Diet Worldwide

Of note, this list was provided to me by child neurologists, parents, and dietitians and does not necessarily constitute endorsement of the particular ketogenic diet center. These sites are outside the United States as most major hospitals in the United States have a ketogenic diet center. This list is continuously updated at www.ilae.org/Commission/medther/keto-centers.cfm. Please ask your neurologist for more information!

NORTH AMERICA*

**For centers in the United States (too many to count!), please go to www.charliefoundation.org/resources-tools-home/resources-find-hospitals/united-states/united-states-list*

Drs. Peter and Carol Camfield
Dalhousie University and the IWK Health Centre
PO Box 9700, Halifax, Nova Scotia, Canada, B3K 6R8
Phone: 902-470-8479
Fax: 902-470-8486

Dr. Elizabeth J. Donner
Division of Neurology, The Hospital for Sick Children
Dept. of Neurology, 555 University Ave., Toronto, ON M5G 1X8, Canada
Phone: 416-813-7037
Fax: 416-813-6334
E-mail: elizabeth.donner@sickkids.ca

Dr. Kevin Farrell and Linda Huh
British Columbia Children's Hospital
4480 Oak Street, Room A303, Neurology, Vancouver, BC V6H 3V4, Canada
Phone: (604) 875-2121
Fax: (604) 875-2285
E-mail: kevin_farrell@telus.net

Drs. Daniel Keene and Sharon Whiting
Children's Hospital of Eastern Ontario
401 Smyth Rd, Ottawa, ON K1H 5L7, Canada
Phone: (613) 523-5140
Fax: (613) 523-2256
E-mail: dkeene@exchange.cheo.on.ca

Dr. Jeff Kobayashi
The Bloorview Macillan Children's Centre
25 Buchan Court, Toronto, ON M2J 4S9, Canada
Phone: (416) 425-6220 Ext. 6276
Fax: (416) 753-6046
E-mail: jkobayashi@bloorviewmacmillan.on.ca

Dr. Anne Lortie
Hospital St. Justine
3175 Cote-Ste-Catherine, Montreal, PQ H3T 1C5, Canada
Phone: (514) 345-4931
Fax: (514) 345-4787
E-mail: lortie.a@sympatico.ca

Dr. Richard Tang-Wai
Stollery Children's Hospital
8440-112 Street, Edmonton, Alberta, Canada T6G 2B7
Phone: 780-407-1083
E-mail: Richard.Tang-Wai@capitalhealth.ca

UNITED STATES

There are centers at most major hospitals.

CENTRAL AMERICA AND THE CARIBBEAN

Sixto Bogantes Ledezma, MD
National Children's Hospital
San José, Costa Rica
E-mail: sixtobogantes@gmail.com

Dr. Pedro Marrero Martinez
University Hospital Juan Manuel Marquez
Calle E N°517, Esquina a 23, Apartamento 11-D, Vedado-Plaza, Havana City, Cuba
Phone: 05-2435205
E-mail: dpduran@infomed.sld.cu

Dr. Chais Calaña Gonzalez, Espec. Nutrition
Pediatric Hospital
Havana City, Cuba
E-mail: chaiscala@infomed.sld.cu

Rocio Rivera, MSc, Nutricionista
Centro Integral de Nutricion
Calle Padres Aguillar No. 421, Colonia Escalon, San Salvador, El Salvador
Phone: 503-2263-4909
E-mail: rocioriverac@gmail.com

Dr. Marco T. Medina
Instituto de Neurociencias
Colonia Tepeyac, Calle Yoro, Edificio Mater Dei, Tegucigalpa, Honduras
E-mail: marcotmedina@yahoo.com

Drs. Deborah Varela and Beatriz Romo
Hospital Español de Mexico
Mexico City, Mexico
Phone: (525) 548-38
E-mail: Debbie.varela@mac.com
E-mail: draromo.neurodesarrollo@gmail.com

SOUTH AMERICA

Dr. Roberto Caraballo
Hospital de Pediatría "Prof Dr Juan P Garrahan,"
Combate de los Pozos 1881, C.P. 1245, Buenos Aires, Argentina
Phone: 5411-4943-6116
E-mail: rhcaraballo@arnet.com.ar

Dr. Maria Vaccarezza
Hospital Italiano
Buenos Aires, Argentina
E-mail: mmvaccarezza@gmail.com

Dr. Maria del Rosario
Hospital de Ninos
VJ Vilela, Rosario, Argentina
Phone: 54-341-480-8134
E-mail: mraldao@arnet.com.ar

Dr. Beatriz Gamboni
Hospital de Ninos
Humberto Notti, Mendoza, Argentina
Phone: 54-261-496-1365
E-mail: bgamboni@nysnet.com.ar

Dr. Semprino Marcos
Clinica San Lucas
Neuquen, Argentina
Phone: 54-299-443-4730
E-mail: marcossemprino@yahoo.com

Dr. Sarisjulis Nicolas
Hospital de Ninos
Sor Maria Ludovica, La Plata, Argentina
Phone: 54-221-427-5115
E-mail: saris@lpsat.com

Dr Marilisa Mantovani Guerreiro
Departamento de
Neurologia—FCM—Unicamp
Rua Tessália Vieira de Camargo, 126
13083-887 Campinas—SP, Brazil
Phone: (19) 3521-7372 (Dep. Neurologia)
Mobile: (19) 99793-9773
E-mail: mmg@fcm.unicamp.bronr

Laura M. F. Ferreira Guilhoto,
Neurologia Infantil
Mestre e Doutora em Medicina
(Neurologia) pela FMUSP
Av. Queiroz Filho, 1.700—Torre E—Cj.510
Alto de Pinheiros—05319-000,
São Paulo, SP, Brazil
Phone: 11-3642-1325
E-mail: lauragui@apm.org.br
Agendamento: 3082-0466/3064-4011

Dr. Ana Paula A. Hamad
CIREP—Centro de Cirurgia
de Epilepsia—HC
Faculdade de Medicina de
Ribeirão Preto—USP
Campus Universitário—
Monte Alegre—14048-900
Ribeirão Preto, SP,
São Paulo, SP, Brazil
Phone: 16-36022613
E-mail: anahamad@fmrp.usp.br

Dr. Letícia Brito Sampaio
Instituto da Criança do Hospital
das Clínicas—Faculdade
de Medicina da USP
Av. Dr Enéas de Carvalho Aguiar,
647, 05403-900 São Paulo, SP, Brazil
Phone: 55-11-2661-8673
Fax: 55-11-3069-8503
E-mail: leticia.sampaio@hc.fm.usp.br

Dr. Marcio M. Vasconcelos
Av. das Americas, 700 sl 229 bl 6
Universidad Federal Fluminese
22640-100 Rio de Janeiro—RJ, Brazil
Phone: (55-21) 2132-8080
E-mail: mmvascon@centroin.com.br

Dr. Ximena Raimann Tampier
and Dr. Francesca Solari
Clinicas Las Condes
Lo Fontecilla 441, Santiago, Chile
Phone: 56-2-6108000
E-mail: xraimann@mi.cl

Carlos Ernesto Bolaños Almeida
Neurologo Pediatra MD,
Medicina del sueño MsC
Profesor Universidad CES—Facultad
de Medicina—Departamento de
Pediatria Medellín, Colombia
CENPI centro de atención
Neuropediatria integral Carrera
48 B # 10 sur—76
Teléfono 574-2667354 o 574-2661321
E-mail: cebolanos@gmail.com

Dr. Luis Carlos Núñez López,
Pediatric Neurologist
Carrera 29 # 47-108, Edificio
Somes. Consultorio 20.
Bucaramanga, Colombia
Phone: 577 6475723
Fax: 577 6436124 Ext. 136
E-mail: lcnl007@intercable.net.co

Dr. Eugenia Espinosa
Hospital Militar Central
Bogota, Colombia
Phone: 0057-348-6868
E-mail: eugeniae@hotmail.com

Dr. Isaac Yepez
Hospital Pediatrico
"Dr. Roberto Gilbert E."
Guayaquil, Ecuador
Phone: 005934 2287572
E-mail: iyepez@intramed.net

Dr. Andrea Avellanal and Dr. Maren Torheim
Hospital Británico
Benito Nardone 2217, 11.300 Montevideo, Uruguay
Phone: 5982-711-91-86
E-mail: cinacina@adinet.com.uy

EUROPE

Eastern Europe

Dr. Artan Haruni
Poliklinica e
Specialeteve nr. 3 Tiranë
Tiranë, Albania
Phone: +355 (0) 68-20-66-561
E-mail: artanharuni@hotmail.com

Nina Barisic, MD, PhD, Professor of Pediatrics and Child Neurology
Department of Pediatrics, Division of Pediatric Neurology
Clinical Medical Center Zagreb
Zagreb Medical School
Rebro, Kispaticeva 12, Zagreb, Croatia
Phone: 00-385-1-23-88-531
Fax: 00-385-1-24-21-894
E-mail: nina.barisic@zg.htnet.hr

Dr. Vladimir Komarek
Charles University Prague, 2nd Medical School
Vuvalu 84, 150 06 Praha 5, Czech Republic
Phone: +420-2-2443-3302
Fax: +420-2-2443-3322
E-mail: Vladimir.komarek@lfmotol.cuni.cz

Dr. Ulvi Vaher
Children's Clinic of Tartu University Hospital, Department of Child Neurology
Lunini 6 51014 Tartu, Estonia
E-mail: ulvi.vaher@kliinikum.ee

Dr. Gia Melikishvili, Consultant Pediatric Neurologist
Children's Hospital
8 Lagidze Street, Tbilisi 0108, Georgia
Phone: 995 32 923429
E-mail: giam@caucasus.net

Dr. Athanasios Evangeliou
4th Pediatric Clinic of the Aristotelian University of Thessaloniki
Papageorgiou Hospital
Ring Road, TK 56403, Thessaloniki, Greece
Phone: +30-2310-693920
E-mail: aeevange@auth.gr

Dr. Argirios Dinopoulos
University of Athens, Attico University Hospital
Athens, Greece
Phone: +30 2105831269
Fax: +30 2105832229
E-mail: argidino@yahoo.com

Dr. Thanos Covanis
Neurology Department, The Children's Hospital "Agia Sophia"
Thivon and Levadis, 11527, Athens, Greece
Phone: +30 2107751637
E-mail: graaepil@otenet.gr

Dr. Minas Kapetanakis, Ped. Neurologist
Phone: +30 6974446553
Fax: +302106383073
E-mail: minas.kapetanakis@yahoo.com

Christina Kondyli, Clinical Nutritionist-Dietitian, RD
Iaso Pediatric Hospital
Kifisias Av. 37-39, PO Box 15123, Marousi, Athens, Greece
Phone: +30 6945564762
Fax: +302106383073
E-mail: christina.kondyli@gmail.com

Dr. Viktor Farkas
University Children's Hospital,
Semmelweis Medical School, Budapest
Bókay 53, H-1083 Budapest, Hungary
E-mail: klissz@yahoo.de

Dr. Diana Fridrihsone and
Dr. Jurgis Strautmanis
Children's University Hospital
Vienibas gatva 45, Riga LV 1004, Latvia
Phone: +371 29832436
E-mails: diana.fridrihsone@inbox.lv;
and jurgis.strautmanis@eeg.lv

Dr. Jurgita Grikiniene
Vilnius University Children's Hospital
Santariskiu st. 4, Vilnius,
LT-08406, Lithuania
Phone: +370 68411405
Fax: +370 52720283
E-mail: jurgita.grikiniene@mf.vu.lt

Dr. Sergey Aivazyan, Head of
Child Neurology
The Child Moscow Research Hospital
Aviatorov Street, 38, Solntsevo,
Moscow, Russia
Phone: (095) 4521022, +79166204051
E-mail: abc1231961@mail.ru

Dr. Bosanka Jocic-Jakubi
Nis Medical University School
Bul. Zorana Dindica 48,
18000 Nis, Serbia
Phone: +381 18 238 706
E-mail: bosajj@yahoo.com

Dr. Nebojsa J. Jovic
Clinic of Neurology and Psychiatry
for Children and Youth
Dr Subotica 6a Street, 11 000
Belgrade, Serbia
Phone: +381 11 2658 355
Fax: +381 11 64 50 64
E-mail: njjovic@eunet.yu

Dr. David Neubauer
Department of Child, Adolescent &
Developmental Neurology
University Children's Hospital
Vrazov trg 1, 1525 Ljubljana, Slovenia
Phone: +386-1-5229-273
Fax: +386-1-5229-357
E-mail: david.neubauer@mf.uni-lj.si

Orkide Guzel MD, Pediatric
Neurology Department
Dr. Behçet Uz Children's Hospital
İsmet Kaptan Mah. Sezer Doğan Sok.
No: 11, 35210 Konak/İZMİR, Turkey
Phone: +90 232 4116000
Fax: +90 232 4892315
E-mail orkideege@hotmail.com

Dr. Meral Topcu, Prof. of Pediatrics
and Pediatric Neurologist
Hacettepe Children's Hospital,
Dept. of Child Neurology
06100 Ankara, Turkey
Phone: 90-312-3051165
Fax: 90-312-4266764
E-mail: mtopcu@hacettepe.edu.tr

WESTERN EUROPE

Dr. Martha Feucht
Universitatsklinik fur Neuropsychiatrie
des Kindes- und Jugendalters
Wahringer Gurtel 18-20, 1090
Wien, Vienna, Austria
Phone: +43-40400-3012
Fax: +43-40400-2793
E-mail: martha.feucht@univie.ac.at

Dr. Barbara Plecko
University Klinik für Kinder-und
Jugendheilkunde Graz
Auenbruggerplatz 30, A-8036
Graz, Austria
Phone: +43 316 385 82813
Fax: +43 316 385 2657
E-mail: barbara.plecko@meduni-graz.at

Prof. Wolfgang Sperl
Department of Pediatrics, Paracelsus
Medical University
Salzburger Landeskliniken (SALK),
Müllner Hauptstraße 48,
A-5020 Salzburg, Austria
Phone: 0043-662-4482-2600
Fax: 0043-662-4482-2604
E-mail: w.sperl@salk.at

Dr. Lieven Lagae
Kinderneurologie—Epilepsie, Klinische Neurofysiologie
University Hospitals of Gasthuisberg
Herestraat 49, B-3000 Leuven, Belgium
Phone: +32 16 34 38 45
Fax: +32 16 34 38 42
E-mail: Lieven.Lagae@uz.kuleuven.ac.be

Dr. Maria Miranda
Danish Epilepsy Centre, Dianalund
Kolonivej 1, 4293 Dianalund, Denmark
Phone: (+45) 58271062
E-mail: MariMn@vestamt.dk

Dr. Peter Uldall
University Hospital of Copenhagen
Neuropaed clinic 5004l Rigshospitalet, Blegdamsvej, 2100, Denmark
Phone: +45 35455096
Fax: +45 35456717
E-mail: peter.uldall@rh.hosp.dk

Dr. Elina Liukkonen
Helsinki and Vusimaa Hospital, Hospital for Children and Adolescents
PO Box 280, Finland
Phone: 011-358-9-4711-4711
Fax: 011-358-9-471-80-413
E-mail: elina.liukkone@hus.fi

Dr. Anne de Saint-Martin, Neuropédiatre
Service de Pédiatrie 1
CHU de Hautepierre
67098 Strasbourg Cedex, France
Phone: 33(0)388127734
Fax: 33(0)388128156
E-mail: anne.desaintmartin@chru-strasbourg.fr

Dr. Olivier Dulac, Hôpital Saint Vincent de Paul, and Nadia Bahi-Buisson, MD, PhD, Service de Neuropédiatrie et Maladies Métaboliques
Hôpital Necker Enfants Malades, 149 Rue di Sevres, Paris 75743, France
Phone: 33 140 488111
E-mails: o.dulac@nck.ap-hop-paris.fr; and nadia.bahi-buisson@nck.ap-hop-paris.fr

Dr. Stéphane Auvin, Service de Neurologie Pédiatrique et des Maladies Métaboliques
CHU Hôpital Robert Debré
48, boulevard Sérurier, 75935 Paris cedex 19, France
Phone: +33 1 40 03 57 07
Fax: +33 1 40 03 47 74
E-mail: auvin@invivo.edu

Dr. Laurence Lion Francois
Centre Hospitalier Lyon Sud, Département de Neurologie Pédiatrique
165 chemin du Grand Revoyet, 69 495 Pierre Bénite cédex, France
Phone: 04 78 86 14 95
Fax: 04 78 86 57 16
E-mail: laurence.lion@chu-lyon.fr

Dr. R. Madeleyn
Filderklinik—Kinderabteilung
Im Haberschlai 7, D-70794 Filderstadt, Germany
Phone: +49-711-7703-0
Fax: +49-711-7703-1380
E-mails: t.reckert@filderklinik.de; and www.filderklinik.de

Dr. Joerg Klepper
Aschaffenburg Children's Hospital
Am Hasenkopf, 63739 Aschaffenburg, Germany
Phone: ++49/6021/32-3601
Fax: ++49/6021/32-3699
E-mail: joerg.klepper@klinikum-aschaffenburg.de

Dr. Friedrich Ebinger, Dept. Pediatric Neurology
Children's Hospital
University of Heidelberg, Im Neuenheimer Feld 430, 69120 Heidelberg, Germany
Phone: 49-6221-56-8488
Fax: 49-6221-56-5744
E-mail: friedrich.ebinger@med.uni-heidelberg.de

Prof. Dr. F. A. M. Baumeister,
Leiter Neuropädiatrie
Klinik für Kinder- und Jugendmedizin
Klinikum Rosenheim,
Pettenkoferstr. 10, 83022 Rosenheim, Germany
Phone: 49-(0)8031-36-3457
Fax: 49-(0)8031-36-4927
E-mail: friedrich.baumeister@kliro.de

Dr. Adelheid Wiemer-Kruel,
leading consultant,
Clinic for Children and Adolescents
Epilepsy Centre Kork
Landstraße 1, D-77694 Kehl-Kork, Germany
Phone: 0049-7851-84-2230
Fax: 0049-7851-84-2553
E-mail: awiemer@epilepsiezentrum.de

Dr. Yr Sigurdardottir
Icelandic Diagnostic Center
Digranesvegi 5, 200 Kopavogur, Iceland
Phone: (354) 510-8400
Fax: (354) 510-8401
E-mail: yr@greining.is

Drs. Bryan Lynch and Aisling Myers
The Children's University Hospital
Temple Street, Dublin 1, Ireland
Phone: 00-353-86-8197831
E-mail: aislingmyers@hotmail.com

Dr. Giangennaro Coppola
Clinic of Child Neuropsychiatry
Second University of Naples, Italy
Phone: 0039-81-5666695
Fax: 0039-81-5666694
E-mail: giangennaro.coppola@unina2.it

Dr. Federico Vigevano
Department of Neurology, Bambino Gesù Children's Hospital
00165 Rome, Italy
Phone: 0039-06-68592262
Fax: 0039-06-68592463
E-mail: vigevano@opbg.net

Prof. Pierangelo Veggiotti
Dipartimento di Clinica Neurologica e Psichiatrica dell'Età Evolutiva
Laboratorio EEG dell'età Evolutiva
Fondazione "Istituto Neurologico Casimiro Mondino"
Via Ferrata 6-27100 – Pavia, Italy
Phone: +39-0382-380-344
Fax: +39-0382-380-286
E-mail: pveggiot@unipv.it

Dr. Volpi Lilia
Ausl Bo, Bellaria Hospital—Neurology, Bologna, Italy
Phone: +39-0516225111
E-mail: lilia.volpi@ausl.bo.it

Dr. Paul Augustijn
Observatie Kliniek voor Kinderen "Primula"
S.E.I.N., Postbus 540, 2130 AM Heemstede, The Netherlands
Phone: 31(0)23-558800
Fax: 31(0) 23-558229
E-mail: paugustijn@sein.nl

Elles van der Louw (dietitian)
Erasmus MC—Sophia
UMC Utrecht Wilhelmina's Children's Hospital
PO Box 2060, Room sp2434, 3000 CB Rotterdam, The Netherlands
Phone: 003110-4636290

Dr. Björn Bjurulf
Ullevål University Hospital
0407 Oslo, Norway
Phone: 47-22118080
Fax: 47-22118663
E-mail: bjorn.bjurulf@ulleval.no

Dr. Anna Bremer and Kathrine Haavardsholm RD
National Centre of Epilepsy
Pb. 53, 1306 Basum post-terminal, Oslo, Norway
Phone: 47-67501000
E-mail: anna.bremer@epilepsy.no
E-mail: Katherine.c.haavardsholm@epilepsy.no

Dr. Maria Zubiel
Dept. of Child Neurology,
Institute of Polish Mother
Memory Hospital
93-338 Lodz, Rzgowska 281/289, Poland
Phone: 004842 2712080
Fax: 004842 2711412
E-mail: mzubiel@op.pl

Dr. Sergiusz Jozwiak, Professor and
Head, Pediatric Neurology
The Children's Memorial Health Institute
Al. DZieci Polskich 20, 04-736
Warszawa, Poland
Phone: 4822-8153417
Fax: 4822-8157402
E-mail: jozwiak@czd.waw.pl

Dr. Magdalena Dudzinska
Chorzowskie Centrum
Pediatrii i Onkologii
Ul. Truchana 7, 41-005 Chorzow, Poland
Phone: 032-34-90-005
E-mails: duzinska@chcpio.pl; and
mdudzinskapl@yahoo.com

Ana Faria RD and Conceição Robalo, MD
Hospital Pediátrico de Coimbra
Avenida Bissaya Barreto, 3000
Coimbra, Portugal
Phone: 351 239 480 606
Fax: 351 239 480 315
E-mail: anafaria@chc.min-saude.pt

Miguel Leão and Mafalda Sampaio
Neuropediatrics Unit, Centro
Hospitalar S. João
Alameda Professor Hernâni Monteiro
4200-319 Porto, Portugal
Phone: +351-225512100
Fax: +351-225513648
E-mail: mjleao2357@gmail.com
E-mail: mafaldansampaio@gmail.com

Dr. Lesley Nairn, Consultant Paediatrician
Royal Alexandra Hospital
Paisley, Scotland
Phone: 0141 580 4460
E-mail: Lesley.Nairn@rah.scot.nhs.uk

Dr. J. Campistol, Cap Servei de Neurologia
Hospital Sant Joan de Déu
Passeig Sant Joan de Déu,
2, 08950-Esplugues
(Barcelona), Spain
Phone: 93 2532153
Fax: 93 2033959
E-mail: campistol@hsjdbcn.org

Dr. Antonio Gil-Nage, Servicio de
Neurología, Programa de
Epilepsia
Hospital Ruber Internacional
La Masó 38, Mirasierra, 28034
Madrid, Spain
Phone: 0034-913875250
Fax: 0034-913875333
E-mail: agnagel@ya.com

Dr. Per Amark and Dr. Maria Dahlin
Astrid Lindgrens Children's
Hospital
Karolinska Hospital, S-171 76
Stockholm, Sweden
Phone: +46 8 5177 7026
Fax: +46 8 5177 7608
E-mail: per.amark@ks.se

Dr. Tove Hallbook
University Hospital
Se-221 85 Lund, Sweden
Phone: 46-46-17-1000
Fax: 46-46-14-5459
E-mail: tove.hallbook@telia.com

Dr. Isa Lundstrom, Department
of Pediatrics
Nordland University Hospital,
SE-901 85 Umeå, Sweden
E-mail: isa.lundstrom@bredband.net

Dr. Oswald Hasselmann,
Neuropediatrics
Ostschweizer Kinderspital
Claudiusstrasse 6, CH-9006
St. Gallen, Switzerland
Phone: +41 (0) 71 243-7-363 bzw. -111
E-mail: oswald.hasselmann@
gd-kispi.sg.ch

Dr. Gabriela Wohlrab
University Children's Hospital,
Neurophysiological Department,
Steinwiesstrasse 24, CH-8032
Zürich, Switzerland
Phone: 0041 1 266 77 01
E-mail: Gabriele.Wohlrab@kispi.unizh.ch

Dr. Helen Cross, Reader and
Honorary Consultant in
Paediatric Neurology
Institute of Child Health and
Great Ormond Street
Hospital for Children NHS Trust,
The Wolfson Centre
Mecklenburgh Square, London
WC1N 2AP, UK
Phone: 44-207-813-8488
Fax: 44-207-829-8627
E-mail: h.cross@ich.ucl.ac.uk
and
Matthew's Friends Clinics for
Ketogenic Dietary Therapies
@Young Epilepsy
St Piers Lane, Lingfield, Surrey
RH7 6PW, UK
Phone: +44 1342 836571
E-mail: info@mfclinics.com

Dr. Colin Ferrie, Department of
Paediatric Neurology
Clarendon Wing, Leeds
General Infirmary
Leeds LS2 9NS, UK
Phone: 0113 392 2188
Fax: 0113 392 5731
E-mail: Collin.Ferrie@leedsth.nhs.uk

Dr. Frances Gibbon, Department
of Child Health
University Hospital of Wales,
Cardiff, UK
Phone: 44 29 2074 3542
E-mail: Frances.Gibbon@
cardiffandvale.wales.nhs.uk

Dr. Jayaprakah Gosalakkal; University
Hospitals of Leicester
CDC/Windsor LRI, Leicester
LE1 5WW, UK
Phone: 011441162585564
Fax: 011442587637
E-mail: Jay2world@aol.com

Dr. Sunny George Philip,
Consultant Paediatric
Neurologist
Birmingham Children's
Hospital, Birmingham,
UK B4 6NH
Phone: 011 441213338149
Fax: 011 441213338151
E-mail: SUNNY.PHILIP@bch.nhs.uk

Dr. Timothy Martland, Consultant
Paediatric Neurologist
The David Lewis Centre
Mill House, Warford, Near
Alderley Edge, Cheshire
SK9 7UD, UK
Phone: +44 161 727 2346
E-mail: Timothy.Martland@
CMMC.nhs.uk

Dr. Jeen Tan, Consultant
Paediatric Neurologist
Royal Manchester Children's Hospital
Manchester, M13 9WL, UK
Phone: 0161 701 2346
E-mail: Jeen.Tan@cmft.nhs.uk

Dr. Ruth E Williams, Consultant
Paediatric Neurologist
Evelina Children's Hospital,
Guy's and St Thomas' NHS
Foundation Trust
Lambeth Palace Road, London
SE1 7EH, UK
Phone: +44-207 188 3998
Fax: +44-207 188 0851
E-mail: Ruth.Williams@gstt.nhs.uk

Dr. Neil H. Thomas, Consultant Paediatric Neurologist
Southampton University Hospitals NHS Trust, Southampton General Hospital
Mailpoint 021, Tremona Road, Southampton SO16 6YD, UK
Phone: +44 23 8079 4457
Fax: +44 23 8079 4962
E-mail: neil.thomas@suht.swest.nhs.uk

MIDDLE EAST

Dr. Omnia Rashidy, Professor of Pediatric Neurology
Ain Shams University Cairo Egypt
Health Care Consultant of Egyptian National Council of Disability Affairs
Mobile: 002 01222164876
E-mail: omniarashidy@hotmail.com

Hameeda Hamad Al-Shammari RD
Kuwait Hospital for Children, Kuwait
E-mail: h.dietitian98@hotmail.com

Dr. Bosanka Jocic-Jakubi
Al Sabah Hospital, Kuwait City, Kuwait
E-mail: bosajj@gmail.com

Dr. Mohammad Ghofrani, Professor of Paediatric Neurology
Shaheed Beheshti University of Medical Sciences and Health Services:
Mofid Hospital, Shariati St., Tehran, Iran
Phone: 98 21 22200041

Dr. M. Mohammadi, Professor of Pediatrics and Neurology
Tehran University of Medical Sciences
56, Najm Alley, North Felestin Avenue, Enghelab 14168, Tehran, Iran
Phone: 9821-9329117568
E-mail: mohamadi@tums.ac.ir

Dr. Bruria Ben'Zeev
Safra Children's Hospital, Sheba Medical Center
Ramat Gan, Israel 52621,
Phone: 97235302577
E-mail: benzeev4@netvision.net.il

Dr. Eli Heyman
Asaf Harofe Medical Center, Tel Aviv University
Zerifin 70300, Israel
Phone: 00972-8-9778466
E-mail: eheyman@post.tau.ac.il

Dr. Tally Lerman-Sagie, Director of Pediatric Neurology Unit
Wolfson Medical Center, Holon, Israel
Phone: 97235028458
Fax: 97235028141
E-mail: asagie@post.tau.ac.il

Dr. Hadassa Goldberg
Schneider's Children's Hospital, Tel Aviv, Israel
Phone: 0507600865
E-mail: hagoldberg@clalit.org.it

Dr. Nabil Al-Macki and Sana Al-Yafaey (Dietitian)
Pediatric Neurologist, Head of Pediatric Neurology
Royal Hospital, Muscat, Oman
Phone: 0096897330258
E-mail: nabilalmacki2010@gmail.com

Dr. Generoso G. Gascon, Dept. of Neuroscience, MBC J-76
King Faisal Specialist Hospital & Research Center
PO Box 40047, Jeddah 21499, Saudi Arabia
Phone: +(966-2) 667-7777 Ext. 5813
Fax: +(966-2) 667-7777 Ext. 5819
E-mail: generoso_gascon@hotmail.com

Mouaz Al-Sbei, MD, Head of Neurology Section
International Medical Center
PO Box 2172, Jeddah 21451, Saudi Arabia
Phone: +966 2 650 9000 Ext. 4712
Fax: +966 2 650 9001
E-mail: msbei@imc.med.sa

Dr. Adel A. H. Mahmoud, Consultant Pediatric Neurologist
Pediatric Neurology Department, Neuroscience Center
King Fahad Medical City, PO Box 365814, Riyadh 11393, Saudi Arabia
E-mail: amahmoud@kfmc.med.sa

Dr. Mohammed Al-Malik and
Ms. Unita Botes (Dietitian)
Johns Hopkins—Tawam Hospital
PO Box 15258, Al Ain, United
Arab Emirates
Phone: 971-3-767-7444
E-mail: mmalik@tawam-hosp.gov.ae

Dr. Dina Saleh
Mafraq Hospital, Abu Dhabi,
United Arab Emirates
E-mail: dsaleh@mafraqhospital.ae

AFRICA

Dr. Satté Amal, Service de Neurophysiologie
Hôpital Militaire d'Instruction
Mohammed V Rabat, Morocco
E-mail: satteamal@gmail.com

Dr. Tuschka du Toit, Registered Dietitian
PO Box 4404, Rietvalleirand,
South Africa 0174
Phone and Fax: +27 12 345 1392
E-mail: tuschka@absamail.co.za

Dr. James Butler and Kath Megaw (RD)
Constantiaberg Mediclinic,
Plumstead (Cape Town area),
South Africa, 0861477776
E-mail: info@nutripaeds.com

Dr. Jo M Wilmshurst, Head of Paed
Neurology, 5th Floor ICH
Department of Paediatrics, Red
Cross Children's Hospital
Rondebosch, Cape Town
7700, South Africa
Fax: 027 21 689 2187
E-mail: wilmshur@ich.uct.ac.za

ASIA

Jianxiang Liao, MD, PhD
Shenzhen Children's Hospital,
China Medical University
7019 Yi Tian Road, Shenzhen,
Guangdong, P R China 518026
Phone: +86-755-83936150
Fax: +86-755-83936148
E-mail: epilepsycenter@vip.163.com

Lai-Wah Eva Fung MRCP,
Department of Pediatrics
30-32 Ngan Shing Street, Shatin,
New Territories
Hong Kong Special Administrative
Region, China
Phone: 852-2632-2981
Fax: 852-2636-0020
E-mail: eva_fung@cuhk.edu.hk

Winsy Leung, RD
818 Health Professionals, Suite 818,
Central Building, 1 Pedder
Street, Hong Kong, China
Phone: 852-2526-6332
E-mail: winsyleung@children818.com

Dr. Chak Wai Kwong
Tuen Mun Hospital
Tsing Chung Koon Road, Tuen Mun,
New Territories, Hong Kong, China
Phone: 852-2468-5111
Fax: 852-2456-9111
E-mail: chakwk@gmail.com

Dr. Ada Yung, Department of Paediatrics
and Adolescent Medicine
University of Hong Kong,
Queen Mary Hospital
Hong Kong Special Administrative
Region, China
Phone: 852-2855-4485
Fax: 852-2855-1523
E-mails: vcnwong@hkucc.hku.hk;
and ayung@hkucc.hku.hk

Deng Yu Hong
Guangzhou Medical College
Chang-Gang-Dong Road 250, Guangzhou,
Guangdong, P R China 510260
Phone: +86-20-34152244
Fax: +86-20-34153378
E-mail: Deng3251@yahoo.com.cn

Dr. Janak Nathan
Shushrusha Hospital
Ranade Road, Dadar W,
Mumbai 400028, India
Phone: +91-22-24446615
E-mail: jsvpnat@hotmail.com
www.ketodietindia.org

Dr. Neeta Naik
Epilepsy Research Centre for Children
111, 1st Floor, Sundaram Bldg., Above Indian Bank, Opp Cinemax Sion, Sion (E), Mumbai 400 022, India
Phone: +91-24038008
E-mail: neetanaik@yahoo.com

Dr. Anaita Udwadia-Hegde
106 Doctor House, Opp. Jaslok Hospital, Peddar Road
Wadia Children's Hospital
Mumbai 400 026, India
Phone: +91 22 23517883
Fax: +91 22 23512922
E-mail: anaitahegde@hotmail.com

Ritu Sudhakar, Chief Dietitian
Dayanand Medical College & Hospital
Tagore Nagar, Ludhiana 141001, India
E-mail: sudhakar_ritu@rediffmail.com

Dr. Suvasini Sharma, Department of Pediatrics
Lady Hardinge Medical College
New Delhi 110011, India
Phone: +91 10234344
E-mail: sharma.suvasini@gmail.com

Dr. Elisabeth Herini
Gadjah Mada University
Dr. Sardjito Hospital, J1. Kesehatan 1 Yogyakarta 55284, Indonesia
Phone: 62-274-561616
Fax: 62-274-583745
E-mail: herini_es@yahoo.com

Dr. Yukio Fukuyama
Child Neurology Institute
6-12-17-201 Minami-Shinagawa, Shinagawa-ku, Tokyo 140-0004, Japan
Phone: +81-3-5781-7680
Fax: +81-3-3740-0874
E-mail: yfukuyam@sc4.so-net.ne.jp

Dr. Katsumi Imai
National Epilepsy Center, Japan
886 Urushiyama, Aoi Ward, Shizuoka City, Shizuoka, 420-8688, Japan
Phone: +81-54-245-5446
Fax: +81-54-246-9781
E-mail: imaik@szec.hosp.go.jp

Yoshiko Hirano, MD, PhD, Assistant, Dept. of Pediatrics
Tokyo Women's Medical University School of Medicine
8-1 Kawada-cho, Shinjuku-ku, Tokyo 162-8666, Japan
Phone: +81-3-3353-8112 (Ext. 31230)
Fax: +81-3-5269-7338
E-mail: yochi@ped.twmu.ac.jp

Susumu Ito, MD, PhD, Assistant Professor, Dept. of Pediatrics
Tokyo Women's Medical University School of Medicine
8-1 Kawada-cho, Shinjuku-ku, Tokyo 162-8666, Japan
Phone: +81-3-3353-8111
Fax: +81-3-5269-7338
E-mail: ito.susumu@twmu.ac.jp

Dr. Tomohiro Kumada
Shiga Medical Center for Children
5-7-30 Moriyama, Moriyama City, Shiga, 524-0022, Japan
Phone: +81-77-582-6200
Fax: +81-77-582-6304
E-mail: tkumada@mccs.jp

Dr. Hirokazu Oguni, Dept. of Pediatrics
Tokyo Women's Medical University
8-1 Kawada-cho, Shinjuku-ku, Tokyo 162-8666, Japan
Phone: +81-3-3353-8111
Fax: +81-3-5269-7338
E-mail: hoguni@ped.twmu.ac.jp

Dr. Teik-Beng Khoo, Consultant
Paediatric Neurologist
Paediatric Institute, Hospital
Kuala Lumpur
Jalan Pahang, 50586, Kuala
Lumpur, Malaysia
Phone: (6)03-261-55555, Ext. 6938
E-mail: khootb@gmail.com

Dr. Sui-Yin Ng, Consultant,
Paediatric Neurologist
Gleneagles Hospital Kuala Lumpur
282, Jalan Ampang, 55000, Kuala
Lumpur, Malaysia
Phone: (6)03-42576998
E-mail: drngsy@gmail.com

Dr. Nor Azni bin Yahya, Consultant
Paediatric Neurologist
Department of Paediatrics,
Hospital Raja Perempuan Zainab II,
Kota Bharu, Jalan Dusun Muda,
15200 Kota Bharu, Kelantan, Malaysia
Phone: (6)09-745-2643
E-mail: drazni@yahoo.co.uk

Dr. Vigneswari Ganesan, Dr. Chee-Ming Teh
Consultant Paediatric Neurologist
Department of Paediatrics,
Penang Hospital,
Jalan Residensi, 10450 Georgetown,
Penang, Malaysia
Phone: (6)04-2225299
E-mail: cmteh1976@yahoo.com

Dr. Alex Khoo, Consultant
Paediatric Neurologist
Department of Paediatrics,
Hospital Raja Permaisuri Bainun,
Jalan Hospital, 30990,
Ipoh, Perak, Malaysia
Phone: (6)05-2085208
E-mail: pengchuan72@gmail.com

Dr. Benilda Sanchez, Head of the Epilepsy
Monitoring Program of St. Luke's
Manila, Philippines
Phone: (632)723-0301 Ext. 5452
Fax: (632)727-5452
E-mail: beni779@hotmail.com

Dr. Derrick Chan Wei Shih
KK Women's and Children's Hospital
100 Bukit Timah Road, Singapore
229899
Phone: 065-6293-4044
Fax: 065-6394-1973
E-mail: Derrick.Chan.WS@kkh.com.sg

Dr. Hian-Tat Ong, Consultant,
Paediatric Neurology and
Developmental Paediatrics
Children's Medical Institute,
National University Hospital
Singapore
Phone: 065-67724391
Fax: 065-67797486
E-mail: OngHT@nuh.com.sg

Dr. Yong Seung Hwang,
Professor, Pediatrics,
Pediatric Neurology
Seoul National University
Children's Hospital
28 Yon Gun Dong, Jong Ro Gu,
Seoul, 110-744, South Korea
Phone: 82-2-760-3629
Fax: 82-2-743-3455
E-mail: childnr@plaza.snu.ac.kr

Dr. Heung Dong Kim, Associate
Professor
Dept. of Pediatrics, Director
in Child Neurology
Yonsei University College of
Medicine, Severance Hospital
134, Shinchondong, Seodaemun-gu,
Seoul, 120-752, South Korea
Phone: 82-2-361-5511
Fax: 82-2-393-9118
E-mail: hdkimmd@yumc
.yonsei.ac.kr

Professor Ranjanie Gamage
Institute of Neurology, Unit One
National Hospital of Sri Lanka
Colombo 10, Sri Lanka
Phone: +094 112691111 Ext. 2262
E-mails: ranjaniegamage@gmail
.com; and oshanif@yahoo.com
or priyanwada@gmail.com

Dr. Huei-Shyong Wang, Division of Pediatric Neurology
Chang Gung Children's Hospital
Chang Gung University, Taiwan
Phone: 886 (0)968 11026
Fax: 886 3 3277295
E-mail: wanghs444@cgmh.org.tw

Dr. Pipop Jirapinyo, Professor of Pediatrics, Pediatric Nutritionist
Nutrition Unit, Department of Pediatrics
Faculty of Medicine Siriraj Hospital
Mahidol University, 2 Prannok Road, Bangkoknoi, Bangkok 10700, Thailand
Phone: (662) 411-2535
E-mail: sipjr@mahidol.ac.th

Dr. Pongkiat Kankirawatana, Director, Clinical Neurophysiology Lab
Pediatric Neurology, CHB-314
The Children's Hospital of Alabama
1600 7th Ave S., Birmingham, AL 35233-1711, USA
(information regarding Thailand experience)
Phone: 205-996-7850
Fax: 205-996-7867
E-mail: PKankirawatana@peds.uab.edu

AUSTRALIA/NEW ZEALAND

Dr. Deepak Gill, Paediatric Neurologist
Children's Hospital at Westmead
Cnr Hawkesbury Rd & Hainsworth St, Westmead, Sydney NSW 2145, Australia
Phone: 02 9845 2694
Fax: 02 9845 3905
E-mail: DeepakG@chw.edu.au

Dr. John Lawson, Child Neurologist
Sydney Children's Hospital
Sydney, Australia
Phone: 61 2 93821658
Fax: 61 2 93821580
E-mail: Lawson@SESAHS.NSW.GOV.AU

Dr. Sophie Calvert, Staff Specialist in Paediatric Neurology
Neurosciences Department, Royal Children's Hospital
Herston, Australia
Phone: 07 3636 7487
Fax: 07 3636 5104
E-mail: Sophie_Calvert@health.qld.gov.au

Dr. Mark T. Mackay, Consultant Neurologist
Judy Nation (Dietitian)
Department of Neurology, Royal Children's Hospital
Flemington Road, Parkville, Victoria 3052, Australia
Phone: +613-9345-5641
Fax: +613-9345-5977
E-mail: mark.mackay@rch.org.au
E-mail: judy.nation@rch.org.au

Dr. Lakshmi Nagarajan
Princess Margaret Hospital for Children
GPO Box D184, Perth WA 6840, Australia
Phone: (08) 9340 8364
Fax: (08) 9340 7063
E-mail: Lakshmi.Nagarajan@health.wa.gov.au

Dr. Thorsten Stanley, Senior Lecturer in Paediatrics
Wellington School of Medicine and Health Sciences
University of Otago
PO Box 7343 Wellington South, Wellington, New Zealand
Phone: +64 4 3855 999
Fax: +64 4 3855 898
E-mail: paedtvs@wnmeds.ac.nz

Tracey Eccles, BSc, MSc Nutrition and Dietetics, NZRD
Dietitian—Medical Nutrition Specialist, New Zealand
Phone: +64-9-213-3308
Mobile: +64-21-259-7940
E-mail: tracey@eatwise4life.co.nz

APPENDIX H

Routine Ketogenic Diet Lab Studies

As part of our follow-up of the children on the ketogenic diet, we suggest that parents obtain the following laboratory tests one week prior to clinic visits. Please fill in your child's name and the date and have the neurologist fill in the rest.

KETOGENIC DIET LAB REQUEST (MUST FAST FOR MINIMUM OF 8 HOURS BEFOREHAND)

Patient Name: ______________________________

ICD9 Dx. Code: 345.01; ICD10 Dx Code: G40.419

Date: ________________

Service or Clinic: Pediatric Epilepsy Center

Urinalysis

CBC with differential

(CMP-SMA20) to include: BUN, albumin, AST, creatinine, calcium, T. Bili, ALT, glucose, phosphorus, direct bilirubin, total protein, uric acid, alkaline phosphatase

Complete lipid profile (fasting)

Selenium level

Carnitine profile (total and free)

1, 25-OH-Vitamin D level

Anticonvulsant levels for these drugs: ________________________________

____

____

____

Physician's Signature: ____________________ DEA # ____________________

Physician's Name (print): ____

PLEASE FAX RESULTS TO: ____

APPENDIX I

Selected References

GENERAL INFORMATION ON EPILEPSY

Freeman JM, Vining EPG, Pillas DJ. *Seizures and epilepsy in childhood*. 3rd edition. Johns Hopkins University Press, Baltimore, MD, 2002.

REFERENCES ON THE EFFECTIVENESS AND ACCEPTABILITY OF DIETS

Amari A, Turner Z, Rubenstein JE, Miller JR, Kossoff EH. Exploring the relationship between preferences for high fat foods and efficacy of the ketogenic and modified Atkins diets among children with seizure disorders. *Seizure* 2015;25:173–177.

Cervenka MC, Terao NN, Bosarge JL, Henry BJ, Klees AA, Morrison PF, Kossoff EH. Email management of the modified Atkins diet for adults with epilepsy is feasible and effective. *Epilepsia* 2012;53:728–732.

Chen W, Kossoff EH. Long-term follow-up of children treated with the modified Atkins diet. *J Child Neurol* 2012;27:754–758.

Farasat S, Kossoff EH, Pillas DJ, Rubenstein JE, Vining EP, Freeman JM. The importance of cognition in parental expectations prior to starting the ketogenic diet. *Epilepsy Behav* 2006;8:406–410.

Freeman JM, Kossoff EH. Ketosis and the ketogenic diet: 2010. *Adv Pediatr* 2010;57:315–329.

Freeman JM, Vining EPG. Seizures rapidly decrease after fasting: preliminary studies of the ketogenic diet. *Arch Pediatr Adolesc* 1999;153:946–949.

Freeman JM, Vining EPG, Pillas DJ, Pyzik PL, Casey JC, Kelly MT. The efficacy of the ketogenic diet—1998: a prospective evaluation of intervention in 150 children. *Pediatrics* 1998;102:1358–1363.

Gilbert DL, Pyzik PL, Vining EPG, Freeman JM. Medication cost reduction in children on the ketogenic diet: data from a prospective study of 150 children over one year. *J Child Neurol* 1999;14:469–471.

Hartman AL, Rubenstein JE, Kossoff EH. Intermittent fasting: a "new" historical strategy for controlling seizures? *Epilepsy Res* 2013;104:275–279.

Hemingway C, Freeman JM, Pillas DJ, Pyzik PL. The ketogenic diet: a 3 to 6 year follow-up of 150 children enrolled prospectively. *Pediatrics* 2001;108:898–905.

Hong AM, Hamdy RF, Turner Z, Kossoff EH. Infantile spasms treated with the ketogenic diet: prospective single-center experience in 104 consecutive infants. *Epilepsia* 2010;51:1403–1407.

Kim DW, Kang HC, Park JC, Kim HD. Benefits of the nonfasting ketogenic diet compared with the initial fasting ketogenic diet. *Pediatrics* 2004;114:1627–1630.

Kossoff EH. More fat and fewer seizures: dietary therapy for epilepsy. *Lancet Neurol* 2004;3:415–420.

Kossoff EH, Cervenka MC, Henry BJ, Haney CA, Turner Z. A decade of the modified Atkins diet (2003–2013): results, insights, and future directions. *Epilepsy Behav* 2013;29:437–442.

Kossoff EH, Hedderick EF, Turner Z, Freeman JM. A case-control evaluation of the ketogenic diet versus ACTH for new-onset infantile spasms. *Epilepsia* 2008;49:1504–1509.

Kossoff EH, Henry BJ, Cervenka MC. Transitioning pediatric patients receiving ketogenic diets for epilepsy into adulthood. *Seizure* 2013;22:487–489.

Kossoff EH, Krauss GL, McGrogan JR, Freeman JM. Efficacy of the Atkins diet as therapy for intractable epilepsy. *Neurology* 2003;61:1789–1791.

Kossoff EH, Laux LC, Blackford R, Morrison PF, Pyzik PL, Turner Z, Nordli DR, Jr. When do seizures improve with the ketogenic diet? *Epilepsia* 2008;49:329–333.

Kossoff EH, McGrogan JR. Worldwide use of the ketogenic diet. *Epilepsia* 2005;46:280–289.

Kossoff EH, Pyzik PL, McGrogan JR, Vining EPG, Freeman JM. Efficacy of the ketogenic diet for infantile spasms. *Pediatrics* 2002;109:780–783.

Kossoff EH, Rowley H, Sinha SR, Vining EPG. A prospective study of the modified Atkins diet for intractable epilepsy in adults. *Epilepsia* 2008;49:316–319.

Kossoff EH, Zupec-Kania BA, Rho JM. Ketogenic diets: an update for child neurologists. *J Child Neurol* 2009;24:979–988.

Kossoff EH, Zupec-Kania BA, Amark PE, Ballaban-Gil KR, Bergqvist ACG, Blackford R, Buchhalter JR, Caraballo RH, Cross JH, Dahlin MG, Donner EJ, Jehle RS, Klepper J, Kim HD, Liu YMC, Nation J, Nordli, DR Jr, Pfeifer HH, Rho JM, Stafstrom CE, Thiele EA, Turner Z, Veggiotti P, Vining EPG, Wheless JW, Wirrell EC, Charlie Foundation, and the Practice Committee of the Child Neurology Society. Optimal clinical management of children receiving the ketogenic diet: recommendations of the International Ketogenic Diet Study Group. *Epilepsia* 2009;50:304–317.

Lord K, Magrath G. Use of the ketogenic diet and dietary practices in the UK. *J Hum Nutr Diet* 2010;23:126–132.

Mady MA, Kossoff EH, McGregor AL, Wheless JW, Pyzik PL, Freeman JM. The ketogenic diet: adolescents can do it, too. *Epilepsia* 2003;44:847–851.

McNally MA, Pyzik PL, Rubenstein JE, Hamdy RF, Kossoff EH. Empiric use of oral potassium citrate reduces symptomatic kidney stone incidence with the ketogenic diet. *Pediatrics* 2009;124:e300–e304.

Neal EG, Chaffe HM, Schwartz RH, Lawson M, Edwards N, Fitzsimmons G, Whitney A, Cross JH. The ketogenic diet in the treatment of epilepsy in children: a randomised, controlled trial. *Lancet Neurol*. 2008;7:500–506.

Nordli DR, Jr., Kuroda MM, Carroll J, et al. Experience with the ketogenic diet in infants. *Pediatrics* 2001;108:129–133.

Patel A, Pyzik PL, Turner Z, Rubenstein JE, Kossoff EH. Long-term outcomes of children treated with the ketogenic diet in the past. *Epilepsia* 2010;51:1277–1282.

Pfeifer HH, Thiele EA. Low-glycemic-index treatment: a liberalized ketogenic diet for treatment of intractable epilepsy. *Neurology* 2005;65:1810–1812.

Rubenstein JE, Kossoff EH, Pyzik PL, Vining EPG, McGrogan JR, Freeman JM. Experience in the use of the ketogenic diet as early therapy. *J Child Neurol* 2005;20:31–34.

Selter JH, Turner Z, Doerrer SC, Kossoff EH. Experience in nutritional and medication adjustment for patients treated with the ketogenic diet. *J Child Neurol* 2015;30:53–57.

Sharma S, Sankhyan N, Gulati S, Agarwala A. Use of the modified Atkins diet for treatment of refractory childhood epilepsy: a randomized controlled trial. *Epilepsia* 2013;54:481–486.

Than KD, Kossoff EH, Rubenstein JE, Pyzik PL, McGrogan JR, Vining EPG. Can you predict an immediate, complete, and sustained response to the ketogenic diet? *Epilepsia* 2005;46:580–582.

Vining EPG, Freeman JM, for the Ketogenic Diet Study Group. A multi-center study of the efficacy of the ketogenic diet. *Arch Neurol* 1998;55:1433–1437.

Wheless JW. The ketogenic diet: an effective medical therapy with side effects. *J Child Neurol* 2001;16:633–635.

THE MEDIUM-CHAIN TRIGLYCERIDE (MCT) DIET

Huttenlocher PR, Wilbourn AJ, Signore JM. Medium-chain triglycerides as a therapy for intractable epilepsy. *Neurology* 1971;21:1097–1103.

Neal EG, Chaffe HM, Schwartz RH, Lawson M, Edwards N, Fitzsimmons G, Whitney A, Cross JH. The ketogenic diet in the treatment of epilepsy in children: a randomised, controlled trial. *Lancet Neurol*. 2008;7:500–506.

Sills MA, Forsyth WI, Haidukwych D. The medium-chain triglyceride diet and intractable epilepsy. *Arch Dis Child* 1986;61:1169–1172.

Trauner DA. Medium-chain triglyceride (MCT) diet in intractable seizure disorders. *Neurology* 1985;35:237–238.

THE LOW-GLYCEMIC INDEX TREATMENT (LGIT) DIET

Coppola G, D'Aniello A, Messana T, et al. Low glycemic index diet in children and young adults with refractory epilepsy: first Italian experience. *Seizure* 2011;20:526–528.

Karimzadeh P, Sedighi M, Beheshti M, Azargashb E, Ghofrani M, Abdollahe-Gorgi F. Low Glycemic Index Treatment in pediatric refractory epilepsy: the first Middle East report. *Seizure* 2014;23(7):570–572.

Kumada T, Hiejima I, Nozaki F, Hayashi A, Fujii T. Glycemic index treatment using Japanese foods in a girl with Lennox-Gastaut syndrome. *Pediatr Neurol* 2013;48(5):390–392.

Larson AM, Pfeifer HH, Thiele EA. Low glycemic index treatment for epilepsy in tuberous sclerosis complex. *Epilepsy Res.* 2012;99:180–182.

Muzykewicz DA, Lyzkowski DA, Memon N, Conant KD, Pfeifer HH, Thiele EA. Efficacy, safety, and tolerability of the low glycemic index treatment in pediatric epilepsy. *Epilepsia* 2009;50:1118–1126.

Pfeifer HH, Theile EA. Low–glycemic-index treatment: a liberalized ketogenic diet for treatment of intractable epilepsy. *Neurology* 2005;65;1810–1812.

OTHER BOOKS OF INTEREST

Bowden Jonny. *Living the low carb life*. Sterling, New York, NY, 2004.

The CalorieKing calorie, fat and carbohydrate counter 2015. Family Health Publications, Costa Mesa, CA, 2015.

Martenz DM, Cramp L. *The keto cookbook*. Demos, New York, NY, 2012.

Neal E, editor. *Dietary treatment of epilepsy: practical implementation of ketogenic therapy*. John Wiley & Sons, West Sussex, UK, 2012.

Snyder D. *Keto kid*. Demos, New York, NY, 2007.

Stafstrom C, Rho J, editors. *Epilepsy and the ketogenic diet*. Humana Press, Totowa, NJ, 2004.

Westman EC, Phinney SD, Volek JS. *The new Atkins for a new you*. Fireside, New York, NY, 2010.

Whitmer E, Riether JL. *Fighting back with fat: A parent's guide to battling epilepsy through the ketogenic diet and modified Atkins diet*. Demos, New York, NY, 2013.

INDEX

Note: Page numbers with *t* indicate tables; those in **bold** indicate illustrations or figures.